CHALLENGES IN INTELLIGENCE ANALYSIS

In *Challenges in Intelligence Analysis*, Timothy Walton offers concrete, reality-based ways to improve intelligence analysis. After a brief introduction to the main concepts of analysis, he provides more than forty historical and contemporary examples that demonstrate what has, and what has not, been effective when grappling with difficult problems. The examples cover a wide span of time, going back 3,000 years. They are also global in scope and deal with a variety of political, military, economic, and social issues. Walton emphasizes the importance of critical and creative thinking and how such thinking can be enhanced. This book provides a detailed and balanced explanation of intelligence work and will be of particular interest to students who are contemplating a career in intelligence analysis.

- Offers a brief introduction to the concepts, vocabulary, and tools of intelligence analysis.
- Features more than forty examples, each with questions for further discussion and recommended reading.
- Includes an instructor's guide with model answers to the "Questions for Further Thought," as well as suggested exercises and additional background information.

Timothy Walton is an adjunct professor of intelligence studies at Mercyhurst College and is on the roster of subject matter experts at Omnis Inc., an intelligence training consulting firm. The author of *The Spanish Treasure Fleets*, he served in the U.S. Navy and spent twenty-four years as an analyst at the Central Intelligence Agency.

Challenges in Intelligence Analysis

Lessons from 1300 BCE to the Present

Timothy Walton

Institute for Intelligence Studies, Mercyhurst College, Washington, DC

CAMBRIDGE UNIVERSITY PRESS
Cambridge, New York, Melbourne, Madrid, Cape Town, Singapore,
São Paulo, Delhi, Dubai, Tokyo, Mexico City

Cambridge University Press
32 Avenue of the Americas, New York, NY 10013-2473, USA

www.cambridge.org
Information on this title: www.cambridge.org/9780521132657

First published 2010

Printed in the United States of America

A catalog record for this publication is available from the British Library.

Library of Congress Cataloging in Publication data

Walton, Timothy R., 1948–
Challenges in intelligence analysis : lessons from 1300 BCE to the present /
Timothy Walton.
    p.   cm.
Includes bibliographical references and index.
ISBN 978-0-521-76441-4 (hardback) – ISBN 978-0-521-13265-7 (pbk.)
1. Intelligence service – History.   2. Intelligence service – Methodology.   3. Military
intelligence – History.   4. Espionage – History.   5. Business intelligence – History.
I. Title.
JF1525.I6.W39   2010
355.3′43209–dc22   2010028670

ISBN 978-0-521-76441-4 Hardback
ISBN 978-0-521-13265-7 Paperback

Contents

Figures

Preface

In recent years there has been much discussion of success and failure in intelligence and many proposals for reform. Much of the focus has been on reorganizations, such as establishing the position of Director of National Intelligence to improve coordination among the various intelligence agencies and creating the Department of Homeland Security, or more advanced technology, such as data mining.

Relatively little attention, however, has been devoted to how to improve analytic thinking in intelligence, especially by examining the historical record to see which analytic approaches have worked – or not worked. To fill this gap, *Challenges in Intelligence Analysis: Lessons from 1300 BCE to the Present* offers examples from the last three millennia. These examples have been drawn from around the world and a variety of disciplines, including national security, law enforcement, and business. The goal is to identify some common approaches and principles; it is hoped that a fact-based understanding of the past will help in generating realistic expectations for the future.

Some people ask – rightly – if there is such a thing as a "lesson of history." Of course, each situation in the past, as well as each new set of circumstances in the future, is unique and different. Details of what we learn from one situation may not be applicable to other situations, especially in a large number of cases. That said, there are similar problems over time, such as fast-moving situations, tightly held decisions made by adversaries, implications of new technologies, and skilled deception. Moreover, over a long period of time analysts trying to understand such difficult situations or solve a problem have found certain ways of thinking about their issues to be helpful. Among the various ways to better understand a problem are factors such as context, evidence, options, risks, and indicators. Therefore, even if the answers are always different, there are questions that, adjusted for each problem, are useful to ask in an effort to make better decisions.

Another lesson of history that is perhaps less prominent, but also worth considering when thinking about intelligence analysis, is contingency – in other words, that events were not necessarily destined to happen the way they did. A different mix of circumstances and decisions, and events could have taken a different path. With better information and analysis, results closer to what leaders aimed at may well have been achieved. When reviewing the examples in *Challenges in Intelligence Analysis*, it is worth remembering that there were a number of possible outcomes. It is also interesting to ponder what factors, such as human decisions, could have been changed and which ones, such as geography and weather, could not.

It is also possible to "overlearn" the lessons of history. There are trends over time and similarities with some past events, but there are also discontinuities and surprises. Sometimes things change from what has happened in the past, and intelligence analysts need to remain alert to that possibility.

The examples included in *Challenges in Intelligence Analysis* have been selected from the perspective of interest for an intelligence analyst, rather than because all of them are major turning points in history. Some of the cases are specific episodes; some are broader and involve ways to think about issues. Each of these examples has a larger context beyond analysis that involves organizational factors, such as gaps in collection or relations with decision makers. Often these factors are outside the control of analysts and have been treated in many other works; they are presented here only briefly to provide context.

By design, each example is short, so that a sizable number can be presented and the focus can remain on the analytic aspects. After two introductory chapters on general issues, the following chapters lay out a problem, give a brief account of what attempts were made to deal analytically with that problem, and then summarize the results. It is hoped that this approach combines (1) the breadth of a theoretical perspective – by considering similarities and differences over a wide range of examples – with (2) the fact-based methods of history.

Each example is, therefore, only a short essay to summarize what is admittedly a much more complicated historical situation, as well as to focus on problems that analysts face. There are no pretensions to having uncovered new information. There was no archival research, and there are no footnotes. Many other analysts and historians provided valuable research and insights, and we are all indebted to them. Readers desiring more details are encouraged to consult the list of recommended reading at the end of each chapter.

It should now be clear that *Challenges in Intelligence Analysis* is not meant to be a history of intelligence analysis, which would require many more examples. In World War II alone, there are many interesting cases that have not been addressed, including the Battle of Midway, D-Day, and the Battle of the Bulge. A complete history of analysis would also require much more context about the circumstances, personalities, technology, and other issues to give a full and balanced account of the role of intelligence analysis in history.

Too many people to name inspired and helped me to prepare this book, and I profoundly and gratefully thank them, as a group, for their assistance. Those to whom I owe a special debt of gratitude are colleagues from the following:

- Mercyhurst College, one of the institutions for which I have taught, which has the oldest academic program in intelligence analysis in the United States;
- Omnis Inc., one of the premier consulting firms in the field of analytic training;
- The many excellent analysts throughout the intelligence community with whom it has been a pleasure and an honor to work over the years;
- Last – but far from least – my students, whose questions and comments have continued to educate me.

The views expressed here are mine, as is the responsibility for any errors. All statements of fact, opinion, or analysis expressed are mine and do not reflect the official positions or views of the Central Intelligence Agency (CIA) or any other U.S. government agency. Nothing in the contents should be construed as asserting or implying U.S. government authentication of information or Agency endorsement of my views. The material has been reviewed by the CIA to prevent the disclosure of classified information.

Part I

Problems and Possible Solutions

T HERE ARE MANY DEFINITIONS OF INTELLIGENCE ANALYSIS, OFTEN USING as a starting point the views of Sherman Kent, the founder of the profession of intelligence analysis in the United States, who wrote that that it can be an organization, a process, or a product. Others see intelligence analysis as solving puzzles. Grappling with conundrums is part of what analysts do, but just finding a solution is not the main goal. Still others emphasize that dealing with secret and tightly controlled information, such as from spies or satellites, is what is important about intelligence analysis. This may have been true during the Cold War but is much less so in the age of the Internet, when vast amounts of data that could be useful are readily available. Moreover, many people in business and law enforcement use analytic techniques effectively without recourse to secret sources or methods.

The perspective in *Challenges in Intelligence Analysis: Lessons from 1300 BCE to the Present*, therefore, is that what is unique and important about intelligence analysis is that it supports decision making. This is especially the case when the decision maker is dealing with difficult problems, high stakes, and intense pressure to get it right. Although having quality data, including possibly secret data, is important, analyses can be effective without any secret input. What is really crucial about intelligence analysis is how one thinks about the problem, including factors such as the identifying the main issues, evaluating the evidence, and laying out the options and risks. Effective intelligence analysis is a complex process and therefore is extremely difficult.

Intelligence analysis as support to high-level decision making has taken place throughout history, and there have been both successes and failures along the way. Indeed, given the difficulties, the analyst is probably more likely to get it wrong than right. There are no guarantees or silver bullets, and the role of luck should not be discounted. For all of its shortcomings, however, intelligence analysis is certainly better than alternatives such consulting an oracle, trusting fate, or ignoring the problem.

1

The Main Challenges in Intelligence Analysis

DECIDING CAN OFTEN BE HARD; THERE ARE SO MANY POSSIBILITIES. What do I want for dinner, or what movie do I want to see? Making a decision can be even more difficult when there are high emotional or financial stakes. Whom do I want to marry? What is the best house or career? Even in marriage, housing, or careers, however, there is usually a finite number of options and a reasonable amount of information about them. How challenging is it, then, when the stakes are huge, the information confusing, the deadlines short, and the outcomes momentous, such as when a law enforcement officer is determining which suspect to arrest, a company is considering a new product, or, even worse, a government is trying to decide whether to go to war?

There are four interrelated aspects of decision making that are particularly troublesome: the uncertainty of the current situation, the unpleasant fact that from time to time there are surprises, the strong possibility that someone is trying to deceive, and the imponderable future.

Uncertainty

One of the main reasons why decisions are so hard to make is the nature of the situation in which choices are made. This is especially the case in the three areas in which intelligence analysis is most widely used: national security, law enforcement, and business. For even a simple decision, the environment can be complex, shifting, and uncertain. There is so much information to consider and so little time to deal with it. What is the situation in a foreign country? What are the capabilities of a new technology? When will an enemy strike or surrender? How many nuclear weapons are there, and where are they? What are the vulnerabilities, if any, of a terrorist group or an international criminal organization? Can we really understand a different culture, society, or viewpoint? In addition to the difficulty of these and similar questions, some crucial things are just unknowable, especially in advance: What is really the motivation or breaking point of a terrorist leader or foreign dictator?

In an effort to cope with uncertainty we seek facts, data that we believe to be true. "Facts" may not always be helpful, however. A search on the Internet yields more than a million hits; what are we supposed to do with that? Even with a flood of data, we often seem not to have the one piece we really need. What if one reliable newspaper says the stock market is about to go up, but another says it is about to go down? How do we understand and defeat an enemy who might have a value system different from our own? All of this is maddening enough in our private lives; what about a military commander or law enforcement officer who is trying to save lives, or CEO of a major corporation who has thousands of jobs at stake and millions of dollars in investment committed?

Accuracy alone is not enough, however; analysts and decision makers also want data that are clear and relevant – that is to say, evidence. The concept of evidence, compelling support for a particular point, is borrowed from the legal world. A court of law has high standards for what constitutes evidence and is able to take the time to get it right. Intelligence analysts, in contrast, rarely have unlimited time and usually have to work with data that do not meet legal standards. As a result, some analysts are reluctant to use the term "evidence." Nonetheless, the idea that some data are better than other data and that analysts should seek the best data available to alleviate uncertainty is a useful one.

Surprise

To deal with uncertainty and take advantage of the information that they do have, people, especially leaders, also make plans. They decide to increase the budget, purchase a new weapons system, or line up a new ally in the hope that such measures will help them to sleep at night. Then comes the surprise – the unanticipated, major discontinuity – the attack, the new weapon, the stock market crash, the hurricane, or some other catastrophe that changes everything. Consideration of trends often helps in understanding what is going on; every now and then it does not. Situations and trends that have been going on for years or even decades shift direction and speed overnight. How does one recognize and assess something new, a situation in which past experience is of little help in understanding what is happening?

One of the main reasons for uncertainty is that situations are often inter-active; there is someone else out there trying to accomplish his or her goals, which may not be the same as yours. As soldiers sometimes like to say, "The enemy has a vote." The fact that other active, smart, and probably scheming individuals are involved means that they will be changing their minds and adjusting their actions in response to your actions. An accurate fact or guess about what they will do quickly becomes irrelevant or even harmful when they change their minds in response to evolving circumstances.

Deception

This interactive nature of decision making is particularly dangerous when the adversary is trying to deceive. Intelligence analysts believe that there are two aspects of the problem: denial and deception. Denial is trying to limit the opponent's access to accurate information, and deception is trying to direct their attention elsewhere. An example of denial is commanders camouflaging their tanks or hiding them in a cave. An example of deception is those commanders placing dummy tanks at a point where they did not intend to attack. Denial and deception are especially attractive to the weaker side as a force multiplier. A cloak of denial and deception is even more effective if it appeals to the target's preconceptions, prejudices, and fears and if the denial and deception contains a core of truth. Deception is also integral to the work of spies and terrorists. How do we detect such dangerous deceivers?

The Future

All of this – uncertainty, surprise, and deception – does little to prepare us for one of the great imponderables: the future. The future is, by its very nature, unknowable. There are so many possibilities and so little evidence; again, the situation is shifting as others respond to our actions. Will a military campaign succeed? What will be the impact of a new technology? Can we accurately anticipate how an opponent will respond? What will we do if something unexpected happens?

More Difficulties in Analysis

All of these challenges would be daunting for anyone, but they are especially demanding for intelligence analysts, whose job it is to cope with them on a daily basis. Some of the difficulties are widely shared by all human beings, whereas others are particular to working on tough and significant problems in large organizations, such as military units or intelligence agencies.

Faced with a flood of data, the human mind tries to make sense of it all with cognitive shortcuts and filters otherwise it would be overwhelmed. Although this method can be quick and efficient, it can also be inaccurate. Analysts need a framework of understanding, but is it the right framework? Tanks and troops are moving out of their depots and barracks; is it a coup, preparations to attack a neighbor, or just the National Day Parade getting started? The mind could not function without forming such patterns, so the issue is not how to get rid of mental categories or filters, but rather how to understand them and assure that they do not become pitfalls. Often the problem is not just the data that the analyst receives – or does not receive – but what the analyst makes of those data.

The process of analysis is, by its nature, prone to some errors. Psychologists say that accurate judgments are most difficult to make when people have been receiving data of varying degrees of quality, a little at a time, over an extended period, and are then pressed to make an assessment in a hurry. This is exactly the world of the intelligence analyst. Some potential pitfalls for analysts, based on the way the brain functions, include the availability bias, which occurs when analysts give vivid data (such as a good story) more value than unfamiliar or dry data (such as statistics); and the pattern bias, which occurs when analysts assume there is a design or plan when there has actually been randomness or coincidence. It is the pattern bias that produces conspiracy theories. Some biases can affect those who assess analysis after the situation has clarified, such the hindsight bias, which occurs when events in retrospect appear clearer and easier to predict than they originally were.

Other potentially distorting filters are built up over time as a result of an analyst's background such as education, professional experience, and travel. These mindsets or frameworks for understanding how the world works are easy to form but difficult to change, and data – even if accurate – that do not fit into a given mindset are often dismissed or devalued. An example is mirror imaging, which occurs when people assume that others, even in a different culture, would deal with a situation more or less the same way in which they would. Another example is the rational actor model, when analysts believe that decisions in an organization are made on the basis of a logical calculation, such as weighing ends and means or risks and rewards. A particular danger for experienced analysts is the paradox of expertise, which occurs when those who have worked intently on an issue for a long time are least able to detect major changes as they have so much invested intellectually in their frameworks of analysis. Moreover, their long experience makes them overconfident about the accuracy of their judgments.

There are also challenges in analysis based on the nature of intelligence. The work of professional intelligence analysts is traditionally portrayed as being part of what is known as the intelligence cycle, a model of the intelligence process that tries to capture the various aspects of producing intelligence and emphasizes responsiveness to decision makers. There are a number of different versions of the elements of the intelligence cycle, but they generally include the following:

- Requirements, or what the decision maker wants and needs to know;
- Planning and directing collectors and analysts to respond to those requirements;
- Collection of the data that will fulfill the requirements;
- Processing the data collected to make it more useful through operations such as decryption or translation;
- Analyzing the processed data to give it meaning and context;
- Putting the analysis into a form the decision maker can use;
- Dissemination, in a timely fashion, of the analysis to those who need it, and
- Obtaining feedback on whether the analysis was effective (and, if necessary, turning that feedback into new requirements).

For an intelligence success, everything in the cycle has to go right; a failure, however, can occur even if only one thing goes wrong.

Like all models, the intelligence cycle provides a general picture but does not necessarily describe all cases. In real life, the model is not always accurate in many of the steps of the cycle. Senior decision makers rarely have the time or interest to provide detailed requirements, analysts can be wrong, and accurate analysis can be too late to be helpful. In addition, actual intelligence work is not linear, as portrayed in the model; there are usually some contacts taking place simultaneously between decision makers, collectors, and analysts. Other important things to note are that intelligence analysts are not the only sources of input for decision making and that analysts are not in control of significant aspects of the overall process.

Another set of difficulties specific to intelligence involves collection. Clandestine technical systems collect whatever images, telephone conversations, and other material they can, rather than only what is needed. In the end, there is probably too much classified data to manage effectively. Quality control is difficult given the huge amounts of material that both clandestine and open collection systems produce. Vulnerability to denial and deception remains significant. The nugget that is both true and illuminating remains elusive.

The final set of challenges is in the wider bureaucratic and political environment in which most analysts work. Although there has been some progress, sharing of information between agencies is not optimal. Budgets for people and equipment increase and decrease, sometimes unpredictably. Concern for security may make it difficult to do things such as approve travel or hire foreign-born linguists. Vertical management review and horizontal coordination of draft products with colleagues certainly takes time, and may result in the lowest common denominator of viewpoint. Criticism from politicians and the press encourages some analysts and managers to play it safe. Analytical assessments might not always be welcomed by decision makers, especially if they differ from strongly held policy preferences. Then, of course, the computer crashes just when the analyst needs it the most.

Given the serious and widespread nature of these problems, is there any hope for dealing with them?

Recommended Reading

Andrew, Christopher, *For the President's Eyes Only: Secret Intelligence and the American Presidency from Washington to Bush*, New York: Harper Perennial, 1996.

Betts, Richard K., *Enemies of Intelligence: Knowledge and Power in American National Security*, New York: Columbia University Press, 2007.

George, Roger Z., and Bruce, James B., eds., *Analyzing Intelligence: Origins, Obstacles, and Innovations*, Washington, DC: Georgetown University Press, 2008.

Kennedy, Robert, *Of Knowledge and Power: The Complexities of National Intelligence*, Westport, CT: Praeger Security International, 2008.

Kent, Sherman, *Strategic Intelligence for American World Policy*, Princeton, NJ: Princeton University Press, 1949.

Lowenthal, Mark, *Intelligence: From Secrets to Policy*, 4th ed., Washington, DC: CQ Press, 2008.

Russell, Richard, *Sharpening Strategic Intelligence: Why the CIA Gets It Wrong, and What Needs to be Done to Get It Right*, New York, Cambridge University Press, 2007.

2

Attempts to Deal with the Challenges

Analysis is as much about questions as it is about answers. It is about understanding various ways to think about a problem and realizing that not every analytic method applies to every problem. The effective analyst has a collection of approaches, techniques, and tools, along with the willingness and patience to apply them. These analytic methods have been accumulated over time and from many different sources.

Uncertainty

To deal with uncertainty, analysts seek to provide context, a sense of the bigger picture. A useful first step in understanding context is problem restatement, also known as bounding the problem, which involves making sure that all relevant and important aspects of the issue are taken into account. Virtually every issue has various aspects, such as economic, social, political, and legal; therefore, analysts need to take the various perspectives into account. Analysts also provide context by looking for abstract linkages such as patterns, relationships, and trends. Understanding such linkages involves asking such questions as whether developments are new, accelerated, or having more impact.

A specific tool for providing context is the chronology, or the listing of events in the order in which they happened. This order may well be different from the order in which reports about the events were received; thus it promotes clarity about where individual events fit into the overall pattern. Briefly summarizing the various events, to fit them into a chronology, also helps analysts to focus on the key elements and the relative value of reports.

Table 1, for example, is a chronology of the dates and locations of early attacks carried out by groups or individuals affiliated with the al-Qaeda terrorist group:

Table 1. Early al-Qaeda Attacks

December 29, 1992	Aden, Yemen
October 3, 1993	Mogadishu, Somalia
August 7, 1998	Nairobi, Kenya, and Dar es Salaam, Tanzania
October 12, 2000	Aden, Yemen
September 11, 2001	New York City and Washington, D.C., USA
October 12, 2002	Bali, Indonesia
May 12, 2003	Riyadh, Saudi Arabia
March 11, 2004	Madrid, Spain
July 7, 2005	London, UK

A variation of the chronology is the timeline, which arrays events against a scale, such as days, months, years, or other intervals (see Figure 1). The timeline makes clusters of activity or gaps in the flow of events more readily apparent and may suggest other questions that an analyst may want to pursue, such as whether gaps mean that nothing was really happening or that there was just no reporting. A refinement is to have two or more parallel timelines, on a related subject, in the same graphic. This kind of presentation helps to highlight the interaction between different factors, such as locations or individuals, in the same time frame.

Figure 2 shows exactly the same data as are given in the chronology, but notice how, by arraying the examples against a scale and on multiple tracks (in this case, geographic), the analyst can get a much clearer picture of the acceleration and spread of al-Qaeda operations over a relatively short period of time in the group's early years. Such a graphic presentation goes a long way in explaining the striking impact the group had.

Both chronologies and timelines can be extremely useful in improving the analysis of cause and effect, as the former has to precede the latter. They can also highlight confirming and contradicting data: what fits into the overall picture and what does not. Organization based on time provides the basis for a coherent narrative, especially of a lengthy or complex series of events, and can be used to suggest hypotheses.

Another way to approach problems that reduces uncertainty is to think in terms of models, or generalizations, of activity based on a large number of observations. A model focuses on the aspects of a situation that are funda-mental, significant, and widely applicable to other situations. For instance, what does a typical terrorist attack, rigged election, economic recession, murder, successful product, or any other issue look like? After a model is

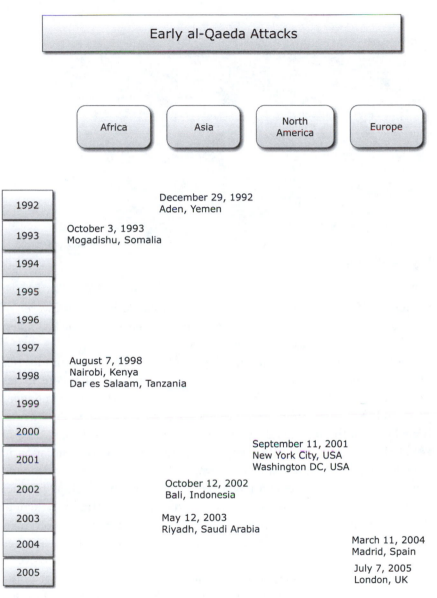

Figure 1. Timeline

constructed, based on known examples, less clear cases can be compared to the model to see if they fit, based on the logic principle of generalization. Generalization is the belief that characteristics that are true of a small, known sample are true of a wider population that may not be as well known or may be more difficult to study. Public opinion polls are examples of using

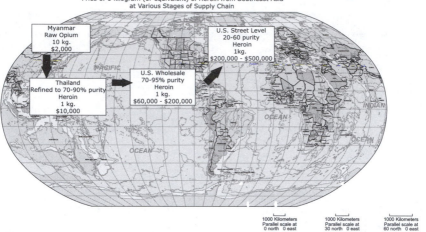

Figure 2. Flow chart

the logical principle of generalization. Analysts should be wary, however, of the logical fallacy of making hasty generalization based on small samples, which is one of the reasons for stereotypes.

Another method by which to get clarity is to look at a problem in terms of flow or process (i.e., how things change over time and what contributes to that change). This approach breaks down a process into its component parts and then seeks to understand how each part functions, the interactions between the parts, and the overall process. Flow can be captured in visual charts, which, like other graphics, can show a complex situation in a single picture. A flow chart, for example, helps the user to understand routine processes that remain much the same over time, such as product development, preparations for a terrorist attack, or industrial production. Another example of a process or flow is how the price and the profit margin of an illegal drug increases as it moves through the supply chain (see Figure 2).

A variation used in competitive intelligence, or intelligence used in the business world to improve competitiveness, is value chain analysis. The value chain portrays the internal processes of a firm – such as research and development; supply of resources; manufacturing, distribution, and marketing of products; and sales and service – and examines particularly how efficiently those procedures are working. Value chain analysis could reveal problems and vulnerabilities, such as whether a firm is too dependent on a few suppliers, has limited plant capacity, lacks well-trained personnel, or is using outdated technology. This emphasis on looking at how efficiently a process works could also be applied to other problems, such government decision making and the production of weapons of mass destruction.

Another variation, used in law enforcement, is an event flow chart, which lays out the times and dates of a specific event, including the origins and consequences. Parallel charts can be used to show events in the lives of victims and suspects. Several similar event flow analyses from unknown subjects may indicate modus operandi or a serial offender.

Another valuable analytic tool for reducing uncertainty and providing context is the matrix, a grid that indicates the relationships between two different sets of data that can readily be broken down into various subcategories. A matrix could be used, for example, to evaluate various weapons systems according to different aspects, such as cost, effectiveness, and production time. Another possibility could be to assess the varying threats from different criminal gangs by comparing and contrasting factors such as manpower, scope of operations, and types of activity. A series of matrices could show changes in these factors over time (e.g., increases or decreases). A matrix is also useful because it is another way – this time through empty cells in the matrix – to show what an analyst does not know, thus helping to guide further research. The computerized spreadsheet is another version that can be used to summarize and manipulate a variety of numeric values.

Matrices do not have to be large, with many cells, to be valuable. A variation used in competitive intelligence that involves only four cells is the analysis of Strengths, Weaknesses, Opportunities, and Threats (SWOT), one of the best-known strategic planning tools taught in business schools (see Figure 3). A SWOT matrix lays out these four forces with which a firm will have to deal, considers the more significant interactions between them, and then prompts the formulation of an appropriate strategic plan. Strengths are what a firm does well and makes it distinctive in the market place, and weakness are what a firm lacks or does poorly. These factors are internal within a company, and management has a degree of control over them. Opportunities, which create demand for a company's products or services, and threats, which are sources of potential harm, are market factors; management has less control over them.

Within each part of the quadrant the analyst lists the 3–5 items concerning the firm that best apply, prioritizes them, and then formulates a strategy for dealing with the situation presented in that quadrant. For example, if the organization has several internal strengths and is facing serious external

SWOT Matrix

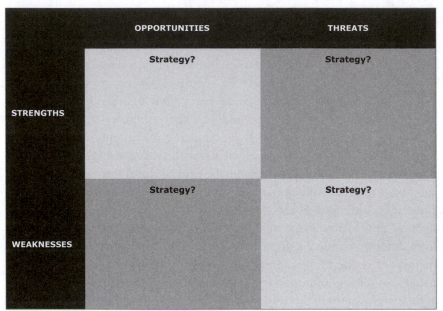

Figure 3. SWOT matrix

threats, it may be facing a decision to either shift resources to weak areas to maintain them or concentrate on preserving strengths and let weak areas go. The most dangerous quadrant is the combination of many internal weaknesses and serious external threats; the fate of the business or organization could be at stake, and a wise and robust strategy is essential.

An analytical approach for dealing with uncertainty based on relationships is link analysis, also known as network or association analysis. Link analysis originated in law enforcement efforts to better understand gangs and espionage networks; later it was used in counterterrorism. The basic elements of link analysis are nodes and links. Nodes can be things such as people, locations, telephones, or bank accounts. Links are the connections between the nodes, which can be pathways for factors such as power, information, or resources. Nodes with more links tend to have more available resources, including information and options, which are key attributes of influence or power.

Network analysis also provides a way to think about problems. Thinking in terms of networks differs from traditional organizational analysis, such as the classic organizational chart or "wiring diagram," which is based on the established hierarchy in organizations such as a business, army, or government. It shows formal relationships, but may not reflect important informal networks or subtle changes over time.

In contrast, in assessing networks the analyst should look at many more potential linkages. Rather than looking at the up and down pathways that are typical in a hierarchy, network analysis looks at multiple possible links, and thus an enhanced capacity for sensing and communicating. This approach is likely to give a different perspective on how an organization functions. For example, the experienced secretary or young computer geek may make a contribution far beyond their place in the formal hierarchy.

A key characteristic of networks is how powerful, flexible, and resilient they can be. Information, funds, or other things can be passed along a variety of different links or pathways. Multiple pathways can enhance the speed of knowledge and reaction, and a variety of potential links also means there are alternatives if some links are damaged. The potential power of multiple links has been greatly enhanced by technology, such as computers, telephones, faxes, and the Internet, all of which make it possible to transmit larger amounts of information much faster. Commercial encryption enhances these capabilities even further by shielding them from outsiders. Terrorists and criminals are increasingly using the network form of organization, as it has distinct advantages in terms of effectiveness and security.

Nonetheless, with careful targeting networks can be weakened or destroyed, and link analysis can help to uncover vulnerabilities. The key is to strike at as many important nodes as possible in a short period of time. This slows the adaptability and resilience that are the main strengths of a network. Ideally, from the point of view of the attacker, the network can be turned on itself by using the many links to more quickly transmit destructive tendencies, such as fear, distrust, and confusion.

Link analysis also lends itself to visual presentation (see Figure 4). The strength or intensity of relationships can be determined through factors such as the number of phone calls or meetings. Strength can be portrayed by varying the width of lines showing the links, with narrow lines representing weak relationships and wider lines representing stronger ones. The nature of relationships can be shown by using unidirectional arrows to indicate one-way relationships, such as control, whereas bidirectional arrows can indicate mutual relationships, such as cooperation or negotiation. Various colors can be used to differentiate between different types of activity, for example, cash transactions, telephone calls, and movement of commodities, such as illegal drugs, weapons, or stolen goods. Portrayal of the links can also be used to show the quality of reporting, with dotted lines showing suspected links,

Link Chart

Basic Elements

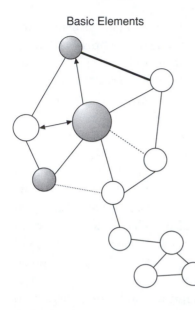

Figure 4. Basic elements of a link chart

dashed lines showing known but unconfirmed ties, and solid lines showing confirmed connections. Like a matrix, a link chart has value as a way to summarize a large amount of data.

These various types of graphics – timelines, flow charts, matrices, and link charts – are valuable to analysts because they take advantage of the power of visualization to show an overall picture, summarize large amounts of data, and indicate gaps. When entering data into charts, however, analysts need to remember that the results depend on the quality of the data used, according to the well-known principle of "garbage in, garbage out." To enhance the quality of results, analysts need to consider factors such as the accuracy, plausibility, completeness, and relevance of the data. Also important are the expertise, access, objectivity, and reliability of the source. The possibility of denial and deception should also be considered.

One of the best ways to compensate for poor data is to seek data from multiple, independent sources. In intelligence analysis, this is accomplished by taking into account reports from human sources (commonly abbreviated in the intelligence world as HUMINT); open sources, such as the media (OSINT); as well as inputs from technical means of collection: signals intelligence (SIGINT), imagery intelligence (IMINT), and measurement and signature intelligence (MASINT). Each of these has its own advantages and disadvantages. An image from a satellite or an intercepted conversation, for example, may be accurate, but they also may be unrepresentative samples of what is happening. Other reports from a human source or a survey of the media can provide context that helps to better understand reporting from technical collection. Thus, with several sources, the strengths of one can be used to compensate for the weaknesses of others.

Reporting from multiple sources helps to reduce uncertainty by providing information about the various aspects of a problem: economic, geographic, technological, political, and – depending on the issue – potentially several others. Some aspects may seem to be less important but are more observable or accessible. The analysts' job is to make valid inferences from what they know to what they do not know. For example, an enemy may have hidden his tanks and other equipment, but some idea of their number and location can be derived by tracking fuel shipments or other support functions.

The fact that available data are rarely complete and of high quality can produce another problem for analysts: Gaps in data are filled by making assumptions. Analysts do not know the intentions of a rival company or the exact strength of a terrorist group, so they assume certain things as they construct their view of the situation. Assumptions are especially dangerous when they play a predominant role in the overall argument, that is to say, when the argument would not stand without them. Assumptions are particularly insidious because they are often not explicit. Analysts have to articulate their assumptions clearly and then examine them for credibility, relevance, and other factors, just as they would for facts. Analysts often make assumptions about the future, and the easiest, and most dangerous, assumptions involve status quo thinking, that is to say, that present trends or conditions will continue more or less unchanged.

Therefore, as part of reducing uncertainty, it is a good idea to do a check of assumptions from time to time. Things to consider include whether there are any data to support the assumptions and are they still valid, what data would undermine or refute the assumptions, and how much of the analysis would be undermined if these assumptions turned out to be false?

A final way to deal with uncertainty is to consider multiple explanations and then try to determine which is the most plausible. Considering a wide range of plausible explanations, or hypotheses, makes it more likely that the best one will be found. As is the case in scientific inquiry, hypotheses in intelligence analysis are preliminary, tentative possibilities, meant to be discussed and tested, rather than a final answer. In fact, accepting a single hypothesis too early can mean that valid data could be devalued or dismissed because they do not fit the hastily chosen conclusion, which is also known as the confirmation bias. If there are too few hypotheses, the analyst might miss the unconventional, barely emerging, or disguised explanation. It is also the case, however, that having too many hypotheses, dozens or even hundreds, is not useful to the decision maker. A large number of hypotheses can probably be better managed by clustering them around central themes.

There are many ways to generate hypotheses, and this is an area in which imagination and creativity can be especially helpful. Two basic strategies are (1) to look at the details of a specific situation (what are the possibilities based on factors such as historic precedents, as well as key plays and their interactions) and (2) to look at a wide range of similar situations (what has been common in other comparable cases). Other ways include tracing cause-and-effect relationships; looking at the situation from another perspective, such as looking at a military issue in an economic context; and determining if there are hidden explanations available only through clandestine information. A final useful tool for generating hypotheses is the anomaly, a fact that does not fit into the existing range of hypotheses and is a warning sign that the analyst needs to come up with more hypotheses. Anomalies should be valued and explored, rather than dismissed as troublesome or inconvenient.

There are also a number of methods for evaluating hypotheses. One of the best is Analysis of Competing Hypotheses (ACH), pioneered by Richards Heuer, a former Central Intelligence Agency (CIA) officer (see Figure 5). ACH uses the matrix format to array the available evidence against the hypotheses and then uses the process of elimination – which hypothesis has the least inconsistent evidence – to determine the strongest one. This method also highlights the diagnosticity of evidence (i.e., which evidence helps to distinguish between hypotheses); some evidence, even if true, is not useful because it supports several different hypotheses. Other methods to evaluate hypotheses include intuition based on experience, Occam's razor (the simplest explanation), cui bono (who benefits, or incentives), plausibility, and quality of evidence. Care should be taken in evaluating whether to use quality of evidence, however, as strong evidence could be used to prove another hypothesis.

Surprise

Formulating multiple hypotheses is also valuable as a way to minimize the chances of being surprised. Analysts who push beyond the traditional or the

Analysis of Competing Hypotheses Matrix

	Hypotheses					
	Hypothesis 1	Hypothesis 2	Hypothesis 3	Hypothesis 4	Hypothesis 5	Hypothesis 6
Evidence A						
Evidence B						
Evidence C						
Evidence D						
Evidence E						
Evidence F						
Evidence G						
Evidence H						
Evidence I						
Evidence J						
Evidence K						
Evidence L						
Total Is						

Which hypothesis has the least inconsistent evidence?

Figure 5. Template for an ACH matrix

obvious and use creativity to envision a range of possibilities are less likely to be caught unaware.

Another useful way to avoid surprise is to provide warning by looking at indicators, a procedure widely used in military analysis. Adversaries will rarely be so accommodating as to clearly announce their intentions, so analysts must look for indirect signs that suggest what might be happening. The basic idea is that when an enemy prepares for an attack – that is, makes the transition from peace to war – it is a complex and lengthy process, and there is a wide range of observable actions that have to take place. For example, troops and equipment have to move, supplies have to be gathered, and communications systems have to be activated. Appropriate indicators are selected based on things such as past operations or exercises, the adversary's doctrine, and the analyst's knowledge of factors such as a country's political system, economy, and infrastructure. There could be dozens, or even hundreds, of indicators to track. This approach of looking for indicators based on an understanding of the overall issue or situation could be used in other fields such as counterintelligence and counternarcotics.

Two other useful frameworks for thinking about surprise and warning are risk and threat. There are many definitions of risk, but in intelligence analysis a useful one is to see risk as a combination of magnitude and impact. If a great deal is at stake and the probability of negative developments is high, then there is considerable risk; if both the stakes and the likelihood are low, the risk is low. Like risk, there are many definitions of threat. Intelligence analysts have often tried to assess the level of threat by looking at a combination of capabilities and intentions. If an adversary both wants to strike and has the ability to do so, the level of threat is high; if both are low, the threat is low. Careful observation and assessment are necessary to calculate risks and threats.

To begin a threat analysis, start by identifying whether the threat actually exists. This seemingly obvious step is often overlooked. Then, when an actual individual or group is identified, ask whether it has the capability to cause harm, in terms of factors such as training, weapons, and organization. Next, determine whether those who constitute the suspected threat have a record of past attacks. Information on past attacks may suggest how the groups might attack in the future. Also, look at whether they have revealed their intentions by issuing specific threats. Finally, be alert to indicators of the actual preparations for an attack, such as purchase of weapons, travel of personnel, or surveillance of potential targets.

Another use of a matrix is to lay out indicators in a grid using a system known as a stoplight matrix, with green indicating normal activity (low risk or threat), yellow indicating caution (something to be investigated), and red indicating the need for immediate attention and perhaps action (see Figure 6). Analysts use large amounts of data, along with their own judgments, to assign the appropriate color to a range of indicators. One of the many benefits of this technique is that the overall situation can be grasped at a glance just by observing which color is predominant. Another benefit is that anomalies that might prompt further investigation could be become obvious.

The greatly simplified hypothetical examples in Figure 6 show the situation on two different days. The top chart clearly shows a nonthreatening situation, as the predominant color is green; but there are several anomalies that call for further investigation: Why have leaves been cancelled at all types of facilities, and why is the situation at the airfields at such variance from that at the army and naval bases? On the bottom chart, the situation is more dire, given the large amount of red; but why haven't all leaves been cancelled, and why aren't naval bases observing radio silence?

Another way to try to anticipate surprise and discontinuity is to look at the situation from the adversary's point of view, to think about what the other

Stoplight Matrix 1				
	Leaves Cancelled	Reserves Called Up	Radio Silence	Extra Supplies Accumulated
Airfields	R	Y	G	Y
Army Bases	R	G	G	G
Naval Bases	R	G	G	G

Stoplight Matrix 2				
	Leaves Cancelled	Reserves Called Up	Radio Silence	Extra Supplies Accumulated
Airfields	Y	R	R	R
Army Bases	Y	R	R	R
Naval Bases	Y	R	G	R

Figure 6. Stoplight matrix

side would do. Analytic expertise regarding the adversary is particularly useful in doing this. There are a variety of ways to generate a different perspective, including:

- Setting up a Red Team, a procedure from military training in which a unit is explicitly assigned the duty of conducting itself the way the enemy would;
- Devil's Advocacy, from the Roman Catholic Church's procedure for considering an individual for sainthood, in which arguments are mustered for and against. More broadly, it is a way to challenge the consensus or conventional wisdom; and
- Team A/Team B, used at the CIA during the Cold War; involves having two different groups look at the same evidence to see if they come to the same conclusion.

All of these techniques can also useful overcoming cognitive shortcomings, but they need to be validated and done properly. For example, Devil's Advocacy can be undercut and become just a "check the box" exercise if the advocate is not sincere or if the job is assigned to the same person over and over.

Deception

Many of the analytic techniques and frameworks already mentioned are also useful for uncovering denial and deception. One of the most valuable is having a variety of independent sources; it may be possible to fool one channel of information, but it is increasingly difficult to mislead as the number of channels is increased. Other useful practices include not jumping to hasty conclusions, considering multiple explanations and outcomes, and being alert to the possible significance of missing information or things that are not happening ("the dog that didn't bark"). Smugness, rigidity, overconfidence, and complacency, in contrast, leave both analysts and leaders vulnerable to being duped. Successful deceivers include an element of reality and play on the preconceptions, biases, and fears of those they are attempting to trick.

   Specific conditions that analyst should be alert to as indicators of possible deception include obvious, neat patterns that point to one option or a small body of evidence that is internally consistent; these could be manufactured with the goal of creating a false impression. Anomalies, facts that do not easily fit into existing frameworks, are also potential indicators of deception.

It is also important to study the adversary, noting whether it has demonstrated a capability for deception, whether it has used it in the past, and how effective past efforts were. This kind of knowledge involves not only awareness of the details of factors such as an opponent's history and doctrine, but also an ability to see the situation from another perspective, sometimes one that is different than one's own. If there is a high likelihood of deception, consider what the opponent's best option is, even if there is, at present, no evidence supporting it.

The Future

For dealing with the future, an effective analytic technique is to construct scenarios portraying a range of outcomes. There can be, of course, a huge number of possible outcomes; therefore, the challenge for the analyst is to come up with a manageable number of plausible ones. One of the best ways to do this is to start with drivers, a procedure that originated in business planning. Drivers are the main forces – political, demographic, technological, or other – that will shape the future. Pick what are, in the analyst's opinion, the two main drivers, and place them on two intersecting axes to create four interactions (see Figure 7).

In Figure 7, it is postulated that the two main forces that will shape China's future are the degree of democracy in the government and the level of freedom in the economy. These drivers provide the basic elements for four plausible scenarios. Based on knowledge of the situation in China, flesh these out with some details of what each scenario would look like. Also, identify some signposts – observable and anticipated events or developments – which would show that events are moving into one or the other of the quadrants. Keep in mind that there might be wildcards – low-probability, high-impact events, such as natural disasters – that might also play a role in shaping the future.

Thinking about future outcomes is often hindered by arguments over which result is most likely. What can get lost in such discussions is consideration of an outcome that may not be likely but would have a serious impact if it did happen. One way to focus attention on an unlikely but still plausible outcome is to use what is known as "What if?" analysis, which is to postulate an outcome, without taking a stand on whether it will actually happen. Constructing a "What if?" scenario is another opportunity for creativity and imagination. After the scenario is laid out in detail, try to come up with plausible steps through which it could happen. If it is possible and could

Scenarios Quadrant

China's Future

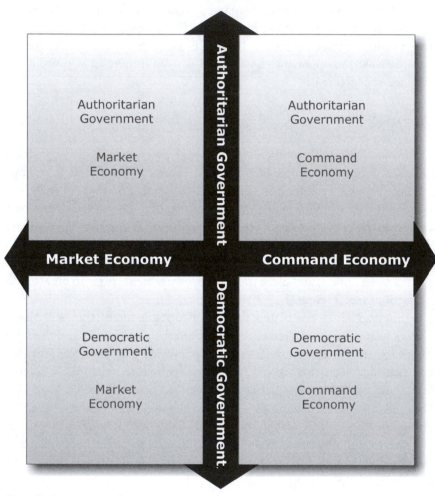

Figure 7. Scenarios quadrant

have a serious impact, it should be included when making plans for dealing with the future.

Based on the nature of the future, with its multiple possibilities, it is also useful for intelligence analysts to think in terms of contingencies: If A happens, then events 1, 2, and 3 are likely to follow; but if B happens, then events 4, 5, and 6 are more likely. Because there is a variety of options for the future and some are more likely than others, analysts sometimes rank the alternatives in terms of probability.

Tracing a Government's Decision to Go to War

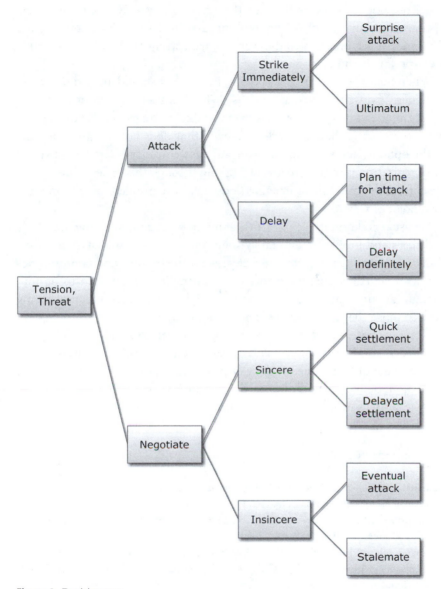

Figure 8. Decision tree

Another way to think about the future is as an outcome of a series of decisions, in what is known as a decision or hypotheses tree (see Figure 8). Begin by laying out the basic logical options or choices that would be available to an individual or organization. Then consider what future choices there would be for each of those options. Construct as many layers as possible, but not so many as to make the exercise unwieldy. Try to make the options mutually exclusive. The resulting chart will aid in understanding the dynamics of the problem, and the end of each string of choices is a possible scenario for the future.

When the hypothesis tree is laid out, the analyst should array the existing evidence against the various options. Where is there the most evidence? Does this mean that this option is the most likely? Are gaps in reporting now more obvious? Is there any valid evidence that does not fit easily into any of the options, and what does that mean? Also consider where an individual or organization is in the process of working through this series of decisions. Be careful to avoid mirror imaging (looking at the problem only from one's own point of view).

Decision makers often complain that intelligence analysts bring them only bad news and problems, and rarely solutions. It is a good idea, then, when thinking about the future to make clear what the options and opportunities are, as well. The scenarios quadrant, for example, can be used to prompt thought about what opportunities there might be in each quadrant, being alert to those that come up in several quadrants.

None of these analytic techniques is guaranteed to avoid an intelligence failure or an unwise decision. To maximize potential benefits, analysts should have a range of techniques at their disposal and keep an open mind. These general guidelines have not been derived in a vacuum, but are based on many examples over a long period of time.

Recommended Reading

Bennett, Michael, and Waltz, Edward, *Counterdeception Principles and Applications for National Security*, Boston, MA: Artech House, 2007.

Clark, Robert M., *Intelligence Analysis: A Target Centric Approach*, 2nd ed., Washington, DC: CQ Press, 2007.

Fleisher, Craig, and Bensoussan, Babette, *Strategic and Competitive Analysis: Methods and Techniques for Analyzing Business Competition*, Upper Saddle River, NJ: Pearson Education, 2003.

Godson, Roy, and Wirtz, James J., *Strategic Denial and Deception: The Twenty-First Century Challenge*, New Brunswick, NJ: Transaction Publishers, 2002.

Grabo, Cynthia M., *Anticipating Surprise: Analysis for Strategic Warning*, Washington, DC: Center for Strategic Intelligence Research, 2002.

Heuer, Richards J., *Psychology of Intelligence Analysis*, Washington, DC: Center for the Study of Intelligence, 1999; available online at: https://www.cia.gov/library/center-for-the-study-of-intelligence/csi-publications/books-and-monographs/psychology-of-intelligence-analysis/index.html.

Heuer, Richards J., and Pherson, Randolph H., *Structured Analytic Techniques for Intelligence Analysis*, Washington, DC: CQ Press, 2010.

Jones, Morgan, *The Thinker's Toolbox: 14 Powerful Techniques for Problem Solving*, New York: Three Rivers Press, 1998.

Peterson, Marilyn, *Applications in Criminal Analysis*, Westport, CT: Greenwood Press, 1995.

Schwartz, Peter, *The Art of the Long View: Planning for the Future in an Uncertain World*, New York: Doubleday, 1996.

Part II

From the Ancient World to Modern Times

A S FAR BACK AS THERE HAVE BEEN ORGANIZED SOCIETIES AND RECORDS of their activities, there have been wars. To achieve victory in those conflicts, military commanders realized that it was to their advantage to have accurate information about factors such as the lay of the land, the strength and location of enemy forces, and the opposing commander's capabilities and intentions.

Looking back from the perspective of the age of the Internet and trying to understand the analytic challenges centuries ago, it is worthwhile to think for a few moments about how different things were.

Records are not always complete or accurate when looking back at the distant past. It is clear, however, that the power, range, and mobility of weapons were quite restricted. The introduction of gunpowder increased capabilities, but muskets and cannons still had limited range. Moreover, armies and fleets could move only at the speed at which a man could march or a ship sail. Providing sufficient supplies also limited the size, duration, and scope of operations.

Information – the lifeblood of intelligence – could move a bit faster than armies or fleets, at the speed of a galloping horse, although this speed was difficult to maintain over extremely long distances.

In the ancient world, the effort to obtain accurate and useful information before making a decision revealed what would turn out to be timeless problems such as how to assess risk, what constitutes reliable evidence, how to uncover and deal with deception, and how to avoid getting caught by surprise.

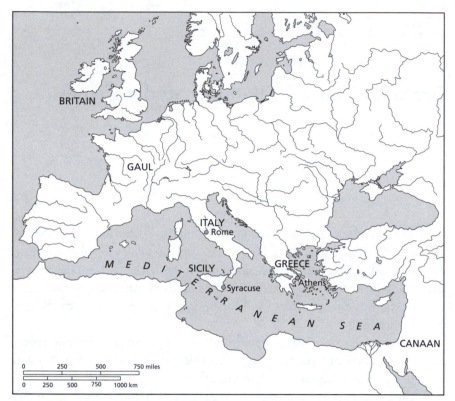

Figure 9. The ancient Mediterranean

3

Moses Sends Spies into Canaan

According to the biblical account in the book of numbers, after leaving Egypt and then spending many years of tribulation in the Sinai desert, the Israelites approached the land of Canaan (modern Israel and parts of the surrounding countries), which had been promised to them by God. Before undertaking the dangerous and important task of launching an invasion, there were certain things that Moses, the commander, wanted to know. Following divine instructions, he sent the leaders of the twelve Israelite tribes on a mission to clandestinely collect information about what lay ahead. According to the King James version of the Bible, Moses' guidance to the spies was:

> ... see the land, what it is, and the people that dwelleth therein, whether they be strong or weak, few or many; and what the land is that they dwell in, whether it be good or bad; and what cities they be that they dwell in, whether in tents, or in strong holds; and what the land is, whether it be fat or lean, whether there be wood therein, or not. And be ye of good courage, and bring of the fruit of the land.

The twelve spies spent forty days in Canaan looking for indicators of the strengths and vulnerabilities of those who occupied the land they wanted. When they returned, the tribal leaders:

> ... brought back word unto them, and unto all the congregation, and shewed them the fruit of the land. And they told him, and said, "We came unto the land whither thou sentest us, and surely it floweth with milk and honey; and this is the fruit of it. Nevertheless the people be strong that dwell in the land, and the cities are walled, and very great ... "

Therefore, in addition to their observations and conclusions, the spies brought back proof – the fruit of the land – to demonstrate its fertility.

Then the discussion began about the implications of the spies' observations so that the Israelites could consider their options and weigh the risks:

> . . . Caleb stilled the people before Moses, and said, Let us go up at once, and possess it; for we are well able to overcome it. But the men that went up with him said, We be not able to go up against the people; for they are stronger than we. And they brought up an evil report of the land which they had searched unto the children of Israel, saying, The land, through which we have gone to search it, is a land that eateth up the inhabitants thereof; and all the people that we saw in it are men of a great stature. And there we saw the giants, the sons of Anak, which come of the giants: and we were in our own sight as grasshoppers, and so we were in their sight.

These differing views caused great consternation, and there was doubt about the leaders, as well as what to do next. Joshua and Caleb pressed again to go forward.

> . . . Joshua the son of Nun, and Caleb the son of Jephunneh, which were of them that searched the land, rent their clothes: And they spake unto all the company of the children of Israel, saying, The land, which we passed through to search it, is an exceeding good land. If the LORD delight in us, then he will bring us into this land, and give it us; a land which floweth with milk and honey. Only rebel not ye against the LORD, neither fear ye the people of the land; for they are bread for us: their defense is departed from them, and the LORD is with us: fear them not.

In the end, the Israelites could not agree to accept the risks of an attack; and given their lack of faith, God sent them back into the Sinai until they were ready.

There is disagreement among scholars about the factual accuracy of this story. Traditionally the flight from Egypt and march to Canaan were thought to have taken place in about the thirteenth century BCE; however, the Biblical accounts may well have been written centuries after the events depicted and may reflect the mental framework of the authors rather than the thoughts, including views on intelligence analysis, of an earlier period. Whereas some scholars continue to see the Israelite takeover of Canaan as a quick, violent conquest, others theorize that it was accomplished peacefully over a longer period; still others see it as a rising of indigenous people. These disagreements were often generated or exploited by the emotional political and religious debate over who, Israelis or Palestinians, has the best claim to the area. Preconceptions have shaped assessments of facts in the Middle East for thousands of years. In any case, the context of the story of Moses sending spies into Canaan is much more likely to be about a test of faith rather than an effort to portray accurately the espionage or analytic methods of the thirteenth century BCE.

Nonetheless, the account of Moses sending spies into Canaan is one of the oldest detailed accounts of intelligence collection and analysis available from the written record. The Israelites did many things right, including asking good questions, seeking solid evidence, and having a debate that considers a variety of points of view. In the short term, however, the mission ended up being a failure, and the Israelites had to wander in the Sinai desert for another forty years before being ready to take over the promised land.

Questions for Further Thought

How many elements of the modern intelligence cycle are reflected in the biblical story?

What was Moses' methodology for assessing risk? What else might he have done?

Why wasn't the evidence – "the fruit of the land" – convincing?

There is no information in the story about whether the Canaanites were aware of the spies' mission. If the Canaanites were aware or were suspicious, what might they have done to protect themselves?

Recommended Reading

Herzog, Chaim, and Gichon, Mordechai, *Battles of the Bible*, London: Greenhill Books, 1997.

Sheldon, Rose Mary, *Spies of the Bible: Espionage in Israel from the Exodus to the Bar Kokhba Revolt*, London: Greenhill Books, 2007.

Yadin, Yigael, *The Art of Warfare in Biblical Lands: In the Light of Archeological Study*, Jerusalem: International Publishing, 1963.

4

The Athenian Campaign on Sicily

A CCORDING TO *HISTORY OF THE PELOPONNESIAN WAR*, BY THUCYDIDES (c. 460–c. 395), who was an eyewitness, there was a stalemate in the war in the late fifth century BCE. After a decade and a half of fighting between Athens and its allies on one side, and Sparta along with its allies on the other, neither side had prevailed and there was a shaky peace in place on the Greek mainland. Then a plea for help arrived from a small city–state in western Sicily, Egesta (also rendered as Segesta), which was an Athenian ally. Egesta was doing poorly in a local conflict with its neighbor Selinus, which was backed by Syracuse, the dominant city–state in the eastern part of the island and a potential ally of Sparta. To make the request for assistance attractive, the Egestaeans offered to pay for Athenian support.

Athens had a democratic government, and when the appeal from Egesta had arrived in Athens there was a vigorous public debate in the assembly about how to respond. Some saw this as an opportunity to expand Athenian influence on Sicily and undermine Sparta. Others were wary about making a serious commitment so far away – Sicily was 600 miles (960 kilometers) from Athens – while the rivalry with Sparta had not been resolved. As the debate continued, it became clear that there was an important question that could be addressed by intelligence analysis: The Egestaeans had offered to make a large financial contribution, but did they really have the means to provide significant assistance?

Athenian diplomats and merchants had long operated on Sicily and were familiar, in general, with conditions there. To get more up-to-date information on Egesta's financial resources, the Athenian assembly decided to send a team of diplomats to investigate the situation. Their instructions were:

> . . . to ascertain on the spot whether the Egestaeans really had the money which they professed to have in their treasury and in their temples, and to report on the on the state of the war with Selinus.

The investigators returned in the spring of 415 BCE and announced that Egesta had plenty of gold and silver; they had seen it with their own eyes. Moreover, an Egestaean delegation had brought some of it with them as a down payment. The arrival of the Egestaean funds prompted a renewal of debate in the assembly. One faction believed that there were many potential allies on Sicily and that the situation on the mainland was not threatening, so it was acceptable to dispatch a large fleet far from home. Success on Sicily might turn the tide in the larger struggle with Sparta. All of this could be achieved at little expense, because the Egestaeans would provide the necessary funds. The opponents of the expedition continued to be cautious, seeing too many uncertainties and too much risk.

In the end, based largely on the assurances of financial support from Egesta, the assembly voted to send a fleet and army to Sicily. Athens contributed 60 triremes (their main warships), 40 other ships to act as transports, and more than 2,500 soldiers; their allies provided more than 30 additional ships and 3,000 troops. It was one of the largest forces any Greek city–state had mustered up to that time. The commanding generals had authority to do what they thought best to promote Athenian interests on Sicily.

This was typical of how Athens, one of the first democracies, conducted its government. Reports on the situation from various sources were presented and discussed openly in the assembly of citizens. This procedure maximized citizen involvement and brought an array of viewpoints and experience to bear on the problem under discussion. Open debate also meant that the most loquacious members of the assembly, as well as those with a specific agenda, could have a disproportionate influence. Moreover, public discussion meant that a democratic government's military plans, along with any doubts or weaknesses revealed in the debate, could easily be learned by enemies.

The fifth century BCE was when the Western intellectual tradition and democratic government was being founded, through the work, of among others, Socrates (469–399 BCE) and Plato (428–348 BCE). The methods to evaluate information that the Greeks used in their public debates were therefore quite sophisticated. Concerns included factors such as the character and motivation of the person providing the report, as well as whether a new report was consistent with other material already received. They valued personal testimony, preferred direct observation to secondhand reporting, and sought a variety of independent reports.

On its way to Syracuse, the fleet stopped in southern Italy for supplies. While they were there, Athenian ships arrived from Egesta with a bit more money and the surprising word that these funds were all that Egesta would contribute. It turned out that that the earlier Athenian delegation had been duped by a clever deception. According to Thucydides:

> The fact was that when the original envoys came from Athens to inspect the treasure, the Egestaeans had practiced a trick upon them. They brought them to the temple of Aphrodite at Eryx, and showed them the offerings deposited there, consisting of bowls, flagons, censers, and a good deal of other plate. Most of the vessels were only of silver, and therefore they made a show quite out of proportion to their value. They also gave private entertainments to the crews of the triremes: on each of these occasions they produced, as their own, drinking vessels of gold and silver not only collected from Egesta itself, but borrowed from the neighboring towns, Phoenician as well as Hellenic. All of them exhibiting much the same vessels and making everywhere a great display, the sailors were amazed, and on their arrival at Athens told everyone what heaps of wealth they had seen.

Athens was already committed, so the commanders decided to continue on to Sicily, and, in time, the army and fleet laid siege to Syracuse. The campaign turned into a disaster, however, even though Athens sent substantial reinforcements. Not as many allies joined as had been hoped, there was no quick victory, and Athenian forces became bogged down in a two-year struggle. In the end, all of the ships in the fleet were lost, and all of the men were either killed or captured.

The decision to launch what would turn out to be a disastrous campaign on Sicily resulted from many factors. The great questions of war, peace, and how to use a government's resources are policy questions, and there were differences of opinion on policy in Athens. It was also clear that the Athenians, who prided themselves on their cleverness and intellectual sophistication, had not made an accurate intelligence assessment and had been deceived. They had fallen victim to common and serious problems in analysis: preconceptions and cognitive biases. The Athenians who favored a campaign on Sicily needed money and, more broadly, were looking for a relatively easy solution; it appeared that the Egestaeans offered both. Analysts need to be alert to the dangers of finding what they are looking for as well as seeing what they expect to see, without considering other possibilities.

To be sure, faulty intelligence was not the only problem. Even the large forces committed were not enough for such an ambitious project. Once on Sicily, there was poor Athenian generalship, and throughout the campaign there were many disagreements and delays that resulted from managing sensitive military issues through the mechanism of a public assembly.

The consequences were much more serious than just a single defeat. The expedition to Sicily did turn out to be a turning point in the Peloponnesian

War, but not in the way that many in Athens had hoped. When the Spartans heard about how badly things were going for the Athenians, they broke the truce. When the war resumed, the Athenians were never able to recover the military advantage, and, in the end, Sparta triumphed in the conflict.

Questions for Further Thought

What did the Athenians do correctly in making their assessment of the situation on Sicily? What did they do wrong?

Why was the Egestaean deception successful?

Was intelligence the decisive aspect of the failure?

Recommended Reading

Kagan, Donald, *The Peace of Nicias and the Sicilian Expedition*, Ithaca, NY: Cornell University Press, 1981.

Lazenby, J. F., *The Peloponnesian War: A Military Study*, London: Routledge, 2004.

Russell, Frank Santi, *Information Gathering in Classical Greece*, Ann Arbor, MI: University of Michigan Press, 1999.

Thucydides, *History of the Peloponnesian War*; Benjamin Jowett, trans., Amherst, NY: Prometheus Books, 1998.

5

Caesar's Campaigns in Gaul

J ULIUS CAESAR (100–44 BCE) IS ONE OF THE MOST FAMOUS AND SUCCESS-
ful military commanders in history, and there are many reasons for his
triumphs. He is well known for his persistence, ruthlessness, and personal
courage, as well as for the careful planning and organization of his military
operations. Caesar was also famous for the close ties with his troops, upon
whom he lavished praise, plunder, and promotions. One of the things that
was most striking to both his fellow Romans and his enemies was the speed
of his decision making and action. Not least of his skills was that he had
an uncanny ability to size up a situation and come up with an appropriate
response; he was, in fact, an excellent analyst.

In the first century BCE, the expanding Roman Empire controlled most of
the northern coast of the Mediterranean. One of the few areas that was close
to the Italian heartland of the empire but not yet conquered was Gaul, which
is now France, Belgium, and parts of the Netherlands and Switzerland.
Roman merchants did business in the region and knew something about
it, but the Roman army had never conducted operations there. For Caesar,
who was looking for ways to enhance both Roman power and his personal
glory, Gaul was a tempting target. What could be gained, however, and could
it be achieved at reasonable cost? A key issue was, therefore, how to conduct
successful military operations on unfamiliar terrain.

The main source on Caesar's methods is his own work, *Commentaries on the
War in Gaul*, also known as *The War in Gaul*. Much of the work is, of course,
propaganda aimed at those in Rome who would determine the political
future of this extremely ambitious man. As a result, much of Caesar's writing
about the fighting in Gaul from 58 through 50 BCE is a self-serving account
of his brilliance in conducting battles and negotiations. The *Commentaries*
also reveal how he dealt with information and made decisions, that is, how
he conducted intelligence analysis.

From the first page of the *Commentaries*, it is clear that Caesar is interested in trying to understand the context in which he will be operating. He notes the sizes and different levels of development of the tribes, their customs, their combat tactics, as well as their leadership. He also notes which might be potential allies. The crucial factor that emerged from his inquiry was that there was no strong, centralized leadership. He concluded, based on his study, that the situation in Gaul was fluid and unstable, thus offering considerable opportunities. In addition to political and ethnographic information, he was concerned about whether the area had the economic resources to provide him with supplies so that he did not have to depend on bringing grain and other essentials from Italy. Caesar paid particular attention to geographic factors, such as rivers and mountains with which his armies, who marched on foot, would have to contend.

In the pages that follow, interspersed among the accounts of speeches, negotiations, fortified camps, and battles, are clues to how Caesar acted as his own intelligence analyst. He refers over and over, for example, to listening to reports and then giving the order to march or take some other decisive action. His main sources were his subordinate officers stationed throughout Gaul and his scouts, and it is clear that he relies on them for speed and accuracy. These scouts were apparently trained observers to whom he had given clear directions about exactly what he needed to know. He also had other sources, and at various times he mentions reports from merchants, prisoners, diplomats, informants among the local people, and captured documents. The advantage of multiple sources was that they could be used for confirmation, and Caesar noted in a variety of places that:

> Such were the reports I received, and indisputable facts confirmed these suspicions...

> Other people, secretly questioned, confirmed the truth of his statements...

> My argument depends not on Ambioix's [a Gaul] advice, but on the facts.

He summed up the usefulness of considering a variety of perspectives as a basis for making a decision by saying the following:

> Now in addition to the information just received, there were many other considerations that led me to believe that I must think carefully about this problem and take action on it.

Information that was false, exaggerated, or not properly understood could be dangerous. During the first year of campaigning in Gaul, while the army was in camp resting between battles, reports arrived from merchants – not Caesar's scouts – that the warriors of a German tribe threatening to move against Rome's Gallic allies were unusually tall, courageous, and skilled. Upon receiving this frightening news, some of the Roman officers panicked, and many soldiers started preparing their wills. Caesar calmed his officers by reminding them of the strengths of the Roman army and his own personal record of success, and then immediately gave the orders to march so that the troops would be too busy to dwell on their fears.

Caesar clearly saw the conflict in terms of the civilization of Rome versus the barbarism of the Gallic tribes, and he contrasted his thoughtful methods with those of his adversaries.

> ... a crowd gathers traders and forces them to say what country they have come from and what information they have gathered there. Influenced by these reports, even when they are hearsay, the Gauls frequently adopt plans about important matters, which they are bound to regret almost immediately, since they are slaves to unsubstantiated rumors and most of the people they question make up answers they think will please them.

Caesar acknowledged the role of uncertainty and the power of luck, and he knew that it was advisable to have several alternative plans or options.

> Although I had not yet discovered what the enemy's plans were ... I prepared to meet any eventuality.

Despite his careful methods of gathering and assessing information, Caesar could be caught by surprise. Tactically the Roman army reduced the risks of surprise by constructing a walled encampment at the end of each day's march. On several occasions, however, units did not detect attacks until they were underway. It was the discipline and training of the soldiers, rather than the alertness of the commanders, that saved the day.

In 55 BCE, Caesar faced an even more daunting version of a familiar problem: military operations in an area unfamiliar to the Romans. This time, however, the target was the mysterious island of Britain. There were certainly people on the island who could be enslaved, and there were also rumors of mineral wealth. Would Britain provide an opportunity for even more of the plunder that was one of the main driving forces behind the expansion of the Roman Empire? Could Britain be made a permanent part of that empire? Again, Caesar had to consider what could be gained and what would be the cost.

As part of his preparations, Caesar summarized the gaps in his knowledge and thus what he needed.

> Even if we should not have enough time for conducting a campaign that season, I thought it would be very useful merely to have visited the island, to have seen what sort of people lived there, and to get some idea of the terrain and the harbors and landing places. The Gauls knew practically nothing about all this. In the ordinary way no one goes to Britain except traders, and even they are acquainted only with the sea coast and the areas that are opposite Gaul. And so, although I summoned traders from all parts, I could not find out about the size of the island, the names and populations of the tribes who lived there, their methods of fighting or the customs they had, or which harbors there could accommodate a large number of ships.
>
> In order to get this information before venturing on an expedition to Britain, I sent Gaius Volusenus there first with a warship. I thought he was a suitable man for the task, and gave him instructions to make enquiries about all these points and come back to me as quickly as he could.

After these preparations, in the summer of 55 BCE Caesar led a sizeable force to Britain to explore the possibilities. With two legions – approximately 8,000 troops – he landed on the southern coast, but unfamiliar tides and bad weather in the English Channel disrupted both operations and logistics. The Romans' experience in the calmer Mediterranean waters had not prepared them for the adverse tides and weather. That year, Caesar and his troops spent only about two and half weeks in Britain. Although they won several battles, they were not able to learn much about the geography, inhabitants, or resources of the island.

The following year, this time with five legions, Caesar made a more serious effort. Again, the weather interfered, and in a serious storm just after landing a significant number of his ships were damaged or destroyed. This time, the Romans were able to march further inland (as far as the site of modern London), make some alliances, and win several battles. None of this, however, produced a quick and decisive victory.

Some of the accounts about Britain were so baffling and outside the Roman experience that Caesar had to leave them as unsolved mysteries, anomalies that did not fit the mental frameworks of the time but might have been indicators of something else.

> ... it is believed that there are several smaller islands, too, where, some writers say, there is continued darkness for 30 days in midwinter. We made numerous inquiries about this, but found out nothing. However, from accurate measurements with a water clock, we could tell that the nights were shorter than on the continent.

After about two months, with the campaigning season coming to a close, Caesar decided to withdraw. It would be another century before Rome established a lasting presence in Britain.

Over the winter of 53 to 52 BCE, while Caesar was in northern Italy and focused on political developments in Rome, tribes in central Gaul who resented Roman encroachment on their status and power began to plot a revolt under the leadership of Vercingetorix. Rome's system of information gathering completely failed to detect the preparations for an uprising, and it was a great shock when obviously organized attacks on Roman merchants and officials in a variety of locations began even before spring.

When it became clear that there was trouble, Caesar quickly returned to Gaul. By this time, he had a firm grasp of the strengths and vulnerabilities of Gallic warriors, and he was able to complete the conquest of Gaul by defeating Vercingetorix through an elaborate siege at Alesia in 52 BCE. Minor fighting continued for another two years. By 50 BCE Gaul was firmly in the Roman empire, and would continue to be for more than 400 years.

As a result of his military campaigns in Gaul, Caesar had the reputation, connections, money, and troops that would be the foundation of his political campaign to take supreme power in Rome. Intelligence analysis was not the only element of Caesar's success in Gaul. He came from a sophisticated culture that knew how to organize great undertakings.

Caesar's main asset in Gaul, apart from his own abilities and considerable resources, was the Roman army – the first professional army in the Western world and a force that would readily carry out even difficult orders. This army included soldiers who were skilled not only in the use of weapons but also in engineering, scouting, and other fields. Scouting was the main form of long-range intelligence gathering and was done by soldiers drawn from the cavalry units. They were to be on the lookout for indicators of the size and location of enemy forces, which could include things such as the number of campfires, clouds of dust thrown up by marching men, and sunlight glancing off shined metal equipment. There were no professional analysts, however. Caesar himself, aided by a small staff, often conducted his own tactical reconnaissance and then made an assessment of all of the various reports available.

Caesar's methods would become an inspiration to military commanders for centuries to come, not least in his ability to analyze a situation. He was, for example, a proponent of cost/benefit analysis as well as taking into consideration both sides of an argument. As an analyst focused on decision and action, Caesar kept in mind multiple explanations and possible outcomes, and sought out indicators of the capabilities and intentions of his adversaries. He was also curious and sensitive to both what he knew and what he did not know.

Questions for Further Thought

What were the factors that Caesar took into account when making his assessments of the situations in Gaul and Britain as he prepared for operations? From the perspective of opportunities, were the ways that the assessments were made consistent or inconsistent?

What kinds of evidence did he find useful? Why?

When Caesar had setbacks, what were some of the reasons?

What are some other examples of the difficulties faced by advanced countries fighting in backward environments? What were the elements of success or failure in these cases?

Recommended Reading

Austin, N. J. E., and Rankov, N. B., *Exploratio: Military and Political Intelligence in the Roman World from the Second Punic War to the Battle of Adrianople*, London: Routledge, 1995.

Caesar, Julius, *The Battle for Gaul*, Anne and Peter Wiseman, trans., Boston: David R. Godine, 1980.

Goldsworthy, Adrian Keith, *Caesar: Life of a Colossus*, New Haven, CT: Yale University Press, 2006.

Goldsworthy, Adrian Keith, *The Roman Army at War, 100 BC – AD 200*, Oxford: Clarendon Press, 1996.

Grant, Michael, *The Army of the Caesars*, New York: Scribner's, 1974.

6

Sun Tzu

THE EXACT DATES OF SUN TZU'S LIFE ARE NOT KNOWN WITH CERTAINTY, although they are traditionally believed to be around the fifth century BCE. Some scholars are not even sure that Sun Tzu was a single individual: They believe instead that the classic work, *The Art of War*, may be a compendium of the work of several authors. In any event, *The Art of War* is a summary of the Chinese perspective on some of the longstanding issues in intelligence analysis, including deception, surprise, uncertainty, indicators, calculation of risk, and anticipation of events.

As was the case in the West, the earliest Chinese works on intelligence analysis are preoccupied with military issues. Sun Tzu wrote before the unification of China and during a time when governments had to deal with shifting alliances and constant conflict. Rulers often faced the prospect of defeat and perhaps the extinction of a dynasty or even the state itself. As a result, a high value was assigned to guidance that could lead to success in war. Sun Tzu's views are expressed in a series of pungent aphorisms, sometimes embodying paradox, such as how to win a battle without fighting. *The Art of War* addresses a wide range of strategic and tactical issues, but gives special attention to intelligence.

Sun Tzu is quite specific about the main thing that a commander needs to know to achieve victory.

> Therefore appraise it [war] in terms of the five fundamental factors and make comparisons of the various conditions of the antagonistic sides in order to ascertain the results of a war. The first of these factors is politics; the second, weather; the third, terrain; the fourth, the commander; and the fifth doctrine...Those who master them win; those who do not are defeated.

> Therefore, I say: Know the enemy and know yourself; in a hundred battles, you will never be defeated. When you are ignorant of the enemy but know yourself,

your chances of winning or losing are equal. If ignorant of both your enemy and
of yourself, you are sure to be defeated in every battle.

With these goals in mind, the commander should remain alert when he
goes into the field, and he should make sure he has information from the
locals, who are the best sources. Clandestine collection is a useful supple-
ment to other reports.

Those who do not know the conditions of mountains and forests, hazardous
defiles, marshes and swamps, cannot conduct the march of an army. Those who
do not use local guides are unable to obtain the advantages of ground.

Now, the reason a brilliant sovereign and a wise general conquer the enemy
whenever they move, and their achievements surpass those of ordinary men,
is their foreknowledge of the enemy situation. This foreknowledge cannot be
elicited from spirits, nor from gods, nor by analogy with past events, nor by
astrological calculations. It must be obtained from men who know the enemy
situation [spies].

And therefore, only the enlightened sovereign and the wise general, who are
able to use the most intelligent people as spies, can achieve great results. Spy
operations are essential in war; upon them the army relies to make its every
move.

There are a number of indicators of troops moving in the distance. Commanders need to keep in mind the possibility that an enemy would try to
deceive them, along with the high likelihood that any situation could become
fluid and uncertain.

If birds start up, there are ambushes there. If the animals are frightened, there
are attackers there. If dust rises high and sharp, vehicles are coming; if it is low
and wide, foot soldiers are coming. Scattered wisps of smoke indicate wood-
cutters. Relatively small amounts of dust coming and going indicate setting up
camp.

All warfare is based on deception. Therefore, when capable of attacking, feign
incapacity; when active in moving troops, feign inactivity; when near the enemy,
make it seem that you are far away; when far away, make it seem that you are
near.

As water shapes its flow in accordance with the ground, so an army manages its
victory in accordance with the situation of the enemy. As water has no constant
form, there are in warfare no constant conditions.

When all of these factors have been taken into account, the commander
should make his assessment, using rational calculation.

Now, if the estimates made before a battle indicate victory, it is because careful
calculations show that your conditions are more favorable than those of your

enemy; if they indicate defeat, it is because careful calculations show that favorable conditions for a battle are fewer. With more careful calculations, one can win; with less, one cannot.

If you estimate the enemy situation correctly and then concentrate your strength to overcome the enemy, there is no more to it than this. He who lacks foresight and underestimates his enemy will surely be captured by him.

Beyond Sun Tzu's observations and calculations, the broader Chinese intellectual tradition independently came up with some of the same principles for dealing with data that the Greeks had originated in the West. Chinese officials believed, for example, that multiple reports were more convincing than a single one and that direct observation was better than secondhand reports. The Chinese, however, were better than the Greeks at recognizing the dangers of cognitive biases. Chinese writers on intelligence warned about the dangers of devaluing data that did not fit into existing analytic frameworks, and they also noted that after assessments are made they are difficult to change.

The Chinese greatly valued being able to assess the character of individuals – what would later be known as leadership analysis – and Confucius said that the essence of knowledge was "knowing men." In addition, Chinese sages believed that a leader's virtue was an important factor to consider in evaluating him and his government. There was controversy among Chinese writers, however, on whether motives and intentions could be accurately determined by a person's appearance or behavior. Could an individual be so self-disciplined that deception could not be detected? Many believed that one's eyes revealed a person's true character. Confucius, for his part, stated that "The virtuous will be sure to speak correctly, but those whose speech is good may not always be virtuous."

When investigating the strengths and vulnerabilities of an adversary, Chinese sages recommended that, in addition to considering the character of the ruler, the analyst should determine whether the ruler employed able officials. Analysts should also carefully observe the state of public works and agriculture, which were useful indications of an effective and formidable government. In contrast, cruel officials, high taxes, and corruption could mean that a government was weak, even if it had a large army.

Ironically, much of what Sun Tzu had to say about how to conduct military operations would be disdained by officials in his own country over the centuries that followed. Scholarly mandarins often did not consider the barbarians on Chinese frontiers to be a serious threat. When the government was concerned, China preferred to believe in cultural superiority as a source of strength or to use manipulation and bribery rather than military campaigns. These attitudes would be especially dangerous when China encountered aggressive and well-armed representatives of Western powers from the sixteenth century onward.

Questions for Further Thought

What are some common elements of intelligence analysis in Europe and in Asia that emerged early in history? Differences?

Sun Tzu puts great emphasis on spying. Why? Is this the only valid source for a commander?

In the Confucian world view, relationships – between son and father and between ruler and subject, for example – are of great significance. What is the appropriate relationship between an intelligence analyst and a decision maker?

Recommended Reading

Kierman, Frank A., Jr., and Fairbank, John K., eds., *Chinese Ways in Warfare*, Cambridge, MA: Harvard University Press, 1974.

Sawyer, Ralph D., *The Tao of Spycraft: Intelligence Theory and Practice in Traditional China*, Boulder, CO: Westview Press, 2004.

Sun-Tzu, *The Art of War*, Ralph D. Sawyer, trans., New York: Barnes & Noble, 1994.

7

The Spanish Armada

U NDER ENGLAND'S QUEEN ELIZABETH I (1533–1603) TENSIONS WITH Spain, which had once been an ally, increased over religion, trade, and other issues. From the mid-1580s there was an undeclared naval war in European waters, as well as in Spain's colonies throughout the world. To resolve the rivalry, King Philip II of Spain (1527–98) decided to build a great fleet (Armada) for an invasion of England.

The method of the attack was fairly well known: It would be carried out by large wooden sailing ships. Since the beginning of the sixteenth century there had been such ships, carrying sizable numbers of cannons and troops anywhere on earth where there was water and wind, which was approximately 70 percent of the planet's surface. This capability to send men and equipment in considerable numbers over vast distances was unprecedented. For the English government, the key questions were to determine (1) what Philip would choose as the target and (2) when an attack an attack might come. The information on which to base planning to resist the Armada came in two separate channels: the experience of the English navy and the country's espionage network.

Spain had a global empire, with territory in Europe, the Americas, and the Philippines. The English navy, which was then an emerging organization, learned about Spain's galleons through direct contact in battles around the world, starting in the 1560s. Mariners, such as John Hawkins (1532–95) and Francis Drake (1540–96), found that Spanish ships were powerful, but also slow and awkward. Spain's galleons sat high out of the water, which made it easier to observe and fire on other ships; height also made it harder for enemy boarders to climb up the sides. Their main tactic was to close with an enemy ship, fire a single broadside from their cannon, and then use the large onboard infantry contingent to try to take their opponent by storm.

In 1577, Hawkins became treasurer of the Navy Board, which was responsible for the procurement of warships for the navy. With the support of Drake
and others, Hawkins sponsored vessels that they thought would be effective
in dealing with the Spanish warships. The English version of the galleon
rode low in the water and was built for speed and maneuverability. English
galleons did not carry large contingents of troops, and therefore sought to
avoid close contact and boarding. Captains of these ships preferred to stand
off from enemy ships and fire their cannons repeatedly.

There were limits, however, to what the English navy could learn through
direct observation and combat, and naval commanders complained about
how little reliable information they received about the nature of an attack
by sea from the other main source available to Elizabeth's government: the
espionage organization that, like the national navy, was also in the early years
of its development.

The man in charge of the English espionage network was Elizabeth's
chief secretary of state, Francis Walsingham (1532–90). His multifaceted
operation brought together under centralized management covert action,
counterintelligence, and espionage. Walsingham's main methods of collection were having his operatives make direct observations and intercepting
written messages, such as letters, military orders, or diplomatic dispatches.
There was no large, permanent organization for intelligence analysis, however. Walsingham's network of spies was made up of part-time amateurs,
and he was his own senior analyst.

Direct observations from merchants trading in Spain was one important
source, but information through commercial channels dropped dramatically
after 1585, when the Spanish seized English and Dutch ships in Spanish
ports in an attempt to stop English support for the ongoing rebellion against
Spanish authority in the Netherlands. It was only a few months later that
Philip started serious planning for the Armada.

Philip had tried to keep preparation of the Armada secret, but the vast
effort of gathering ships, men, and supplies from all over Europe provided
indicators that were fairly easy to track. As early as 1586 one of Walsingham's
agents intercepted a piece of official Spanish correspondence that provided
an accurate account of the intended strength of the Armada, as well as the
plan to have it sail up the English Channel, link up with the Spanish army in
the Netherlands, land near the mouth of the Thames River, and then march
on London.

Accurate forecasting of Spanish actions was made difficult, however,
by the fact that Philip kept changing his mind. At one time he considered sending his fleet from Spain to Ireland; at another time there was

discussion of a direct assault from the Spanish-controlled provinces in the Netherlands.

Despite reports that the Spanish intended to land at the mouth of the Thames – which turned out to be accurate – some English military leaders had another scenario for the future and believed that it made more sense to land on the southern coast and attack one or more of the ports and naval facilities there. Indeed, some on the Spanish side had urged that a harbor be seized soon after arriving in English waters so that the huge fleet could have a secure base.

A more difficult question was "When would the Armada leave on its mission?" Although the fleet's capabilities were reasonably clear, Philip's intentions for landings and other key factors about how the Spanish galleons would be used were harder to determine. Detecting a fleet when it was out on the broad ocean was almost impossible, given the technology at the time, except through luck. Answering the question of when the Armada would depart (and, therefore, when to reasonably expect it to arrive) was a difficult challenge because coverage by English agents was spotty and the departure date kept changing.

There were also a series of reports from the English ambassador in Paris claiming that the Armada had been disbanded or assigned another mission. Walsingham knew that there was some hesitancy and indecision in Madrid, but he recommended against giving any credence to the reports from Paris because the ambassador had a poor record for reliability and his loyalty was suspect.

In addition, messages providing indirect indicators came from Rome. The Pope, for example, was making preparations for the return of England to the Catholic fold. Walsingham believed these reports, seeing them as confirmation of the strength and ambition of the Armada.

Given the variety of reports on the Armada and their mixed quality, there were several false alarms. A large Spanish fleet set sail from Lisbon in the summer of 1587, but Walsingham was able to learn that it was bound for the Azores to try to find Drake. Toward the end of 1587, Walsingham received news that the departure of the Armada for England was imminent, and he recommended mobilizing the English fleet. When Drake heard about the report, he urged a naval raid to disrupt preparations. Still uncertain, Elizabeth assessed the risks and then decided to mobilize only part of the fleet and to spread it out to cover a variety of potential threats in Ireland, Scotland, and the Channel. From a purely military point of view, this disposition of forces was extremely risky: It violated the principle that forces should be concentrated, hopefully at the decisive point. A major goal of the ruler, however, was to avoid an expensive full mobilization and save money for future contingencies. Luckily, this gamble proved to be the right decision, because, in fact, the Armada was not yet ready to sail.

Philip continued to make changes, and he did not decide on the final plan for the Armada – to sail up the Channel and rendezvous with an army coming over from the Netherlands in smaller boats – until early in 1588. This plan was a revival of an earlier one. Reports of any other plans, however accurate they may have temporarily been, did not reflect what the final operation would look like.

Meanwhile, the English navy continued to use more direct methods to learn about and exploit the vulnerabilities of its Spanish enemies. In April 1587, Drake led a squadron to Cadiz, one of the ports where Armada ships were gathering, where he destroyed Spanish ships and supplies. In the months that followed, Drake sank more Spanish vessels at sea and set up a temporary blockade of Lisbon, Portugal, which was the headquarters of the Armada preparations.

There was one last series of delays that could not have been anticipated. The Armada, made up of galleons and a host of other ships, approximately 130 in all, sailed from Lisbon at the end of May 1588 and, with good weather, could have expected to approach the Channel approximately a month later. There were contrary winds and storms, however, and the fleet had to regroup at Corunna, in northwest Spain, in the middle of June and then remain there a month to restock and make repairs.

By June 1588 Elizabeth had an accurate idea of the size of the Armada and concluded that its main mission was to engage the English fleet in the Channel. She was wrong, however, about where the combined force would land, believing it would be on the north bank of the Thames. In fact, Philip had decided on the south bank.

Although Walsingham provided an accurate strategic warning about the nature of the Armada, he failed at the harder task of giving a tactical warning of when it would arrive. When the Spanish fleet first came within sight of England toward the end of July 1588, the English were surprised and most of their warships were still in port. Only a quick response by their skilled commanders and sailors got the English ships to sea in time to face the Armada.

The weeks that followed tested the British assessment of the Armada's strengths and weaknesses. English galleons were able to avoid being boarded, but they were unable to sink significant numbers of Spanish ships. In the end, it was the weather that did most of the damage to the Armada.

Walsingham was one of the pioneers of modern intelligence, and when King Philip received a report of Walsingham's death in 1590 and the accompanying sorrow in London, the king scribbled in the margin, "There, yes! But it is good news here."

The story of the Armada demonstrates the important difference between strategic and tactical intelligence. Indicators and evidence regarding strategic questions (such as whether there is a change in trends and a country is becoming hostile) can be subtle, but they typically happen over an extended period, and analysts have a chance of recognizing them. In contrast, tactical issues, such as the exact time, location, and method of an attack, often become clear only at the last minute and are much harder to anticipate. Regarding both strategic and tactical questions reporting can be inaccurate for a variety of reasons, and decision makers with different interests and perspectives can interpret information differently.

Attempts to anticipate the arrival date of the Armada also showed the difficulties of trying to fathom an authoritarian government. Rulers are often trying to hide or disguise their intentions, and clandestine collection that reaches behind appearances is essential. In addition, such rulers can be capricious, making accurate analysis difficult. Last, there are some things, such as the weather, that are beyond the control of even the most powerful ruler but can still have an impact on operations.

The British response to the Armada is also an early example of trying to understand new technology and to design countermeasures. Oared vessels, like the Greek triremes, with limited range and firepower, had been the main type of warships for centuries. The galleon represented a dramatic expansion of capability at sea and the context of naval warfare. Failure to be able to assess those capabilities and find an effective response could lead to defeat.

Questions for Further Thought

How might the intelligence needs of commanders at sea be different from those of their counterparts on land?

Given the uncertainties of the situation, what might have been some of the assumptions that the British were making? Did these turn out to be correct?

Were there other possible channels of information or methods of analysis that the English might have used, given the technology at the time?

What are some ways to anticipate the actions of a government with a single, dominant leader?

Recommended Reading

Budiansky, Stephen, *Her Majesty's Spymaster: Elizabeth, Sir Francis Walsingham, and the Birth of Modern Espionage*, New York: Viking, 2005.

Fernandez-Armesto, Felipe, *The Spanish Armada: The Experience of War in 1588*, Oxford: Oxford University Press, 1988.

Haynes, Alan, *The Elizabethan Secret Services, 1570–1603*, New York: St. Martin's Press, 1992.

Hutchinson, Robert, *Elizabeth's Spy Master: Francis Walsingham and the Secret War that Saved England*, London: Phoenix, 2006.

Parker, Geoffrey, *The Grand Strategy of Philip II*, New Haven, CT: Yale University Press, 1998.

8

George Washington

Like commanders for centuries before, General George Washington (1732–99) served as his own intelligence officer. Although he had no formal training in intelligence, Washington developed an impressive understanding of how to use information to assist decision making. Because he was the leader of the weaker force, it was in his interest to place a high value during the War of Independence on many aspects of intelligence, including espionage, counterintelligence, and analysis.

Assisted by only a few close aides, Washington personally organized the work of those who could bring him useful information. He employed the traditional uniformed scouts who operated more or less openly. He himself had performed this task during the French and Indian War. As commander, he also selected soldiers for short-term clandestine missions behind enemy lines, such Nathan Hale (1755–76), whose first mission ended in disaster. Finally, Washington recruited civilians to remain in place for long-term missions, such as the Culper Ring in New York City. When relaying to his agents what he needed to make decisions, he typically asked detailed questions and gave precise guidance.

Washington's correspondence has numerous references to intelligence matters, and, like many other commanders, he appreciated the importance of speed, accuracy, and secrecy in delivering reports.

> ... the good effect of intelligence may be lost if it is not speedily transmitted – this should be strongly impressed upon the persons employed as it also should be to avoid false intelligence. (April 8, 1777)

> ... do not spare any reasonable expense to come at early and true information; always recollecting, and bearing in mind, that vague and uncertain accounts of things [are] ... more disturbing and dangerous than receiving none at all. (August 8, 1778)

I wish you to take every possible pains in your power, by sending trusty persons to Staten Island in whom you can confide, to obtain Intelligence of the Enemy's situation & numbers . . . The necessity of procuring good intelligence is apparent & need not be further urged – All that remains for me to add is, that you keep the whole matter as secret as possible. For upon Secrecy, Success depends in Most Enterprizes [sic] of the kind, and for want of it, they are generally defeated, however well planned & promising a favorable issue. (July 26, 1777)

In time, Washington learned, in detail, how to conduct many aspects of clandestine operations, including the use of cover companies and secret ink.

I would imagine that with a little industry, he will be able to carry on his intelligence with greater security to himself and greater advantages to us, under cover of his usual business, than if he were to dedicate himself wholly to the giving of information. It may afford him opportunities of collecting intelligence that he could not derive so well in any other manner. It prevents also those suspicions which would become natural should he throw himself out of the line of his present employment. (September 24, 1779)

[Use of secret ink for reports from one of his agents in New York City] . . . will not only render his communications less exposed to detection, but relieve the fears of such persons as may be entrusted in its conveyance . . . [they could be written] on the blank leaves of a pamphlet . . . a common pocket book, or on the blank leaves at each end of registers, almanacks, or any publication or book of small value . . . A much better way is to write a letter in the Tory stile [sic] with some mixture of family matters and between the lines and on the remaining part of the sheet communicate with the Stain [secret ink] the intended intelligence. (February 5, 1780)

Nonetheless, Washington was not always successful in intelligence matters. The plot by Benedict Arnold (1741–1801) to betray the American fortress at West Point to the British was uncovered only as a result of a lucky break, when a random patrol of patriots stopped Arnold's British contact and found incriminating documents on him.

Washington also operated according to excellent principles of analysis, including making evidence convincing through attention to details, identifying indicators and making inferences from them, and focusing on the importance of multiple sources.

. . . as we are often obliged to reason on the design of the enemy, from the appearances which come under our observation and the information of our spies, we cannot be too attentive to those things which may afford us new light. Every minutiae should have a place in our collection, for things seemingly trifling in nature, when enjoined with others of a more serious cast, may lead to valuable conclusion. (October 6, 1778)

... by comparing a variety of information, we are frequently enabled to investigate facts, which were so intricate or hidden, that no single clue could have led to the knowledge of them ... intelligence becomes interesting which but from its connection and collateral circumstances, would not be important. (April 1, 1782)

He understood that assessing threats was a matter of understanding both capabilities and intentions.

It is a matter of great importance to have early and good intelligence of the enemy's strength and motions, and as far as possible designs, and to obtain them through different channels. (May 3, 1779)

As already suggested in some of this chapter's quotations, Washington knew that an important method for mitigating risk was to understand the overall picture.

... besides communicating your information as it arises ... you might make out a table, or something in the way of columns, under which you might range, their magazines of forage, grain and the like, the different corps and regiments, the Works, where thrown up, their connexion, [sic] kind and extent, the officers commanding, with the number of guns ... This table should comprehend in one view all that can be learned from deserters, spies, and persons who may come out from the enemy's boundaries. And tho' it will be a gradual work, and subject to frequent alteration and amendment yet it may be, by attention and proper perseverance made a very useful one. Transcripts may be drawn occasionally from it as you advance ... (November 18, 1778)

Washington did not provide an illustration of exactly how he wanted the table laid out to understand the overall pattern of British capabilities but Figure 10 is a guess at what he had in mind.

The last quote is an especially insightful summary of some of the key aspects of intelligence analysis: Look at both the tactical and the strategic, put data into some kind of framework to give it meaning, use a variety of sources, and update periodically.

Washington's skilled use of other aspects of intelligence also played a role in his successes. Late in 1776, for example, when confidence was at a low point, he used surprise at Trenton to great advantage. Then in 1781, at the climax of the struggle when it was imperative to keep British forces occupied in New York, he built expensive new ovens for baking bread to make it look like he intended to keep his army in the north and allowed fake orders to fall into the enemy's hands. These deceptions were meant to convince the British that he was still planning on attacking their headquarters in New York. British commanders accepted the false indicators as real, and allowed

	Magazines	Corps and Regiments	Works	Officers	Guns
Location A					
Location B					
Location C					
etc.					

Figure 10. Washington's intelligence spreadsheet

the American and French armies to slip away on their march southward to Yorktown and victory.

Of course there were many elements that contributed to winning the War of Independence and founding the United States of America, including an outstanding generation of leaders, an inspiring cause, support from France, and numerous British mistakes.

Questions for Further Thought

How is Washington's approach to intelligence analysis similar to Caesar's and Sun Tzu's? How is it different?

How could an analytic tool like Washington's spreadsheet help in formulating requirements for intelligence collectors?

What are some ways in which Washington's principles of intelligence analysis, derived from military campaigns, could be used in law enforcement and business?

Recommended Reading

Ferling, John, *Almost a Miracle: The American Victory in the War of Independence*, New York: Oxford University Press, 2007.

Flexner, James Thomas, *Washington: The Indispensable Man*, Boston, MA: Little Brown, 1974.

Ketchum, Richard M., *Victory at Yorktown: The Campaign that Won the Revolution*, New York: Henry Holt, 2004.

Rose, Alexander, *Washington's Spies: The Story of America's First Spy Ring*, New York: Bantam, 2006.

Searchable online versions of Washington's papers are available from the Library of Congress at http://memory.loc.gov/ammen/gwhtml/gwhome.html and from the University of Virginia at http://gwpapers.virginia.edu.

Part III

The First Half of the Twentieth Century

I N STARK CONTRAST TO THAT OF THE PREVIOUS 3,000 YEARS, INTELLIGENCE
analysis in the nineteenth and twentieth centuries was transformed by
three factors: bureaucracy, technology, and psychology.

From the nineteenth century onward, support to decision making in government was increasingly done by large, permanent organizations. These
large organizations were characterized by hierarchical structure and division
of labor, and they had both strengths and weaknesses. As demonstrated in
factories, they could handle massive volumes of work, especially of a routine
nature, but the flow of information up and down through the various layers
of hierarchy could also lead to distortion and delay. Soon the bureaucratic
style of organization was being used in armies, governments, political parties, and other functions. It was only a matter of time before it spread to
intelligence analysis.

Another significant development in the nineteenth century was the
increasing application of science to business, weaponry, law enforcement,
and other fields. There were various versions of the scientific method, but
basically the main steps were to formulate a question, propose one or
more hypotheses that could answer the question, gather relevant facts, use
those facts to test the hypotheses, and then accept, adjust, or abandon
the hypotheses based on the results of the tests. This procedure produced
a number of benefits, including new medicines and commercial products.
Such systematic inquiry could also be of assistance in intelligence analysis.

Improved knowledge of psychology helped analysts to better understand
thinking and decision making in their own work, as well as the leaders for
whom they worked and their adversaries. The human mind has great power
to organize and store data, as well as to recognize abstract patterns and
relationships, but it can also construct connections that have little basis in
reality and jump to hasty conclusions. Analysts would come to realize the

great potential dangers of succumbing to cognitive shortcomings, such as assumptions and biases, and the importance of finding ways to overcome such shortcomings.

These developments were just getting underway when World War I broke out in 1914. There were some interesting and influential intelligence episodes in this war, such as the Zimmermann telegram, that helped to bring the United States into the conflict. World War I, however, was not a war in which intelligence played an important role. In contrast, World War II, which began in 1939, would be full of challenges and lessons for analysts.

9

Wilson and the Paris Peace Conference

THE CHALLENGE FOR PRESIDENT WOODROW WILSON (1856–1924) AS WORLD War I came to an end was to promote American interests in a unique environment. The United States was playing a much more active role in the international scene than it had previously. Moreover, it found itself in a position of great military, economic, and political power, and its resources of manpower, equipment, and money were being applied on an unprecedented, global scale.

Wilson believed that the contribution that he and the United States could make to a peace settlement was to bring a perspective that was enlightened, rational, and progressive. Wilson's Fourteen Points made clear his vision of a settlement based on openness, freedom, justice, self-determination, disarmament, and a League of Nations to settle future disputes. Not everyone agreed with these goals, but the principles, along with American power, framed the debate.

In 1917, only a few months after the United States entered the war, Wilson set up a semi-official commission, known as the Inquiry, to gather information that would be useful for supporting him in the eventual peace negotiations. Financial support for the commission came from a presidential national security contingency fund provided by Congress. This was one of the earliest examples of bureaucratic analytic support for a senior decision maker.

Drawing on his extensive experience in academia, including obtaining a doctorate in history and political science, as well as serving as president of Princeton University, Wilson took a decidedly academic approach to the work of the Inquiry. He wanted geographic, economic, ethnographic, historical, and other types of information about the many and complex issues that a peace conference would face. Wilson also wanted to be "scientific" – that is, objective and organized. Because neither the Department of State nor the existing Army or Navy intelligence units had what he wanted, he recruited researchers from the academic world, although usually only relatively junior scholars were available. The Inquiry also drew on expertise in government, business, and nongovernmental organizations.

The staff of the Inquiry believed that their work had four aspects: planning, collection, digesting, and editing. Their goal was to produce reports that were brief and could be organized in a filing system so that the information could be easily retrieved. In addition to statistics and narrative, they also prepared hundreds of maps. Besides reporting the facts, they also made recommendations for action. As the Inquiry's researchers grappled with their work, they found that it was not always easy to balance objectivity with their own views or U.S. national interests, and they also struggled with the difficulty of mastering the details while also seeing the larger overall picture.

The Paris Peace Conference was one of the great gatherings of world history, with a cast of characters that, in addition to the senior figures of the various delegations, included, among many others, Bernard Baruch, Edvard Beneš, Winston Churchill, John Foster Dulles and his brother Allen, Herbert Hoover, John Maynard Keynes, T. E. Lawrence, Tomáš Masaryk, Jean Monnet, IgnacPaderewski, Jan Smuts, Arnold Toynbee, Chaim Weizmann, and (on the sidelines) Ho Chi Minh.

The conference faced many challenges, but the main ones were arranging security for France, finding a way to restrain Germany, dealing with the breakup of the Austro-Hungarian Empire, and figuring out how to work with the new communist government in Russia. Many of these problems involved the related issues of borders and the aspirations of various ethnic groups. In trying to settle the many conflicting claims, Wilson's progressive idealism and logic would be at odds with the traditional European diplomacy of secret treaties and territorial adjustments made with little concern for the wishes of the populations.

The Paris Peace Conference, which convened on January 18, 1919, was the first major international gathering abroad that was attended by an American president. Of the 125 or so people who had been involved with the Inquiry, Wilson took 23 with him to join the U.S. delegation – which would eventually number of total of more than 1,000. The Inquiry staff who participated included Walter Lippmann (1889–1974), who would become an influential journalist, and Samuel Eliot Morison (1887–1976), who would write the official history of the U.S. Navy in World War II. It was the first time a sizable group of civilian scholars were intimately involved in diplomatic negotiations.

At the conference, the Inquiry personnel became the Division of Territorial and Political Intelligence in the U.S. delegation. Although the experts found Wilson to be aloof and never really established a close working relationship with him, they were able to provide some useful services beyond strictly research. In the spirit of openness and over the objections of Secretary of State Robert Lansing (1864–1928), the division provided bulletins to the press corps at the conference, making clear that they, as researchers, did not necessarily represent American policy. Scholarly experts also provided a forum in which lobbyists for various nationalist causes could express their views without taking up the time of the more senior members.

The Division of Territorial and Political Intelligence was not the only source of information and advice for the American delegation. U.S. embassies provided a flow of reports on conditions in countries around the world and supported a number of fact-finding delegations, including one to Germany that was told that, if the treaty was too harsh, "a leader, as yet undiscovered, would be found to lead a great popular uprising." Army and Navy intelligence also supplied reports to the delegation from their sources. Finally, a large number of private individuals, such as businessmen and labor leaders, offered their views on issues of concern to them.

Among other things, the Division's experts, backed by a representative of the U.S. Navy, argued against allowing Japan to take control of islands in the Pacific that were former German colonies but could perhaps be used as naval bases in the future. The U.S. scholars also supported including the Sudeten Germans in Czechoslovakia, for historical and defense reasons, along with the belief that the German ethnic minority in Czechoslovakia themselves preferred this. Another recommendation was that the multiethnic Russian Empire be broken up into a number of independent states.

Even with all of its power, the United States would not be able to get everything it wanted at the conference. Compromises and alliances would have to be made. For its part, the Division of Territorial and Political Intelligence made tentative efforts to cooperate with experts in other delegations. There was some success in dealing with the British, but many Europeans thought that the Americans had little regard for political realities.

The Treaty of Versailles, embodying the work of the conference, was signed on June 28, 1919. The treaty stipulated that Germany be reduced in size, with significant loss of territory in Europe to France and Poland, as well as the loss of its colonies. There were also stringent limits on the size of its armed forces and huge reparations to be paid, and the new democratic government of the country had to accept responsibility for having caused the war. Austria and Hungary were separated and reduced in size, with the territorial remnants assigned to several new states that were created in Central Europe and the Balkans. The conference was unable to agree on a way to cope with the ideological challenge from Russia, so the treaty did not address Russian issues. In addition, outside of the framework of the treaty the victorious allies had already sent troops to try to protect their interests there. Acknowledging that many problems had not been resolved, the conferences acceded to Wilson's wishes and established the League of Nations as a forum for dealing with international controversies in the future.

The 1919 Treaty of Versailles was widely criticized, at the time and later, for not abiding by the principles of Wilson's Fourteen Points. It did not end the fighting, which continued in Poland, Russia, and Turkey, among other places. Moreover, the settlement contributed to many of the causes for World War II twenty years later.

Wilson's Inquiry was an effort, however modest, to bring scholarship to bear on important decisions. It was temporary and had only a limited impact on the Versailles settlement. In retrospect, the work of the Inquiry scholars was of mixed quality because of inexperienced personnel, a limited budget, and tight deadlines.

Nonetheless, the American scholars did take a multidisciplinary look at complex problems. Their research and advice proved to be of some value: Quite a few of their recommendations were adopted by Wilson, and some of these ended up in the final treaty. Moreover, their work raised some important issues, not only about how to perform intelligence analysis, but also about the future of Europe and Asia. They saw some things clearly, others less so.

Questions for Further Thought

In what ways did the work of the Inquiry anticipate the later intelligence cycle?

To what extent are political questions, such as the territorial issues dealt with at the Versailles conference, amenable to rational, objective solutions?

What else might the U.S. scholars have done to deal with the challenges they faced at Versailles?

How could the scholarly methods of the Inquiry – such as reports, files, maps, statistics, and such – be applied to counterterrorism and to other problems?

Recommended Reading

Ferrell, Robert H., *Woodrow Wilson and World War I*, New York: Harper & Row, 1985.

Gelfand, Lawrence E., *The Inquiry: American Preparations for Peace, 1917–1919*, New Haven, CT: Yale University Press, 1963.

MacMillan, Margaret, *Paris 1919: Six Months that Changed the World*, New York: Random House, 2001.

Walworth, Arthur, *Wilson and His Peacemakers: American Diplomacy at the Paris Peace Conference, 1919*, New York: W. W. Norton, 1986.

10

Estimating the Strength of the *Luftwaffe* in the 1930s

A IR POWER HAD NOT BEEN A DECISIVE FACTOR IN WORLD WAR I, BUT technological improvements in the 1920s and 1930s had made it a matter of great concern. Theorists, such as the Italian Giulio Douhet (1869–1930), believed that massive bombing attacks from the air would be the decisive weapon of the next war. In Britain, the leader of the Conservative Party, Stanley Baldwin (1867–1947), claimed that "the bomber will always get through." Even in popular culture, movies such as *The Shape of Things to Come* envisioned a world in which airpower would be of decisive importance. Military planners trying to design and implement defenses, as well as civilian officials with budgetary responsibilities, grappled with how to assess a technology that had never been used extensively and was constantly advancing. The problem was particularly acute when trying to estimate the threat from Germany.

One of the provisions of the Treaty of Versailles had been that Germany was not to have an air force. Given the increasing importance of air power, however, the postwar German democratic governments fostered a limited secret aerial rearmament in defiance of the treaty. In 1933, Adolf Hitler (1889–1945), the head of the National Socialist (Nazi) Party who had made criticism of the treaty a key element of his foreign policy, became Chancellor of Germany and soon established a dictatorship. In addition to other rearmament efforts, he continued and accelerated clandestine efforts to build war planes.

The year that Hitler came to power, the new German Air Ministry, ostensibly a civilian organization, drew up a secret plan to produce 244 military aircraft over the next twelve months. Less than a year later, in January 1934, with a massive infusion of resources for rearmament underway, a much more ambitious plan was adopted to produce more than 800 bombers and approximately 250 fighters, along with hundreds of support aircraft for functions such training and reconnaissance. By 1935 the German goal was eventually to have more than 3,800 combat aircraft. It should be noted that if outsiders had been able to obtain any of these impractical plans, even though authentic, the documents by themselves would not necessarily have provided an accurate guide to future German capabilities.

What the Nazi government had in mind for this early phase of rearmament was to establish deterrence against attack by quickly producing a large number of aircraft, many of which might quickly become outmoded; improvements in quality would come later. The Germans themselves soon realized that this large, quickly built force was unrealistic. Nonetheless, an ambitious, if more restrained, program continued. In March 1935, Hitler, in an effort to gain British respect, ended the policy of secrecy and publicly announced that Germany had an air force, the *Luftwaffe*. Moreover, he claimed in talks with visiting British politicians that German air power was already roughly equal to Britain's Royal Air Force (RAF), which then had nearly a thousand aircraft.

In Britain at the time, there was a governing cabinet led by Prime Minister Ramsay MacDonald (the former head of the Labour Party) and supported by Baldwin's Conservatives as well as the Liberals. This coalition cabinet was dedicated to peace abroad and spending restraint at home. In 1935 Baldwin took over as prime minister and followed similar policies. As the Nazis consolidated their position at home and became bellicose abroad, anxiety and uncertainty increased in the international arena. In response, British leaders were willing to expand and modernize the RAF, but they wanted to do so in a restrained fashion. For professional assessment of the threat from Germany, so that they would not spend more than necessary, the leadership looked to a relatively new intelligence bureaucracy: the intelligence staff at the Air Ministry and the Industrial Intelligence Centre.

The Air Ministry's main doctrine was that strategic bombing would be the decisive element in any future war, and the cabinet's fiscal restraints meant that the ministry had to compete with the army and navy for a significant share of a limited defense budget. Their main fear, which became their main prediction, was that Germany would launch a "knockout blow" early in any conflict, which would devastate British cities. Therefore, in the ministry's view, Britain must have a large force of bombers to act as a deterrent in peace and, if necessary, a force that could strike back in war.

The Air Ministry made its first assessment of the implications of Hitler coming to power in the spring of 1934. Coming up with an accurate picture was made difficult by a shortage of reliable information, given German secrecy. There was also uncertainty about the implications of Hitler's extremist views; could he really be as ready to go to war as he said? In May of that year, French military intelligence gave their British counterparts a report that officials in Paris had received from Germany suggesting that the Nazis were planning an initial air division of some 500 first-line aircraft, planes of the latest technology that would comprise the main fighting force in the air. Over an unspecified time, it was alleged that the Germans planned to have three or four such divisions. Later in the year, the French provided a follow-on report claiming that the Germans planned to have a force of some 1,300 first-line aircraft by 1936. Nonetheless, despite their bureaucratic interest in hyping the threat, British analysts were not especially worried at this point about the pace of the *Luftwaffe*'s growth and the uses to which any increase in strength might be put. Analysts believed, on the basis of stereotypes of national behavior, that the Germans would favor quality over quantity. As a result, the Air Ministry initially estimated that it would take the Germans until 1939 to build a force of two air divisions and that it would not have a force of about 1,600 until 1945.

The Industrial Intelligence Centre, operating outside of the structure of the service ministries, made its own estimates of German aircraft production. Analysts there based their assessments on statistical compilations of factors such as the number of workers in the German aviation industry and the size of factories. In a more alarming analysis than that of the Air Ministry, the Centre concluded that from 1934 through 1935 German capacity for aircraft production had increased dramatically from 60 or 70 per month to approximately 200 per month.

From the back benches of Parliament, Winston Churchill (1874–1965), eloquent and forceful, but out of power and believed by many to be well past his prime, sounded the alarm about the rising power of Germany. He argued that Britain needed to do much more to improve its defenses. As early as 1934, Churchill had claimed in a parliamentary debate on defense spending that the Germans were violating the Treaty of Versailles, had a clandestine air force that was nearly two thirds the size of the RAF, and that by 1936 this air force would surpass its British rival. In response to those who believed that "the bomber will always get through," he urged the government to investigate new technologies that might enhance Britain's defensive capabilities.

In challenging what he regarded as a complacent leadership, Churchill often drew on information from individuals in the military and the bureaucracy who supported his views. Some of these private alarmist views were based on clandestine reports from British businessmen with contacts in the

German aviation industry, as well as from human sources in the German government. In 1934, for example, an informant in the British Foreign Office had passed Churchill an internal report claiming that within two years the Nazis planned to have an air force of 1,000 planes. Churchill was prone to exaggeration in some of his charges and had some misconceptions (including one that warships at sea were virtually invulnerable to attack by aircraft), but his general point that Nazi Germany represented a serious threat, especially from the air, was accurate.

From 1936 on, the British were able to expand the number of sources reporting on the *Luftwaffe*. Now that the German air force was no longer a secret, foreign attachés were permitted to visit bases and factories, although these visits were still carefully controlled. Reporting on the 1936 *Luftwaffe* exercises, for example, suggested that the bomber force's main mission was to support army operations. Other information, from a British business-man with good contacts in Germany, indicated that the Germans planned on having just over 2,000 first-line war planes by the end of 1938. The businessman's source also indicated that the *Luftwaffe* had abandoned the development of heavy bombers in favor of medium bombers. As a result of such reports, it became clear that the rapid expansion of the *Luftwaffe* was continuing, and the British Air Ministry adjusted its estimates of likely German strength by 1939 to a total of 2,500 aircraft.

In response to Churchill's criticisms, improved information, and actual threatening German behavior, such as the failure of arms control talks and the remilitarization of the Rhineland in 1936, British intelligence assessments became more alarmist. In 1936, the British cabinet reluctantly agreed to a further increase in spending on air defense. Back in 1934 they had planned for a 1,200-aircraft force; by 1937 the goal was to have more than 1,700 planes. The expanded construction programs included the new Hurricane and Spitfire fighters, which had all-metal exteriors and included new features such as eight guns, a closed cockpit, retractable landing gear, high-frequency radios for communications between aircraft and ground controllers, and a transmitter that identified them as friendly.

The cabinet also supported the proposals from the new head of Fighter Command, Air Chief Marshal Sir Hugh Dowding (1882–1970). He called for more aircraft, pilots, and bases. There would also be a network of sites housing the newly developed radar to detect incoming hostile aircraft, a network of civilian observers, and hardened communications links. All of this would feed data to an operations room where air defense could be centrally managed. No other country in the world – not even Germany – had such a system.

Thousands of miles away, the United States was much less threatened by the *Luftwaffe*, but there were many American civilian and military aviation enthusiasts who were interested in learning more about German capabilities. In 1936, Major Truman Smith, the military attaché at the U.S. embassy in Berlin, invited Charles Lindbergh (1902–74), the hero of the first solo flight across the Atlantic in 1927 and probably the best-known aviator in the world, to Germany. Smith hoped that Lindbergh's celebrity status would give the embassy better access to accurate information about the new *Luftwaffe*. In addition, the attaché believed that Lindbergh's technical expertise would enable embassy personnel to better evaluate what they saw and heard.

The Nazis, acutely aware of the value of propaganda, rolled out the red carpet for the American hero. The German government made it possible for Lindbergh to meet Air Minister Hermann Goering (1893–1946) and to tour facilities that were not normally open to foreigners. Lindbergh was impressed with the modern bases and factories, as well as the competent personnel of the *Luftwaffe*. Although some of the existing planes he saw were out of date, it was clear that new and planned aircraft were much more capable. Smith believed that Lindbergh's visit had helped greatly in getting American officials to see the *Luftwaffe* as a significant emerging factor in European power politics.

Over the next two years Lindbergh made a series of further visits to Germany. A November 1937 report, drafted by both Lindbergh and Smith, began:

> Germany is once more a world power in the air. Her air force and her air industry have emerged from the kindergarten stage. Full manhood will still not be reached for three years. The astounding growth of German air power from a zero level to its present status in a brief four years must be accounted one of the most important world events of our time.

In that report, Lindbergh and Smith estimated the strength of the *Luftwaffe* to be at least 1,800 first-line planes, with another 600 in reserve. They concluded that Germany had surpassed France in technical development and was closing in on Britain. Within four to five years it would achieve parity with the United States. The *Luftwaffe's* greatest weakness, in their view, was the inexperience of its personnel. In Washington, such opinions were unwelcome. Civilian officials there – like their British counterparts, mindful of tight budgets – believed that this assessment was alarmist and that Smith had been swayed by German propaganda.

In subsequent reports, Smith and his colleagues in Berlin refined their analysis. The attachés suspected, for example, that obsolete bombers that were still being produced were probably intended to transport airborne troops. They also reported that the *Luftwaffe* gave a higher priority to supporting infantry at the front than to long-range bombing, meaning that, for the time being at least, the *Luftwaffe* was less of a threat to America.

The *Luftwaffe* provided a demonstration of its capabilities during the Spanish Civil War. At the beginning of the conflict, in the summer of 1936, German aircraft transported troops commanded by fascist General Francisco Franco (1892–1975) from the Spanish colony of Morocco to the mainland. Aided by small numbers of Spanish and Italian planes, the *Luftwaffe* moved more than 20,000 soldiers, along with substantial amounts of equipment, in less than three months – an unprecedented logistics feat at that time. In the months that followed, *Luftwaffe* personnel and aircraft also took part in combat operations, including the infamous air raid on Guernica in April 1937. Much of the work of the *Luftwaffe* units in Spain was tactical support to ground units. In total, Germany provided more than 100 aircraft, supported by some 5,000 personnel at any one time, to the effort, making an important contribution to the eventual fascist victory and gaining valuable combat experience.

In the late 1930s, as the fighting continued in Spain, the *Luftwaffe* continued to grow and modernize, introducing its own first-line, all-metal, single-wing aircraft, including a range of medium bombers, the Stuka dive bomber, and the Messerschmitt 109 fighter. The rate of growth was slowing, however, as the shortage of skilled labor began to have an impact.

In 1938, British analysts concluded that total German production of warplanes was pulling ahead not only of British production, but also of British and French production combined. Another assessment suggested that Germany had far more bombers than both Britain and France, although overall strength, considering all types, was less worrisome. In response to a question from Prime Minister Neville Chamberlain (1869–1940), a planner claimed that the current strength of Britain and its allies was insufficient to prevent the Germans from taking over Czechoslovakia. Moreover, it would take many months to produce the military equipment, including aircraft, that would give Britain a fighting chance if a war came. These dire assessments were part of what was on the mind of Chamberlain and other British leaders when they decided, during the September 1938 Munich crisis, not to go to war to protect Czechoslovakia from German aggression.

In November 1938, after the Munich crisis had highlighted the increasing danger and likelihood of war with Germany, the cabinet in London authorized yet another increase in fighter strength to a level that was about as much as British factories, maintenance facilities, and training schools could support.

By 1939, as war became more likely, British analysts believed that increased preparations in their country, and emerging vulnerabilities in the German rearmament program, provided grounds for hope. With more intelligence sources from which to draw, as well as a political leadership uniting behind strengthening the RAF, British assessments became more accurate and relevant. In early 1939, for example, Air Ministry analysts believed that the *Luftwaffe*'s short-term goal was a total of approximately 3,700 aircraft of all types. When war came in September, the total order of battle for the German air force was 3,750 planes of all types. Analysts in Britain believed that the pace of German aircraft construction was now reaching a peak and that expanding British production had a chance of catching up over the next year or so. In addition, they were becoming more aware that a relatively low number of German planes were actually ready for operations on any given day. Increased British optimism about their strength in the air relative to Germany was part of a wider official judgment that the country's defenses as a whole were strong enough that the country could survive any initial attempt at a knockout blow. Once the early days of any war had been weathered, the strategy was for Britian to use its, superior economic strength to survive and prevail in a long war.

Churchill became prime minister on May 10, 1940, the same day on which German troops started moving into Belgium and the Netherlands on their way to France. In little more than a month, French resistance collapsed; on June 17, the French government asked for an armistice. When the Battle of Britain began a few weeks later, the *Luftwaffe* actually had available approximately 1,000 bombers and some 800 fighters to strike at Britain, although they claimed to have more. Against this force, the RAF had some 700 Hurricanes and Spitfires (British bombers would play virtually no role in the Battle of Britain).

The British cabinets of the 1930s do not always get the credit they deserve for the decisions they made to build up the RAF and other aspects of air defense, such as radar and the infrastructure for centralized command. They may have been slow and wrongheaded at times, but British officials closed enough of the gap with Germany to give Britain a fighting chance when it stood alone in 1940. Intelligence analysts played a significant, but mixed, role in this accomplishment.

Analysts trying to assess the *Luftwaffe* ran into several problems. It was hard to judge the capabilities of new technology; fighters capable of 350 or more miles (560 kilometers) per hour were replacing the multiwinged, fabric-covered aircraft of World War I. Although the Germans had used modern aircraft when assisting the fascist side in the Spanish Civil War, little was known about the capabilities of the new fighter and bomber aircraft. In addition, the Germans covered the growth of the *Luftwaffe* with a cloak of secrecy and changed their plans over time. Finally, Nazi officials tended to exaggerate what they wanted and what they had.

Despite all of this, over time, British and American analysts were able to come up with quite accurate estimates. Initially, in an example of mirror imaging, the British Air Ministry staff, heavily influenced by their own views of bombing strategy, had an inaccurate view and grossly underestimated the future strength of the *Luftwaffe*. There were also early faulty assumptions, based on stereotypes, that the Germans would give top priority to efficiency and take a longer time to build up a technically capable force. In contrast, the Industrial Intelligence Centre got closer to the mark by using a more methodical, fact-based approach. Later, clandestine reports from human sources with contacts in the business world were fairly accurate, as were Lindbergh's views based on direct, albeit controlled, observation. By 1938, the strength of the *Luftwaffe*, from a numbers point of view, was fairly well understood.

That said, there were some important aspects of German airpower that the analysts, preoccupied with numbers, missed. Serviceability – the actual numbers of aircraft ready to fly on any given day – was a more accurate criterion for strength than was the distinction used at the time between first-line and reserve planes.

More broadly, although there were some accurate indicators, analysts did not understand Hitler's airpower doctrine – how he intended to use his military aircraft. In peacetime, the German leader saw large numbers of planes as a way to intimidate rival governments; he was not overly concerned with quality. When war actually came, he intended to use most aircraft to support "lightning war" (*blitzkrieg*), which would be short, violent blows by the army stressing surprise and mobility. He had no intention to launch the great knockout blow from the air that so many feared; and when, in the autumn of 1940, Germany tried to carry out a bombing offensive against Britain, it found itself inadequately prepared and unable to succeed.

Any criticism of the analysts of the 1930s needs to be careful, however, to avoid another cognitive shortcoming: the hindsight bias, in which events seem much clearer and easier to predict when one looks back with the advantage of knowing how things turned out.

Questions for Further Thought

How was trying to figure out how Hitler would use the *Luftwaffe* a problem that was similar to – and different from – uncovering how Philip II would use the Armada?

What would have constituted reliable evidence, if it could have been obtained, about the current status of the *Luftwaffe* in the 1930s? About its future strength in the 1940s?

The analysts' work on the *Luftwaffe* in the 1930s is an example of how intelligence judgments contrary to what decision makers want to hear can become part of policy debates. What are some other examples, and did they play out in ways similar, or dissimilar, to what happened in Britain?

Besides numbers, what might be some useful criteria for assessing the capabilities of other weapons systems besides aircraft?

Recommended Reading

Berg, A. Scott, *Lindbergh*, New York: G. P. Putnam's Sons, 1998.

Hessen, Robert, ed., *Berlin Alert: The Memoirs and Reports of Truman Smith*, Stanford, CA: Hoover Institution Press, 1984.

Homze, Edward, *Arming the Luftwaffe: The Reich Air Ministry and the German Aircraft Industry, 1919–1939*, Lincoln, NE: University of Nebraska Press, 1976.

May, Ernest, ed., *Knowing One's Enemies: Intelligence Assessment Before the Two World Wars*, Princeton, NJ: Princeton University Press, 1984, chapter 9.

Wark, Wesley K., *The Ultimate Enemy: British Intelligence and Nazi Germany, 1933–1939*, Ithaca, NY: Cornell University Press, 1985.

Figure 11. Europe in 1939

11

Stalin Assesses Hitler

B Y 1940, JOSEPH STALIN (1879–1953) SAT ATOP A TOTALITARIAN SYSTEM THAT gave him unchallenged control of the Soviet Union. The ideological fervor and effort to spread the communist faith around the world during the first years after the revolution of 1917 had given way to consolidation of power at home and a foreign policy in which protection of national interests was the main priority. Brutal purges of the late 1930s had demonstrated the price of disloyalty, or even suspicion of disloyalty, to Stalin. As recently as July 1940, the head of military intelligence had been removed (and was later shot) after disagreeing with Stalin.

All of this had implications for the bureaucratic structure of intelligence that supported Stalin's decision making. There were two main intelligence organizations. The civilian service was reorganized multiple times and had several different names, but from the mid-1930s through the mid-1940s, it was usually referred to as the People's Commissariat for Internal Affairs (*Narodnyy Komissariat Vnutrennikh Del*; NKVD). The military service was the Chief Intelligence Directorate (*Glavnoye Razvedyvatelnoye Upravleniye*; GRU) of the General Staff. Both used sympathy for Communism and effective tradecraft to forge a system that was one of the best collectors of information in the world at that time. There were Soviet spies in crucial positions in the United States, Britain, and even Nazi Germany (although at least one of the Germans would turn out to be a double agent). As that copious, and often accurate and significant, flow of data moved upward, however, it tended to become distorted to fit Stalin's preconceptions and prejudices. Stalin was his own senior intelligence analyst, and alternative points of view were not welcome.

The key challenge for Stalin and his intelligence system in 1940 was to assess the degree of threat from Hitler's Germany. Germany badly needed the oil, grain, and coal of the USSR; but at the same time, Germany would never be secure until it dealt with any powerful neighbors. Hitler often had expressed his hatred for Communism and his determination to conquer "living space" for the Germans beyond their eastern borders.

Stalin, for his part, was well aware of the fundamental differences with Nazi Germany but desperately wanted to avoid a German attack for which he was not prepared. Many of his assumptions about how best to head off a strike by Hitler were based on his understanding (or, more accurately, misunderstanding) of history. His strategic assessment was that German governments had to give a high priority to avoiding a two-front war, so he assumed that Hitler would be reluctant to open a second front with the USSR until the war with Britain had ended either through a German victory or a negotiated peace. Moreover, Stalin did not want to make any military preparations that might provoke an attack, as he believed mobilizations had done in 1914. Stalin was also confident that there would be other indicators of a possible attack besides the status of the war between Germany and Britain, and these would give him time to react. For example, he assumed that any German attack would be preceded by an ultimatum. To support his assessment, Stalin could draw on the reassuring tone of the remarks that were being made by the German ambassador in Moscow. Stalin did not realize, however, that the ambassador was not part of Hitler's inner circle, and thus not a reliable source regarding the German leader's intentions.

Hitler began preparations to give himself the option to attack the Soviet Union in the summer of 1940, after France had fallen and it was clear that there would be no quick victory over Great Britain. Initially the emphasis was on long-term projects that could be used to support an invasion, such as building bases and improving transportation facilities. On December 18, 1940, Hitler issued formal orders to his armed forces to prepare for a quick campaign to crush the USSR without waiting for peace with Britain; these preparations were to be completed by the spring of 1941. Within two weeks, an accurate account of the order, from a source in the German Foreign Ministry, was in Moscow, courtesy of Soviet intelligence. As it was winter, actual preparations continued at only a modest pace.

By the spring of 1941 German military preparations, including the movement of millions of troops throughout Eastern Europe, had become too large to conceal. Therefore, Hitler, his generals, and civilian officials came up with a deception campaign that included a number of false explanations. These had a degree of plausibility because Germany was very much at war with Britain at the time and had a mutually advantageous relationship with the Soviet Union. For example, the Germans explained away the presence of their forces along the border with the USSR as training for an invasion of Britain that was being conducted outside the range of the Royal Air Force. To support this deception, English-language interpreters and maps of Britain were sent to *Luftwaffe* units in Eastern Europe. In discussions with Moscow, Berlin characterized its seizure of the Balkans in the spring of 1941 as a response to local events and efforts to aid its Italian ally and improve Germany's position in its struggle with the British in the Mediterranean, which, again, was plausible. In early June, Propaganda Minister Joseph Goebbels wrote an editorial in the Nazi Party newspaper claiming that the recent airstrike on Crete had been practice for an invasion of Britain. After enough copies were out to guarantee that foreign reporters had them, the issue was ostentatiously confiscated, as if a state secret had been revealed.

Warnings of a likely German attack came from outside normal Soviet reporting channels. In March 1941, President Franklin Roosevelt (1882–1945) authorized the American ambassador in Moscow to pass a message that was based on reports from the American Embassy in Berlin, as well as decrypted Japanese diplomatic cables. The content was carefully worded to avoid revealing the communications intercepts.

> ...the Government of the United States, while endeavoring to estimate the developing world situation, has come into the possession of information which it regards as authentic, clearly indicating that it is the intention of Germany to attack the Soviet Union.

Stalin wrote "Provocation!" on the report when it reached his desk, and took no action.

In Britain there was an elaborate – and extremely successful and sensitive – program to intercept and decrypt high-level German communications. The British assigned this material the codeword "Ultra" and sometimes also referred to it as "Enigma," which was the German name of the encoding machine. In late March 1941, there was an Ultra report about the movement of German forces in Eastern Europe. Several panzer divisions had been diverted to deal with the situation in the Balkans – but their original destination had been Poland. Churchill believed that this showed that the Germans were serious about invading the USSR. After several weeks of debate within the British government over whether it was wise and useful to inform the Soviets, Churchill, in an unprecedented move, sent the following carefully phrased personal message to Stalin on April 21:

> I have sure information from a trusted agent that when the Germans thought they had got Yugoslavia in the net, that is to say after March 20, they began to move three out of the five Panzer divisions from Roumania to Southern Poland. The moment they heard of the Serbian revolution this movement was

countermanded. Your Excellency will readily appreciate the significance of these facts.

Stalin, ever suspicious, believed that Churchill was trying to push the USSR into a war that would relieve the pressure on Britain. In addition, he had some reporting through his own intelligence channels that appeared to support this hypothesis, so he assigned no importance to the warning from Churchill.

Stalin's scenario for the future in the spring of 1941 was that he probably had another year before relations with Germany deteriorated to the point that war would be likely. He told his intelligence collectors that his primary requirements were: (1) advanced warning about what terms Germany might demand for future cooperation, or (2) indications that Britain would make a separate peace. Any assessment that war was imminent and inevitable was made harder by mixed input from Soviet intelligence. Some reports suggested, for example, that Hitler had not yet made up his mind about how to handle the Soviet Union and was still interested in a deal, especially one that would give Germany privileged access to the USSR's economic resources. There were also indications that Hitler wanted to forge a great continental diplomatic bloc, including the USSR, that would convince the British that it was impossible for them to find allies; and therefore they could come to an agreement with Germany to end the war. Naturally, Stalin gave great credence to reports, like these, that confirmed his preconceptions.

These reassuring indicators were supported by some of Moscow's best spies. Anthony Blunt (1907–83), one of the "Cambridge five" spies who, had been recruited by Soviet intelligence in the 1930s, passed along analyses from the British Foreign Office stating that there was no evidence that a German attack was planned for the summer of 1941. Another member of the Cambridge five, Kim Philby (1912–88), reported that the mysterious flight to Scotland in May 1940 by Deputy Fuhrer Rudolf Hess was an attempt by Britain and Germany to make a deal at the Soviet Union's expense.

Those closest to the German buildup, however, saw clear indications that something major (suggesting the possibility of an attack) was going on. Soviet border patrol units worked for the NKVD, and in April 1941 a unit protecting the border in the Ukraine reported:

> Agent reporting and debriefing of border crossers establishes that the Germans are intensively preparing for war with the USSR, for which purpose they are concentrating troops on our borders, building road and fortifications, and bringing in munitions.

Red Army commanders also received tactical information on German activity through their own channels, and senior officers became increasingly alarmed in the spring of 1941. The Germans were dramatically increasing the number of reconnaissance flights, large numbers of troops and vehicles were moving closer to the border, and German deserters claimed that their units were preparing for an assault. The Germans, in an effort to maintain the deception, explained that the suspicious flights were inexperienced crews who had made navigational errors. Stalin ordered his forces not to fire on the aircraft. Soviet military commanders made limited preparations to repel an attack but felt they could not disobey Stalin's order to avoid provocative actions. Those in Moscow who did not believe Hitler would order an assault acknowledged the military buildup but asserted that it was only a means to apply pressure on Moscow for territorial and economic concessions.

Richard Sorge (1895–1944), a German national and Communist Party member operating as a Soviet spy under journalist cover, had managed to ingratiate himself with the German embassy in Tokyo. The Japanese were allied with the Germans, and there was much that an observant agent could learn in the Japanese capital, even though it was on the other side of the world. Throughout the winter of 1940–1941, Sorge had been reporting on a German buildup of troops and equipment in Eastern Europe.

By May 1941 the indicators in Tokyo were becoming more alarming, and on May 6 Sorge told Moscow:

> Possibility of outbreak of war at any moment is very high, because Hitler and his generals are confident that war with USSR will not hamper conduct of war against Britain in the least. German generals estimate the Red Army's fighting capacity is so low that they believe the Red Army will be destroyed in the course of a few weeks . . .

On May 21, he reported:

> New representative who arrived here from Berlin said the war between Germany and USSR may start at the end of May, because they are under orders to return to Berlin by then. However, they also said that it is possible the danger may blow over in this year. They reported that Germany had nine army corps composed of 150 divisions.

Stalin's response to this report was to belittle Sorge as a man preoccupied with women and his private business interests in Tokyo. In other reports, however, Sorge had said that his sources maintained that Hitler still wanted to finish the war with Britain before dealing with the USSR, and a peaceful resolution of differences between Berlin and Moscow was still possible. As might be expected, Stalin paid more attention to the latter reports.

On June 1, Sorge followed up with two separate messages:

> Berlin informed [Ambassador] Ott that German attack will commence in latter part of June . . . The technical department of German Air Force in my city [Tokyo] received orders to return home without delay. Ott instructed military attaché not to send any important reports via USSR. Shipment of rubber through USSR reduced to minimum . . .

> Expected start of German–Soviet war around June 15 is based exclusively on information which Lieutenant-Colonel Scholl brought with him from Berlin, which he left on May 6 . . .

Intelligence officials in Moscow characterized them as a "provocation."

By mid-June, the Soviet military leadership was so concerned about German troop movements and reconnaissance activities that Minister of Defense General Semyon Timoshenko (1895–1970) and Chief of Staff General Georgy Zhukov (1896–1974) recommended putting their forces on full alert. Stalin rejected their proposal, saying that he did not want to provoke a war. Stalin asked how many German divisions were along the border, and they replied approximately 150. Stalin said that his information was that there were fewer and that the Germans did not yet have enough forces for an attack. The officers pointed out that their information was that German divisions were larger than Soviet ones, but Stalin replied that intelligence could not always be believed.

With a few exceptions, such as Churchill, most senior British officials had not believed that a German attack on the USSR was imminent, but by early June the weight of evidence concerning troop movements and the enhancement of communications networks had convinced many of them to change their minds. On June 16, the British gave the Soviet ambassador in London a summary of German deployments in Eastern Europe, based on all their sources, including Ultra decrypts. The ambassador passed it along; but, well aware of Stalin's views (as well as that his job as ambassador and perhaps even his life were at stake), noted in his comments that military intelligence reports were not always accurate and it was in the British interest to have the USSR come into the war against Germany. The ambassador did go so far as to suggest that the British material was food for thought, corroboration should be sought, and the forces on the USSR's border should be put on alert.

A day later, in Moscow, in a rare example of a contrary report making it all the way to the top, senior Soviet intelligence officials told Stalin that one of their prized sources, who worked the German Ministry of Aviation, had said:

> ...the leading circles of the German Ministry of Aviation and the Staff of the Air Force are convinced that the issue of the attack by Germany on the Soviet Union is definitely decided. Regardless of whether any demands are put to the Soviet Union in advance – we should take into account the possibility of a surprise attack.

Stalin replied that this was disinformation.

Even the fact, reported on June 18, that the German Embassy in Moscow was sending home members of the staff and their families and destroying its papers did not shake Stalin's belief in the correctness of his analysis.

On the evening of June 21, Timoshenko and Zhukov made another trip to the Kremlin and asked Stalin to put Soviet forces on alert, as they had compelling information that an attack was imminent. Tactical reports from the border about suspicious German activities, anomalies that could not be accounted for by the prevailing mindset, had been arriving in disturbing numbers. Stalin was concerned by these reports but still maintained that to respond would be premature and would provoke Hitler. He believed that there was still time for a peaceful settlement of differences with Germany. Stalin did agree, however, to send out a warning that hostile German actions were possible in the coming days but that Soviet commanders should try to avoid anything that would increase tensions. He authorized a few defensive measures, but no further actions should be taken without specific orders. The message went out at 30 minutes after midnight.

Early on the morning of June 22, 1941, there were famous scenes of German officers, standing by to give the order to strike, watching in utter disbelief as trains carrying Soviet goods to feed the German war machine continued to cross the border. At 4:00 A.M., German artillery opened fire. Even after the first reports came in of guns firing, instructions from the Soviet military command, still operating in Stalin's framework, saw the German actions as unprovoked and minor, rather than as indicators of war. Orders assuming that Hitler's intentions were still peaceful went to the foreign ministry to contact Berlin for an explanation of the firing. In the months that followed, massive losses of Soviet men and equipment would be one of the greatest defeats in history, and a tremendous effort was required to avoid losing the war.

Stalin's role as dictator required him to appear all-knowing and infallible, but his shortcomings as an analyst demonstrate many of the cognitive pitfalls that analysts face. These included faulty assumptions about what the start of a war would look like and giving more credence to reports that confirm one's point of view while undervaluing contradictory information. Stalin also used a variant of the rational actor model, believing that it would not make sense for Hitler to undertake a war on two fronts.

These natural pitfalls were exacerbated by the fact that the Germans were conducting a skillful deception campaign. The events of 1941 show that, when dealing with deception, tactical indicators are more likely to be true than are long-held strategic assessments. A sizable number of indicators received through different and independent channels can form a better basis of assessment than strategic judgments that could be false or out-of-date.

Stalin's failure to accurately assess Hitler in 1941 was not caused by a lack of information. In fact, in the 1930s – and for decades after – the USSR had one of the best espionage organizations in history. Although there were false and misleading reports in the mix, overall sufficient indicators were present to have made possible a conclusion other than the one Stalin reached. There is some controversy regarding Sorge, as not all of his reports may have been sent, and those that did reach Moscow varied in accuracy and importance. Moreover, later (after Stalin had died), it was very much in the interest of Soviet intelligence to discredit Stalin and emphasize the competence of Soviet operatives. Nonetheless, the clandestine collection system overall performed admirably; it was what Stalin made of those reports that was the problem.

Questions for Further Thought

Why were the Germans so successful in their deception?

Is it an example of the hindsight bias to believe, now that we know the outcome, that it was inevitable that Hitler would attack the USSR? What was the quality of the evidence available at the time both for and against this view?

What might have been some better ways to organize Soviet intelligence to mitigate the problems associated with having Stalin serve as the senior intelligence analyst? Would these have been practical?

What other countries currently might have similar systems and vulnerabilities?

Recommended Reading

Barros, James, and Gregor, Richard, *Double Deception: Stalin, Hitler, and the Invasion of Russia*, DeKalb, IL: Northern Illinois University Press, 1995.

Gorodetsky, Gabriel, *Grand Delusion: Stalin and the German Invasion of Russia*, New Haven, CT: Yale University Press, 1999.

Murphy, David, *What Stalin Knew: The Enigma of Barbarossa*, New Haven, CT: Yale University Press, 2005.

Read, Anthony, and Fisher, David, *The Deadly Embrace: Hitler, Stalin, and the Nazi-Soviet Pact, 1939–1941*, New York: W. W. Norton, 1980.

Whaley, Barton, *Codeword BARBAROSSA*, Cambridge, MA: MIT Press, 1973.

Whymant, Robert, *Stalin's Spy: Richard Sorge and the Tokyo Espionage Ring*, New York: St. Martin's Press, 1998.

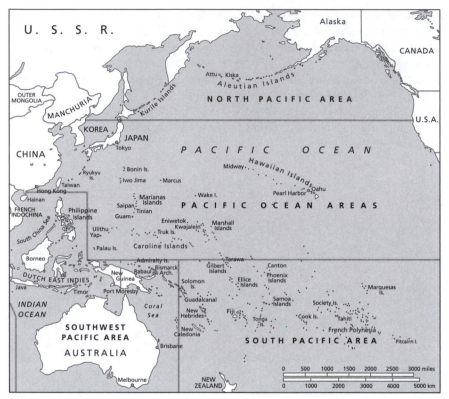

Figure 12. The Pacific in World War II

12

Pearl Harbor

I N 1941 MUCH OF THE WORLD WAS AT WAR, WITH THE UNITED STATES THE only major power still on the sidelines. American public opinion was strongly isolationist, but many in the government, including President Franklin Roosevelt, believed that U.S. involvement was inevitable. Roosevelt's focus, however, was on and across the Atlantic Ocean, where Nazi Germany's army had overrun most of Europe and its navy was threatening Britain's maritime lifelines. In October 1941, in two separate incidents, U.S. warships escorting shipments to Britain were torpedoed by German submarines. If either – or worse, both – of the two remaining German opponents, Britain or the USSR, were defeated or sued for peace, the United States would be in an extremely unfavorable strategic position. To prepare for a likely war, Roosevelt provided armaments to the British and Soviets, and set in motion a new building program for the U.S. Navy, among other preparatory measures.

Asia, in contrast, seemed less dangerous. Japan had been fighting to take over part of China for a decade, but the situation there had settled into a stalemate. The Japanese also appeared interested in taking advantage of Germany's victory over France and the Netherlands in 1940 and its continuing heavy pressure on Britain, to perhaps take over some of the European colonies in Southeast Asia; but it was not clear when or where this might actually happen. The U.S. government did not want a new and expanded round of fighting in Southeast Asia. Washington hoped to stop Japanese aggression by taking advantage of the fact that the United States was Japan's largest source of vital raw materials and imposed an embargo on exports of oil and scrap steel to Japan. To further increase pressure on Japan, officials in Washington also moved much of the Pacific Fleet from bases in California to Hawaii.

Priorities, threats, and opportunities looked different from Tokyo's point of view. The main driver, or determinant, for Japanese leaders was the fact that they governed a collection of modestly sized islands with a large and growing population and few natural resources. Japanese ministers, generals, and admirals saw expansion into Southeast Asia as a way to restrict outside help to China as well as to obtain badly needed commodities such as oil, rubber, rice, and tin. They saw this as a life or death issue; time, in their view, was not on their side, so they had to act quickly.

There were some doubts and disagreements in Tokyo about the risks involved in a new campaign in Southeast Asia. In time, however, senior officials decided that Japan had to seize control of the area. They also concluded that U.S. bases in the Philippines and Hawaii could pose a threat along their eastern flank that would have to be weakened or removed. Japanese leaders had no intention of invading the continental United States, but instead hoped that a sharp blow would give them an opportunity to consolidate their position in eastern Asia to such an extent that Washington would calculate that it was not worth its while to interfere. As a result, starting late in 1940 a small team of Japanese naval officers began working in secret on a bold plan to attack Pearl Harbor by using warplanes launched from aircraft carriers.

As this threat quietly took shape, American decision making regarding the Pacific region was based on virtually no information about what was going on at the senior levels of the Japanese government. The United States simply had no clandestine collection capability in Japan. In any case, gathering accurate information about Japanese capabilities and intentions was extremely difficult, as the Japanese were conducting an elaborate denial and deception campaign to cover their next moves. Nonetheless, the American embassy in Tokyo had considerable insight into Japanese psychology, noting at one point, when assessing the chances of a conflict between Japan and the United States, that "National sanity would dictate against such an event, but Japanese sanity cannot be measured by our own standards of logic." The embassy, however, did not realize the extent to which Japanese leaders saw the United States as a threat.

In one intriguing report in January 1941 the embassy told Washington that it had heard from contacts in the Peruvian embassy that if relations between Washington and Tokyo deteriorated the Japanese would attack Pearl Harbor. The embassy was incredulous but passed the information on to the State Department. Those who read the report in Washington wondered how the Peruvians, of all people, could possibly have reliable information on such a sensitive topic, so they discounted it. In fact, nothing happened in the months that followed, so there was little further interest in the report until much later.

Americans had conducted a strategic assessment of the threat from Japan but had concluded that there was little reason to be concerned. The personnel of the now-reinforced base at Pearl Harbor in Hawaii were confident that it could handle any developments. In addition to the new warships, it had large numbers of fighters and bombers, as well as extensive supplies and fortifications. In war games over the years, American commanders had considered the possibility of a Japanese attack but had assumed that it was virtually impossible because, among other things, Japanese warships could not carry enough fuel to carry them across the more than 4,000 miles (6,400 kilometers) that separated Japan from Hawaii. Even if the Japanese made it that far, torpedoes would not function properly in the relatively shallow waters of Pearl Harbor. What they did not realize was that, in 1941, the Japanese navy solved both of these problems.

Other aspects of American thinking reinforced such complacency. Hawaii itself – beautiful, peaceful, and isolated – contributed to the sense of calm. More broadly, American analysts believed that Japan would never be so foolish as to undertake what would obviously be a suicidal attack against an enemy that had ten times the industrial production. Moreover, racial attitudes at the time meant that many believed that the Japanese were inherently inferior.

A final advantage inspiring confidence that the situation was not threatening, known only to a few, was that American cryptographers had successfully broken some Japanese codes and were reading many of the diplomatic cables that Tokyo exchanged with its embassies abroad. American planners assumed that the insights from the intercepted messages, plus public events, such as an ultimatum or breaking diplomatic relations, would give them several days warning, during which time the fleet could be put to sea and thus be much harder to find and attack.

In Hawaii from June 1940 through October 1941, the base was put on alert several times in response to the deteriorating diplomatic and military situation in East Asia. These alerts generated considerable disruption and expense, but nothing happened. Many began to believe that the alerts were a waste of resources.

As the autumn of 1941 passed, communications intercepts and other reports tracked the tensions in Asia. One of the intercepted messages, which had been transmitted from Tokyo in late September but was not processed until October 9, contained instructions to a Japanese spy in Honolulu. His orders were to break Pearl Harbor into five reporting zones and then to collect information on each.

> With regard to warships and aircraft carriers, we would like to have you report on those at anchor (these are not so important), tied up at wharves, buoys, and in docks. (Designate types and classes briefly. If possible, we would like to have you make mention of the fact when there are two or more vessels alongside the same wharf.)

Analysts in Washington, who tended to have communications backgrounds, interpreted the new Japanese zone-based reporting framework as a way to shorten messages. Shorter messages were easier to handle, and short transmissions meant that the sending station was harder to detect using direction finding equipment, such as that employed by counterintelligence units in the military and the Federal Bureau of Investigation (FBI). Analysts also saw that similar messages were sent to several ports in addition to Honolulu, thus they believed that they could be an indication of Japanese thoroughness and attention to detail.

During November, the intercepted diplomatic cables took on a more ominous tone. On November 2, for example, Tokyo told its embassy in Washington:

> ... We have carefully considered a fundamental policy for improving relations between Japan and America, but we expect to reach a final decision in a meeting on the morning of the 5th and will let you know the results at once. This will be our Government's last effort to improve diplomatic relations. The situation is very grave ...

Also throughout November there was a stream of reports regarding a convoy of Japanese warships and transports heading south from the home islands. This information seemed to indicate an increasing threat to areas such as French Indochina, the Dutch East Indies, and Hong Kong. The convoy was real, but concern about it attracted attention from other possible scenarios for the future.

The Japanese continued with their extremely effective denial and deception campaign. On November 16, American analysts noted that high-frequency, long-range communications intercepts from the Japanese carriers had ceased and assumed that this meant that the warships were in port and using only low-frequency communications. In fact, the Japanese were imposing radio silence. When the fleet that was to attack Pearl Harbor left northern Japan at the end of November, it traveled through some of the least-traveled maritime routes in the world to minimize the chance of detection. On December 1, American listening posts noted that the Japanese fleet changed its call signs, a precaution that was normally done every six months – but had just been done on November 1. Back at Japanese naval bases, a higher percentage of the remaining sailors were allowed to go on liberty so that it would not be obvious that so many had departed.

Senior commanders in Washington were focused on the deteriorating diplomatic situation. On November 24, the Chief of Naval Operations sent out the following message:

> Chances of favorable outcome of negotiations with Japan very doubtful. This situation coupled with statements of Japanese Government and movements their naval and military forces indicate in our opinion that a surprise aggressive movement in any direction including attack on Philippines or Guam is a possibility. Chief of Staff has seen this dispatch concurs and requests action adees to inform senior Army officers their areas. Utmost secrecy necessary in order not to complicate an already tense situation or precipitate Japanese action. Guam will be informed separately.

Three days later there was an even more urgent warning from the naval command staff, including instructions to be especially concerned about sabotage.

> This dispatch is to be considered a war warning. Negotiations with Japan looking toward stabilization of conditions in the Pacific have ceased and an aggressive move by Japan is expected within the next few days. The number and equipment of Japanese troops and the organization of naval task forces indicates an amphibious expedition against either the Philippines, Thai, or Kra Peninsula, or possibly Borneo. Execute an appropriate defensive deployment reparatory to carrying out the tasks assigned in WPL 46. Inform district and Army authorities. A similar warning is being sent by War Department.

> ... inform British. Continental districts Guam, Samoa directed take appropriate measures against sabotage.

That same day, November 27, the headquarters of Army intelligence in Washington sent guidance to the ground forces commander in Hawaii, again emphasizing the danger of sabotage.

> Japanese negotiations have come to practical stalemate stop Hostilities may ensue stop Subversive activities may be expected stop Inform commanding general and Chief of Staff only.

Intercepted Japanese diplomatic cables appeared to confirm that a break in diplomatic relations was imminent. Officials in Tokyo were concerned that this break might interfere with their ability to send encrypted messages to their embassies, so alternative means to send important messages in the clear were advisable. On November 28, U.S. intelligence distributed a recently processed Japanese message that had been sent nine days earlier.

> Regarding the broadcast of a special message in an emergency.
>
> In case of emergency (danger of cutting off our diplomatic relations) and the cutting off of international communications, the following warning will be added in the middle of the daily Japanese language short wave news broadcast.
>
> (1) In case of Japan–U.S. relations in danger: east wind rain.
> (2) Japan–U.S.S.R. relations: north wind cloudy.
> (3) Japan–British relations: west wind clear.
>
> This signal will be given in the middle and at the end as a weather forecast and each sentence will be repeated twice. When this is heard please destroy all code papers etc. This is as yet to be a completely secret arrangement.
> Forward as urgent intelligence.

Such an emergency message was never intercepted by American intelligence, and it may never have been sent, but the fact that the Japanese government was preparing for a break in diplomatic relations between Tokyo and other capitals was ominous.

Japan was also keeping its allies informed, although only in general terms. On November 30, the foreign ministry told its embassy in Berlin to inform the German leadership that:

> . . . there is extreme danger that war may suddenly break out between the Anglo-Saxon nations and Japan through some clash of arms and add that the time of the breaking out of this war may come quicker than anyone dreams.

In early December, most of the attention was still on diplomatic tensions and Southeast Asia. On December 3, the naval command staff in Washington noted the standard preparations for an imminent break in diplomatic relations.

> Highly reliable information has been received that categoric and urgent instructions were sent yesterday to Japanese diplomatic and consular posts at Hongkong, Singapore, Batavia, Manila, Washington, and London to destroy most of their codes and ciphers at once and to burn all other important confidential and secret documents.

Three days later, the FBI in Hawaii confirmed that, in fact, the Japanese consulate there was burning its papers.

On December 6, Tokyo began sending its embassy in Washington a long message in fourteen parts. Important segments read:

> ... Thus the earnest hope of the Japanese Government to adjust Japanese–American relations and to preserve and promote the peace of the Pacific through cooperation with the American Government has finally been lost.

> The Japanese Government regrets to have to notify hereby the American Government that in view of the attitude of the American Government it cannot but consider that it is impossible to reach an agreement through further negotiations.

> ... Will the Ambassador please submit to the United States Government (if possible to Secretary of State), our reply to the United States at 1:00 p.m. on the 7th, your time [7:30 a.m. December 7 in Hawaii].

> ... please destroy at once the remaining cipher machine and all machine codes. Dispose in like manner also secret documents.

As of the morning of Sunday, December 7, Washington time, American analysts had concluded that, probably as a result of imminent offensive action in Southeast Asia, Japan was about to break diplomatic relations with the United States.

As a result of the lack of urgency in both Hawaii and Washington, last-minute, tactical indicators were not understood. That morning American patrol vessels sighted and attacked submarines at the entrance to Pearl Harbor. In addition, a unit using new radar technology actually detected the incoming planes an hour before the attack, but planes were thought to be U.S. bombers coming from California that were expected at about the same time. A few minutes before 8:00 a.m., the bombs started falling.

Pearl Harbor is, of course, one of the most famous and consequential examples of failure in intelligence analysis. As a result, the United States was thrust into a war it had hoped to avoid, with the serious initial disadvantage of having a large proportion of its fleet sunk or badly damaged (see Figure 13).

One of the main reasons the United States was caught by surprise was that analysts and decision makers in Washington and Hawaii did not understand the viewpoint of decision makers in Tokyo. Japan's leaders were strongly influenced by a distorted version of samurai culture, in which a military solution was readily contemplated, especially in response to an external threat, and a glorious defeat was an acceptable outcome. In the leaders' system of values, spirit was more important than material strength, and death was preferable to humiliation. Japanese military leaders believed that

Figure 13. Wreckage of the *USS Arizona*, Pearl Harbor, December 1941 (U.S. Navy photograph, Library of Congress)

continuation of an unsatisfactory status quo would, in fact, be a defeat, so they had to strike before their oil reserves were exhausted and the United States grew even more powerful. Moreover, steps that Washington saw as part of the normal diplomatic procedure of signaling concern and peaceful pressure, such as embargoing the sale of raw materials and moving part of the fleet, were seen in Japan as serious threats to vital interests. The U.S. embassy in Tokyo pointed out that defiance rather than restraint was a more likely response to American pressure, but this did not bring a change in Washington's approach. Without an appropriate analytic framework, even accurate information would not be understood correctly.

From the perspective of collection, U. S. analysts and decision makers did not realize the seriousness of the gaps in the information that they were collecting on Japan. The American embassy in Tokyo did not have access to decision making at the top levels of the Japanese government and military. Although they were intercepting Japanese diplomatic cables, the most important naval and military codes had not been broken. As a result, in the last weeks before the attack, crucial events were not detected. For example, the Japanese navy stopped the normal rotation of senior officers so that experienced personnel would remain in key positions. The dispatch of operational orders to the Japanese fleet in early November 1941, the final attack order two weeks later, and the actual departure of the warships at the end of the month also were not detected.

Some have suggested, with the benefit of hindsight, that if all of the available indicators had been gathered at one place the attack could have been anticipated. Most, if not all, of these indicators have been provided in this summary. It is true that American analysts and decision makers in 1941 did not fully understand that there were important things that they were not seeing and that there could be other explanations and possible outcomes for what they were seeing. A review of the most valuable information, the intercepted Japanese diplomatic cables, shows, however, that none of them, singly or in combination, clearly gave the precise timing, target, or method of the attack. Finally, as noted, there was significant information, such as Japanese technical improvements and the departure date of the strike force, that was not collected.

The bureaucratic difficulties of processing intelligence in a large organization were also an important contribution to the Pearl Harbor failure. There was poor cooperation between army and navy. In addition, the distribution of significant signals intelligence was limited. There seems to have been little effort to step back and reassess the big picture.

It is worth noting that, despite the tactical brilliance of the Japanese attack, there was also a huge strategic intelligence failure on the part of decision makers in Tokyo. They do not seem to have understood that a surprise attack on U.S. territory would rally a divided America in favor of war and that, if their original gamble failed, they had virtually no chance of victory in a long conflict against a United States with vastly superior resources. There appears to have been no serious, well-informed Japanese assessment of risks or options.

Questions for Further Thought

What were some of the cognitive shortcomings that undermined American analysis of Japanese plans and activities in 1941? How central were they to the overall failure?

Pearl Harbor and Barbarossa are two of the best examples of successful and significant deception in war. What are some analytic techniques that might have overcome these deceptions?

What are some current situations in which diplomatic signals might be misunderstood and actually exacerbate tensions?

In the years since World War II, has technology made it easier to prevent a
surprise such as Pearl Harbor?

Recommended Reading

Feis, Herbert, *The Road to Pearl Harbor: The Coming of the War Between the United States
and Japan*, Princeton, NJ: Princeton University Press, 1950.

Ike, Nobutako, trans. and ed., *Japan's Decision for War: Records of the 1941 Policy Conferences*, Stanford, CA: Stanford University Press, 1967.

Prange, Gordon W., *At Dawn We Slept: The Untold Story of Pearl Harbor*, New York:
Penguin, 1991.

Wohlstetter, Roberta, *Pearl Harbor: Warning and Decision*, Stanford, CA: Stanford University Press, 1962.

13

Targets for the Allied Bombers

TECHNOLOGICAL DEVELOPMENTS IN THE FIRST THIRD OF THE TWENTIETH century brought an entirely new military capability: the long-range strategic bomber that could deliver a large payload over hundreds of miles. Advocates of strategic bombing claimed that this capability had the potential to defeat an enemy without the traditional need to destroy forces in the field. Now commanders could hope to achieve a strategic goal of striking at the enemy's capacity to wage war, such as industrial production, transportation links, and the population. After the fall of France in the spring of 1940, strategic bombing was the only way Britain could hope to inflict damage on Germany, until a cross-Channel invasion could be organized.

During World War II, the main problem for Allied bombers was one of efficiency, or how to have the most impact on the German war effort with the fewest bombs. The solution was to target a limited number of facilities based on their importance to the German war economy and their vulnerability. Analysis was done in two steps: Suitable targets were identified, then results of the bombing were evaluated to determine if further strikes were necessary. Intelligence analysis could play a crucial role in this process, but British and American targeters came up with quite different ways to go about it.

The Royal Air Force's (RAF) doctrine for strategic bombing concentrated on massive, nighttime attacks on large targets, mainly cities. British planners believed that this was the only effective approach because bombing from a high altitude was inherently inaccurate, making it difficult to hit specific facilities, and flying at night to reduce vulnerability to enemy fighter aircraft and antiaircraft artillery made bombing even less reliable. The British also found out that some specific targets, such as the concrete U-boat pens along the coast of occupied France, were virtually impossible to destroy. As a result, the British gave priority to striking cities, hoping that they would damage important industrial targets in urban areas. They believed that an additional benefit would be that any damage to civilian facilities, such as housing, would undermine the population's morale. According to strategic bombing's most ardent advocates, a successful air campaign might even make it unnecessary to undertake a risky invasion.

To select targets and assess damage, British analysts drew on a wide variety of sources, including aerial reconnaissance, communications intercepts, interviews with refugees and captured prisoners, professional and technical journals, and building plans held by banks and insurance companies.

Starting in 1942, the Americans were in the war in Europe bringing vast resources, but also another approach, to strategic bombing. The U.S. Army Air Force (USAAF) had an Air War Plans Division that selected targets. American planners preferred precision bombing of specific facilities, which they believed could be effectively done only during daylight hours. They were willing to accept the risk of high losses to do more significant damage. The difficulty was that, with Nazi Germany in control of much of Europe, there were thousands of potential targets.

American planning drew on the expertise of civilian analysts in the Research and Analysis (R&A) branch of the Office of Strategic Services (OSS). An R&A unit in London supported the American approach of precision bombing by conducting detailed studies of the German economy. The London R&A staff included Charles Kindleberger (1910–2003), who would later be a renowned professor of economic history at the Massachusetts Institute of Technology, and Walt Rostow (1916–2003), who would be President Lyndon Johnson's National Security Advisor. These analysts used a form of cost/benefit analysis. They calculated the cost of American aircraft, fuel, bombs, and so forth, then tried to find targets the destruction of which would bring a higher cost to Germany – hopefully considerably higher– than the cost to destroy them, including losses of planes and crews.

Both the Americans and the British agreed that the initial priority was to establish air superiority over Western Europe. The goal was to destroy the ability of German fighters to shoot down Allied bombers by either defeating the fighters in air battles or destroying their bases, production facilities, and supplies on the ground. After the threat from the fighters was removed or sharply reduced, it was hoped that the Allied bombers could fly anywhere they wanted. Over time, planners identified approximately 150 factories as key targets to undermine the German fighters because these facilities produced aircraft, fuel, and crucial parts, such as ball bearings.

By the end of 1943, Allied strategic bombings had produced only modest results. Serious damage had been inflicted on a number of important targets, such as factories where fighters and ball bearings were produced,

Figure 14. American B-17 bombers over Germany in 1943 (U.S. Army Air Force photograph)

the Peenemünde rocket test facility, and the Ploesti oil fields in Romania. Losses of British and American personnel and planes had been high, however, and bad weather had hindered operations (see Figure 14). Although production and transportation had been made more difficult for the Germans, these crucial functions were continuing, even increasing. The Germans found effective ways to deal with the air attacks by making repairs and dispersing production. It was clear that not enough damage had been done to convince the Germans to surrender. A major part of the problem continued to be an inability to identify a few targets the destruction of which would have a decisive impact.

A major assumption underlying the Allied assessment was that the German economy was fully mobilized for war; with few resources in reserve, and therefore only limited damage to factories and other facilties through bombing could have a significant effect on production. What Allied analysts did not realize was that, in fact, there were many inefficiencies in the German wartime economy. As late as 1943, for example, Germany was not on a wartime footing. Hitler had his own set of assumptions that also turned out to be mistaken, including that the war would be a short one. As a result, well into the war, significant German resources were still devoted to consumer production and, for ideological reasons, women were not used for factory work. Moreover, widely used German techniques of looting and slave labor were not efficient.

Early in 1944, the Allied debate over priorities for strategic bombing was focused on the coming amphibious attack across the English Channel to begin the liberation of Europe, Operation Overlord. The British had a proposal, developed by an English academic, to focus on transportation, particularly key railroad facilities in France, such as marshalling yards and repair depots. These targets were large, easy to find and hit, and involved a wide variety of assets, such as buildings, tracks, and rolling stock. The idea was to strike fewer than a hundred key targets but also to spread them over a wide area so that the Normandy area would not be revealed as being of importance to the Allies. It was hoped that disrupting rail transportation would keep the Germans from using their local superiority in numbers against the Allied landing force while the beachhead was still vulnerable.

The Americans, in contrast, proposed, with support from the OSS analysts, that oil-related facilities should be a high priority. Germany had no domestic sources of natural oil and was dependent on synthetic fuel and imports from Romania and other countries. U.S. analysts claimed that there were just fourteen plants that produced more than three quarters of Germany's synthetic fuel and a further thirteen refineries that produced more than half of Germany's oil. OSS analysts were concerned that the results produced by the alternative plan targeting transportation would not be as quick or as important because the rail network was large, with many possible routes. Moreover, they believed that the railroad lines were easy to repair and bridges would be difficult to hit.

General Dwight Eisenhower (1890–1969), the Supreme Allied Commander, not only had to carry out a successful invasion, but also had to keep the alliance together, so he made a compromise decision in March 1944. Priority would go to attacking the key rail yards in France, but when operations there were restricted because of bad weather, the bombers could attack oil facilities in Germany. To support the decision to give transportation top priority, the Americans attacked more and more bridges in the weeks before D-Day.

By the spring of 1944, another distraction in selecting bombing targets was the discovery that the Germans were building facilities in France for launching their V-weapon. Hitler and other Nazi leaders had publicly boasted that they had a new, powerful weapon that would be used as a "retaliation weapon" (*Vergeltungswaffe*) in response to the Allied strategic bombing of

German cities. Although the exact nature of the V-weapon was mysterious, it was clear from the way in which the sites were laid out that they were aimed at London. It was impossible to ignore this threat, and some of the bombers had to be diverted to strike the launch sites.

The D-Day landings in June 1944 were, of course, a success, so in the autumn of 1944, after Allied control of France was clearly established, transportation, oil, and cities were all being heavily attacked in a mutually reinforcing campaign that crippled the German war machine. The Germans tried classic denial and deception techniques, such as camouflage, dispersion, and decoy facilities. They were also skilled at repairs, but disruption increased. Intercepted communications revealed to the Allies that the Germans were increasingly concerned about fuel shortages. Although the Germans were able to achieve surprise in the opening phase of the Battle of the Bulge in December, they could not exploit their initial advantage because of low reserves of fuel for their tanks.

By the beginning of 1945, the combined effects of the attacks on transportation and oil had reduced weapons production to about a third of what it had been at its peak the summer before. Many factories, refineries, and mines were still intact, but the ability to move goods and fuel had been sharply curtailed. At the end of January, Armaments Minister Albert Speer (1905–81) told Hitler that, from an industrial point of view, the war was virtually over.

After the war actually did end in May 1945 and Germany was occupied, the United States conducted a strategic bombing survey to assess the results of the air campaign. The survey determined that, although the damage inflicted was extensive, until the spring of 1944 the planners had not always selected targets that would have had the most impact on the economic assets that supported the German war effort. When the attacks became more focused on oil and transportation, bombing had a greater impact. Nonetheless, some other German vulnerabilities, such as power stations, were not fully appreciated.

Viewed more broadly, looking at the pros and cons of strategic bombing, the air campaign against Germany in World War II remains controversial. More than 2,000,000 tons (1.8 billion kilograms) of bombs were dropped, and the war was probably shortened, but this was a huge expense in money, lives, and property. There were tens of thousands of casualties on both sides, including many civilians. Significant damage was inflicted on many historic cities, again including heavy losses to homes and cultural sites, in addition to whatever military and economic targets were destroyed. In the end, it was not strategic bombing that brought the war to a close. Germany's surrender came only after Allied ground forces had occupied most of the country.

Questions for Further Thought

What were the best targets for the bombers? What are the best criteria for selecting targets?

What was the quality of the data available to the targeting analysts? What other information would have been helpful?

What role did strategic bombing have in hastening the end of World War II? Any war? Would better targets have made the strategy more effective?

Recommended Reading

Ehlers, Robert S., Jr., *Targeting the Third Reich: Air Intelligence and the Allied Bombing Campaigns*, Lawrence, KS: University Press of Kansas, 2009.

Hinsley, F. H., *British Intelligence in the Second World War*, abridged version, Cambridge: Cambridge University Press, 1993, chapters 25, 26, and 36.

Katz, Barry M., *Foreign Intelligence: Research and Analysis in the Office of Strategic Services, 1942–1945*, Cambridge, MA: Harvard University Press, 1989.

Levine, Alan J., *The Strategic Bombing of Germany, 1940–1945*, New York: Praeger, 1992.

Neillands, Robin, *The Bomber War: The Allied Air Offensive Against Nazi Germany*, New York: Overlook Press, 2001.

14

The German V-Weapon

I N THE MIDST OF WORLD WAR II, WHEN IT WAS FAR FROM CLEAR WHO WOULD win the conflict, analysts in Britain faced the especially difficult problem of how to find and understand something they had never seen before and determine the level of danger it represented. The challenge was, in the face of German denial and deception, to assess new weapons and to do so in time to produce countermeasures. It would be easiest to develop countermeasures early on during the design phase of a new weapon, but during that phase the nature of the threat is hard to detect because most of the work is done in someone's head or in an office. There is a greater chance of understanding a new weapon during its testing phase, when prototypes are out in the open – but is this too late? When the new weapon is actually operational, it is difficult to develop countermeasures.

During World War II, Hitler from time to time in his speeches mentioned new weapons that Germany was developing, but he gave no details. British and American intelligence analysts were aware that Germany was working on a number of projects, such as the atomic bomb and jet aircraft, that could be a serious threat. Could there be something else?

Starting in late 1942 operatives working on the European continent for the British Secret Intelligence Service (SIS) reported that the Germans were building a new long-range weapon, often referred to as a "rocket" (*Rakete* in German). Over time, other similarly vague but ominous accounts referring to a rocket came from other sources. These reports provided differing (and sometimes contradictory) data on significant details such size, range, fuel, warhead, and – most importantly – when the rocket would be operational. One of the few concrete and common elements of the reports was that the new weapon was being tested at Peenemünde, on the Baltic coast.

The information, however vague, was enough to prompt increased collection, and, in April 1943, photo reconnaissance missions over Peenemünde revealed recently completed construction. The purpose of the new structures was unknown, but analysts believed that Germany could be testing facilities for a new weapon. By June, after further reconnaissance flights, analysts had identified a wingless, cylindrical object, not seen before, that they estimated to be some thirty-five to forty feet (approximately eleven to twelve meters) long. Was this the rocket, and how dangerous was it?

British leaders had to decide if the work at Peenemünde was a serious enough threat to justify a Royal Air Force (RAF) attack. Before they diverted bombers from other important targets and ran the risk of high casualties by conducting a raid so deep into Germany, the British government needed to know more about the capabilities of the German rocket. Therefore, a number of analysts with scientific backgrounds began looking at the problem.

Some experts in London based their assessments on their knowledge of British rockets – rockets that had been used for tactical purposes by their army for more than a century – including "the rockets' red glare" made famous to Americans by the 1814 attack on Fort McHenry in Baltimore. These rockets had only a limited range and a small warhead; as a result, they usually had more psychological impact than destructive power. Over time, artillery, with its greater range, accuracy, and payload, became more useful to commanders.

The British experts in rocketry were uncertain, but initially they concluded that because so much of the weight of a solid fueled rocket was made up of the propellant, a German long-range rocket of the size being discussed (approximately forty feet) would be impractical because it could have only a modest range and carry only a small warhead. The experts acknowledged, however, that they would need many more details from intelligence collectors before making a definitive assessment. As more reports came in, one from a human source claimed that the German rocket's propellant was "liquid air," which only confused the situation further.

Others thought that the mysterious cylinder might not even be the reported rocket. Additional hypotheses included that it could be a torpedo or even some kind of decoy.

Some British scientists believed that attention should also be given to the hypothesis that the rocket might be a radically new weapon with unfamiliar characteristics and capabilities. They noted that the cylinders photographed at Peenemünde might be such a weapon. Because so little had been learned from human sources and aerial reconnaissance focused on Peenemünde, the scientists suggested widening intelligence collection to cover other indirect indicators of a weapons program, such as the communications of military units that might be responsible for monitoring.test flights.

With collectors energized, more reports came in; but they still did not clarify the situation. Some sources, for example, suggested that the rocket was smaller and might have wings. The photo interpreters trying to make sense of the results of aerial reconnaissance missions were hampered by not knowing exactly what they were looking for. Large construction sites, which included long ramps, were increasingly showing up on the aerial photographs of France. These sites were markedly different in layout from the usual facilities of the Atlantic Wall defenses. Were these hardened operations centers, as some in the military believed, or launch sites for the large rocket?

By August 1943, the level of concern, despite the uncertain reporting, was high enough that the British government finally ordered air raids on the construction sites in France and on the test site at Peenemünde, causing considerable damage. In France, German occupation forces continued work on the sites after the raid, and antiaircraft defenses in the area were strengthened. This response suggested that the facilities were important. After the raid on Peenemünde, damage assessments based on photo reconnaissance indicated that substantial damage had been done. In fact, as a result of the raid, the Germans decided to move the testing ground farther east and production facilities underground. A few of the bombers in the August raid missed their targets and hit a camp near the test site where foreign laborers conscripted for the project lived. Some of these laborers had been the sources of the descriptions of activity at Peenemünde sent through intelligence channels to London. For whatever reason (perhaps the British agents were killed in the bombing, perhaps they were discovered and arrested by the Germans), the British received no further reports from the foreign workers.

At the end of August 1943, a report came in from a human source that began to clarify what the Germans were doing. A senior German official said that there were two programs: a rocket, with a large payload, and a pilotless aircraft. There were some technical problems with some of what the source said, however, and at least one senior British scientist remained unconvinced that that a rocket only about forty feet long could carry both a large warhead and enough fuel to carry it all the way to Britain. Therefore, in his view, the smaller pilotless aircraft, also referred to as a flying bomb, if it existed (none had yet been photographed), should be the greater concern. There was a general belief that use of the new weapons was not imminent, so there was more time to collect further information and to consider countermeasures.

During the fall of 1943, it finally became obvious that there were, in fact, two programs; thus the results of photo reconnaissance, communications intercepts, and reports from human sources could be put into a more accurate context. In November a reconnaissance mission finally captured a flying bomb on one of the launch ramps at Peenemünde, making it clear that the construction of ramps in France were linked to the pilotless aircraft. By the end of 1943, the growing body of intelligence reporting strongly suggested which of the characteristics reported over the years were associated with each project.

- One new weapon was what would later become known as the V-1, sponsored by the *Luftwaffe*. This pilotless aircraft was about 27 feet (8.2 meters) long, with wings and an external engine, and required an elaborate launch site. Its maximum speed was approximately 400 miles (644 kilometers) per hour, and its range was up to approximately 150 miles (250 kilometers).
- The other weapon was the V-2, sponsored by the army, which was much more revolutionary. This rocket was almost 46 feet (14 meters) long, with a sophisticated onboard inertial guidance system and propulsion using a liquid fuel that was a mixture of alcohol and liquid oxygen. The V-2 did not require extensive launching facilities. Its range was just over 200 miles (320 kilometers), and, because of the speed and height at which it traveled, there was no effective defense, given the technology at the time.

With the threat clarifying, bombing of the sites in France intensified, especially against V-1 launching ramps that were oriented toward London. In response to the bombing, the Germans continued repairs on the older sites as a deception that would attract further bombing, while constructing a new type of launch site that was harder to detect from the air. British and American bombers concentrated on the launch sites as targets because they lacked detailed knowledge of other aspects of the program, such as the precise location of manufacturing facilities, which the Germans had dispersed and placed underground.

British experts did not get their first opportunity to see an actual V-1 until May 1944. Two test versions without warheads that had been launched from Germany over the Baltic Sea crashed accidentally in Sweden and in nearby waters, and the neutral Swedes quietly allowed experts from the Britain to examine them. The examination confirmed that the V-1 was a pilotless aircraft, not a rocket. Because the V-1 had flight characteristics not unlike a fighter aircraft, the British felt that existing defense measures dating back to the Battle of Britain in 1940 – radar and observers to spot, and then fighters, antiaircraft artillery, and balloons to destroy – could probably cope with the V-1.

It remained uncertain when the V-1 or the V-2s might be launched. British experts made various estimates that a launch could occur later in 1943 or early in 1944. When these dates came and went, it was obvious that no one on the Allied side really knew the date the weapons would become operational or had an effective way to find out. A major part of the problem, not fully understood at the time, was that on the German side the date kept changing because of factors such as technical glitches and shortages of supplies.

In May 1944, after many delays, Hitler ordered the V-1 attack to begin the following month. This order was reiterated during the evening of D-Day, June 6, after the Allies landed successfully in Normandy. The first pilotless aircraft, or flying bombs, were launched on June 13. They were not particularly accurate, but their main target, London, was a huge area; and the purpose was as much to create psychological strain as to cause physical damage. Although the beginning of the V-1 attacks led to casualties and destruction, it also meant that the British could observe and even capture the weapons, and thus get a much clearer idea of their technical details. Another important countermeasure, the bombing of the launch sites, continued, as this appeared to be a more effective choke point in the system leading from factories to launch sites. With the Allied armies on the continent from June on, countermeasures in the fall of 1944 also included capturing actual or potential launch sites.

In the meantime, the British anticipated that attacks would eventually come using the V-2, but they had little information on the rocket's capabilities that could help in planning countermeasures. A test V-2 had gone astray in Sweden in June 1944, and the wreckage made it clear that this was a machine that was quite different from the V-1 and indeed from any other known weapon. Questions remained unresolved about many important issues, such as fuel, size of the warhead, how the rocket was controlled, and how many of these complicated devices could be produced.

On September 8, just as the British were congratulating themselves on having largely mastered the V-1 threat, they were surprised when the V-2s began arriving. As the V-2s had a somewhat longer range, they could easily be launched from Germany itself or areas still under German control in the Netherlands. Because the rocket was able to travel high into the atmosphere before turning toward its target and it moved so fast that it could not be detected, there was no warning and no way to stop an attack after it had been launched. The only way to prevent V-2 strikes was to capture potential launch sites, and this was one reason why the September 1944 offensive planned by Field Marshal Bernard Montgomery (1887–1976) was launched toward Arnhem, in the Netherlands, rather than directly into Germany.

The launching of both V-1s and V-2s continued until March 1945. In addition to the main target of London, thousands were fired at Antwerp and Liege in Belgium in an effort to disrupt Allied logistics support. In total, more than 12,000 V-1s and 3,000 V-2s were fired over a nine-month period, causing some 13,000 deaths and extensive property damage. They also produced considerable psychological tension, as intended, and led to the diversion of significant resources to deal with them. The attacks by new types of weapons did not keep Germany from losing the war, however. One of the most significant results of the German V-weapon programs was the missile technology that German scientists involved in the projects transferred to the United States, and to a lesser extent to the Soviet Union. The V-1 was the predecessor of the cruise missile, and the V-2 design eventually became the design of the intercontinental ballistic missile.

Understanding the V-weapons was a difficult problem, made even more difficult by the fact that there were no precedents from which to learn. There was a limited amount of information of uncertain quality, and, at least initially, the nature and dimensions of the problem were misunderstood. The keys to a solution were coming up with an accurate framework of understanding and then collecting data that would flesh out that framework.

Initially, cognitive malfunctions (including faulty assumptions) were the main impediments to an accurate assessment of the V-weapons. The case of the V-weapons is also an example of another mental shortcoming that is common in intelligence analysis: the anchoring bias, which occurs when the mind finds it difficult to move beyond a limited number of facts or pre-existing judgments – in this instance, old-fashioned solid fueled rockets – when processing data. The key factor that the British experts were late in understanding was that the rockets had a much more efficient liquid, rather than solid, fuel. In addition, at first the British were beset by the paradox of expertise (i.e., it is exactly the experts, with their long experience with an issue, who find it difficult to detect a major change and are overconfident about their judgment).

Although collection was incomplete, significant clues that were found were not appreciated because of the cognitive filters and lack of appropriate context. In retrospect, some of the clandestine reporting had been inaccurate. Other reports, including at least two that specifically referred to the existence of two different programs, had been accurate but not always properly understood. A third category of reports was so mysterious and difficult to link to existing knowledge that it was initially not given much weight. This category included the reference to a propellant made of "liquid air," which was, of course, liquid oxygen, which, along with alcohol, was the fuel for the V-2.

Although there were bureaucratic rivalries and misunderstandings among the British analysts and decision makers, in the end there was sufficient cooperation to lead to the uncovering of most of the capabilities of the V-weapons. The British system, unlike the Soviet one, made it possible to consider minority viewpoints and multiple hypotheses.

Questions for Further Thought

Based on the British experience in dealing with the V-weapons, what are the steps that intelligence analysts should take to recognize and understand something important that is new and outside their experience?

How helpful was it for the British to have reporting from a variety of sources? What are the limitations of the different kinds of sources, such as human reporting and aerial reconnaissance?

How did the British system of analyzing problems such as the *Luftwaffe*, bombing targets, and the V-weapons compare and contrast with the Soviet system for assessing the threat from Nazi Germany?

Recommended Reading

Hinsley, F. H., *British Intelligence in the Second World War*, abridged version, Cambridge: Cambridge University Press, 1993, chapters 26 and 35.

Jones, R. V., *The Wizard War: British Scientific Intelligence, 1939–1945*, New York: Coward, McCann & Geoghegan, 1978.

King, Benjamin, and Kutta, Timothy, *Impact: The History of Germany's V-Weapons in World War II*, Rockville Centre, NY: Sarpedon, 1998.

Part IV

The Cold War

U NFORTUNATELY, DESPITE ALL OF THE SACRIFICES MADE IN THE MOST destructive war in history, the end of World War II did not bring an era of peace. Instead there was a tense rivalry between the superpowers – the United States and the Soviet Union – and their allies. For nearly half a century, these two coalitions maneuvered against each other on a global basis. This competition was exacerbated by ideological differences, with the Western powers mainly capitalist, and the Eastern bloc communist.

To cope with this new and more threatening environment, the government of the United States, under the 1947 National Security Act, carried out a major reorganization. The 1947 legislation created a unified Department of Defense to coordinate the air force, army, and navy; and it established the Central Intelligence Agency to conduct espionage, covert action, and analysis. To manage the entire structure the president would have a new National Security Council.

The risks in this Cold War struggle for power were greater than ever before because of the existence of nuclear weapons. For the first time, the survival of whole countries, or even the entire planet, was threatened because of the technology of warheads and missiles.

There was also a significant intelligence component to the rivalry between the superpowers. Both sides developed huge and expensive intelligence organizations, including high-technology collection systems. There was also extensive deception and espionage. Despite all of its tensions and dangers, the Cold War never deteriorated to the point of a direct conflict between the superpowers; and in this, too, intelligence played a role.

Figure 15. Atomic bomb explosion (Office of War Information photograph, Library of Congress)

15

Atomic Bomb Spies

O N AUGUST 6 AND 9, 1945, THE UNITED STATES DROPPED TWO ATOMIC bombs on Japan. Less than a month later, on September 2, Japan surrendered. The awesome power of atomic bombs had been decisive in bringing World War II to an end, and the fact that the United States was the only country that had atomic weapons was expected to be a decisive factor in shaping the postwar world.

A few days after the end of the war, on September 5, 1945, Igor Gouzenko (1919–82), a Chief Intelligence Directorate (*Glavnoye Razvedyvatelnoye Upravleniye*; GRU) code clerk at the Soviet embassy in Ottawa, Canada, defected. The documents that Gouzenko brought with him to support his story had the potential to undermine the U.S. monopoly of atomic weapons. He claimed that the intelligence agencies of the USSR, working through local communist parties, had built up an extensive network of informants in the United States, Great Britain, and Canada. Moreover, he alleged that Soviet intelligence had successfully targeted the Manhattan Project, which had produced atomic weapons. Gouzenko was able to provide the name of at least one Canadian who had worked on the Manhattan project and had reported to the Soviets. He also alleged that there were Soviet spies in the U.S. government, but he had no names.

The Canadian government began a series of investigations based on Gouzenko's information. One of the persons whose name emerged as a suspect was Klaus Fuchs (1911–88). Fuchs was one of the British scientists who worked at the Los Alamos, New Mexico, laboratory where the atomic bombs were assembled, and he had been present for the first successful test of an atomic bomb at Alamogordo, New Mexico, in July 1945. If it were true that Fuchs was involved in espionage, even as just a target – and the nature and degree of his involvement was not yet known – it would be a serious breach of security.

The Canadians passed Gouzenko's allegations and information to the Federal Bureau of Investigation (FBI) in the United States, and the Bureau immediately began to review its files. FBI investigators found out that, shortly before Gouzenko's defection, Elizabeth Bentley (1908–63) had volunteered information to the FBI field office in New Haven, Connecticut. She was a former member of the American Communist Party who claimed to have been a courier for a Soviet spy ring in the United States, but, unlike Gouzenko, she had no documents to support her accusations. One of her contacts was an engineer she knew only as "Julius," but it was not clear whether that was his real name or a pseudonym. The leads provided by Gouzenko and Bentley prompted the FBI to begin what would become one of its most extensive investigations up to that time.

As the FBI pursued the allegations about a Soviet spy ring in the United States, the Cold War was getting underway, and Moscow was changing from a wartime ally against Nazi Germany to an ideological and political rival. From 1945 through 1948 pro-USSR governments took over throughout Eastern Europe. During the same time, a communist government come to power in North Korea, and in 1949 communist rebels seized control of China.

Meanwhile, others had joined the investigation in America. U.S. military cryptographers, for example, took another look at hundreds of encrypted cables from Soviet diplomatic and consular posts in the United States that had been intercepted during the war. Little effort to uncover their contents had been made while the fighting was going on, but, with the Cold War underway, working on the cables became a higher priority and was assigned the codeword "Venona." Some of the material in the wartime Soviet cables was intelligence related, and some of those messages appeared to confirm allegations made by Gouzenko and Bentley.

- One message going to Moscow contained technical details of atomic bomb research that could only have come from inside the Manhattan Project. Further investigation revealed that the report had been written by Klaus Fuchs.
- Another report said that Soviet intelligence had an agent operating in the United States who was a scientist (presumably foreign born) whose sister had gone to an American university.
- A third cable discussed one agent's activity but gave only his cover name. The message did note, however, that his wife's true name was "Ethel," that she was then (1944) twenty-nine years old, and that they had been married for five years.

In September 1949, U.S. patrol aircraft detected evidence that the Soviets had recently tested an atomic bomb, and later that month President Harry Truman (1884–1972) revealed the test publicly. The U.S. monopoly of atomic weapons was over, having lasted only four years. This revelation was a shock to the government and public opinion. By early 1950, Republican Senator Joseph McCarthy of Wisconsin (1908–57) began his public campaign claiming that Soviet spies operated throughout the U.S. government.

Public and private concerns about the USSR having an atomic bomb led to many urgent questions: Had Soviet spying in the United States made it possible for the USSR to develop its own atomic weapons so quickly? Who had been the spies, and what had they passed? Pressure mounted on the U.S. and British authorities to accelerate their inquiries into espionage in the atomic bomb program.

As part of the FBI's more intense investigation, its agents now took a closer look at Harry Gold (1910–72), who had been mentioned in the Canadian investigation of Gouzenko's allegations. In the early years of the inquiries, there were more prominent names on the investigators' list, and nothing had been known about Gold, so security officials had taken little notice of him. Gold was a Jew who had been born in Switzerland then moved to Philadelphia with his parents and became a naturalized American citizen. Although he had never joined the Communist Party, he was sympathetic to the USSR, which he saw as a strong and effective enemy of the anti-Semitic Nazis.

During its investigation, the FBI found out that in the 1930s Gold had worked as a commercial chemist and agreed to pass technical data from American companies to the Soviets. Bentley claimed that Gold replaced her as a courier for the Soviet spy ring. FBI agents arrested Gold in May 1950. After a few days of questioning, he identified Fuchs as a spy for Moscow and admitted that he, Gold, had passed on material from Fuchs to Soviet intelligence officers. Such a serious allegation would require confirmation.

In Britain, the domestic intelligence service, MI5, was also closing in on Fuchs. The British had the Venona decrypts from their American colleagues, including the one containing the technical report from the Manhattan Project. The fact that Soviet intelligence officers had a report by Fuchs, however, did not mean that he had provided it; they could have obtained it from someone else. It turned out that Fuchs had been a communist in his native Germany before World War II. His sister had immigrated to the United States and gone to Swarthmore College. The British began interrogating Fuchs on the basis of these leads, and in January 1950 he confessed to being a spy for the Soviets. He also revealed that he had turned sensitive information from Los Alamos over to a courier whom, in accordance with Soviet intelligence tradecraft, he knew only as "Raymond." One of the few other details about "Raymond" that Fuchs provided was that he appeared to know something about chemistry. Later the FBI sent a team to Britain to interrogate Fuchs. The agents showed him pictures of Gold, and Fuchs confirmed that Gold was "Raymond."

As his questioning continued, Gold surprised the FBI and also confessed that he had passed other information about atomic bomb designs from an enlisted man in the U.S. Army who worked at Los Alamos. Gold could not remember his source's name, but he had learned that the soldier was from New York and his wife's name may have been "Ruth." In time, the FBI suspected that the Army man was David Greenglass (1922–), who had worked at Los Alamos and was suspected of involvement in thefts from the laboratory. Greenglass was a Jew from New York City who had been a member of a Communist Party youth group. During the war, Greenglass had been drafted, trained as a machinist, and then posted to Los Alamos.

The FBI arrested Greenglass in June 1950, and he immediately admitted that he had smuggled information about the atomic bomb out of Los Alamos and passed it to Gold for further transmission to Soviet intelligence. Moreover, Greenglass claimed that he had been recruited by his sister Ethel's husband, Julius Rosenberg (1918–53). Ethel had been born in 1915, and she and Julius had been married in 1939. The FBI believed that it was the Rosenbergs who passed reports from Greenglass to Soviet intelligence officers in New York City.

Rosenberg and his wife were New York Jews who had been members of the Communist Party. Like some others, they saw Communism as a potential alternative to the weaknesses of capitalism, as revealed in the Great Depression. During World War II, Julius was a civilian electrical engineer who had worked for the U.S. Army. After the war, he and Greenglass had been business partners, but their company had failed, leading to recriminations on both sides.

Ten days after Greenglass was arrested, North Korean troops poured into South Korea, starting the Korean War. Many in the United States feared that this was the beginning of World War III, which would be between the United States and the communists and could lead to the use of nuclear weapons by both sides. Five months later it became clear that Chinese forces were also sending troops into the Korean peninsula, which increased tensions even more.

In July 1950 the FBI arrested Rosenberg, and then his wife a month later. They were both charged with conspiracy to commit espionage, but they denied any involvement in spying. The investigations and trials of the accused American atom bomb spies – the Rosenbergs, Gold, Greenglass, and several other alleged accomplices – were a media sensation at a time of growing fear and suspicion.

Many observers consider these trials to have been a travesty, with confused charges and much hearsay evidence, among other problems, but the government believed the intercepts of Soviet intelligence communications, which would have supported its case, to be too sensitive to be admitted in court. In March 1951 the Rosenbergs were convicted and sentenced to death, based largely on testimony from Greenglass. In return for his assistance to prosecutors, Greenglass got only fifteen years. Gold was given a thirty-year sentence. In the UK, Fuchs pled guilty and was sentenced to fourteen years. He was released in 1959 and moved to East Germany.

It was the death sentences for both Julius and Ethel Rosenberg that generated the greatest controversy. Unlike Fuchs, Gold, and Greenglass, the Rosenbergs never admitted to espionage. They appealed their convictions, and there were demonstrations of support for them all over the world; even the Pope asked for leniency. All pleas for clemency were rejected, and the Rosenbergs went to their deaths in June 1953 still proclaiming their innocence.

- Were the Rosenbergs innocent victims of war hysteria who had been persecuted for their political beliefs, and perhaps because they were Jewish? Had they, at worst, done nothing more than help a wartime ally, not realizing that the USSR would later become a serious threat to U.S. security?
- Were they clever and dangerous spies who were happy to give Moscow a significant advantage in the Cold War, die as martyrs, and become a global embarrassment to the U.S. government?

There was also controversy over the value of what the Soviets got. Their scientists had been working on an atomic bomb for years, and the information from Fuchs and Greenglass may only have confirmed what Moscow already knew and speeded up production. Would the Soviets have gotten the bomb only much later – perhaps never – if the Rosenbergs had not acted as a conduit for material from the Manhattan Project?

Although the outcome of the atomic bomb spies' case was controversial, the investigation that uncovered them had been a model of thinking

clearly, gathering information patiently, and overcoming institutional challenges. Investigations – trying to establish personal, legal responsibility for
something that has already happened and then being able to prove it in
court – are different kinds of problems from the military-related issues, such
as threat, intentions, and deception considered so far. Analytic techniques
such as hypotheses, relationships, and source evaluation are still helpful,
however. The public release of the Venona material and records from the
Soviet archives decades later in the 1990s vindicated the methods of Bureau
agents who worked to uncover the atomic bomb spies.

   Because of the complexity of the case, with many individuals and a variety
of relationships (including family, ethnicity, and ideology), the FBI found it
useful to construct an elaborate chart showing the key players and the various ways in which they were linked. Although originally conceived of as an
investigative tool, the chart also helped to support the prosecutor's presentation in court. This chart was one of the earliest examples of what would
later become known as link or network analysis, which has now become a
standard part of the intelligence analyst's toolkit.

Questions for Further Thought

Why might counterintelligence issues be difficult for analysts?
What was the quality of the information available to the FBI? What were
   some of the problems with it?
Are the techniques in counterintelligence any different from those that are
   used in dealing with other analytic problems?

Recommended Reading

Feklisov, Alexander, and Kostin, Sergei, *The Man Behind the Rosenbergs*, Catherine Dop,
   trans., New York: Enigma Books, 2001.
Halloway, David, *Stalin and the Bomb: The Soviet Union and Atomic Energy, 1939–1956*,
   New Haven, CT: Yale University Press, 1994.
Haynes, John Earl, et al., *Spies: The Rise and Fall of the KGB in America*, New Haven, CT:
   Yale University Press, 2009, chapter 2.
Haynes, John Earl, and Klehr, Harvey, *Early Cold War Spies: The Espionage Trials that
   Shaped American Politics*, New York: Cambridge University Press, 2006.
Haynes, John Earl, and Klehr, Harvey, *Venona: Decoding Soviet Espionage in America*, New
   Haven, CT: Yale University Press, 1999.
Lamphere, Robert J., and Shachtman, Tom, *The FBI – KGB War: A Special Agent's Story*,
   New York: Random House, 1986.

Radosh, Ronald, and Milton, Joyce, *The Rosenberg File: A Search for the Truth*, New York: Holt, Rinehart and Winston, 1983.

Roberts, Sam, *The Brother: The Untold Story of Atomic Spy David Greenglass and How He Sent His Sister, Ethel Rosenberg, to the Electric Chair*, New York: Random House, 2001.

Romerstein, Herbert, and Breindel, Eric, *The Venona Secrets: Exposing Soviet Espionage and America's Traitors*, Washington, DC: Regnery, 2000.

Williams, Robert Chadwell, *Klaus Fuchs, Atom Spy*, Cambridge, MA: Harvard University Press, 1987.

Figure 16. The Korean peninsula

16

Outbreak of the Korean War

I N 1950, COMMUNISM WAS ON THE MARCH AROUND THE WORLD, AND THE Cold War was well underway. Between 1945 and 1948, Soviet-sponsored regimes had come to power throughout Eastern Europe. In Asia, Kim Il-Sung (1912–94) dominated politics in North Korea as early as 1946, and then proclaimed the founding of the Democratic People's Republic of Korea in the north in 1948. In October 1949, Mao Zedong (1893–1976) took over China. These developments were made even more ominous when the Soviet Union successfully tested an atomic bomb in August 1949, ending the brief U.S. monopoly on this destructive weapon. If the global communist offensive had brought war, there would have been a high probability that the conflict would be of unprecedented scope and destructiveness.

In response to the Pearl Harbor disaster and the start of the Cold War, the United States undertook a major reorganization of its security apparatus, in which intelligence played a new and prominent role. The National Security Act, signed by President Harry Truman on July 26, 1947, established a new structure that included the National Security Council (NSC), a unified Department of Defense (DoD), and the Central Intelligence Agency (CIA).

The leaders of this new security establishment saw the contest with Communism as a global challenge. Their main concern was in Europe, an area of great economic potential; the response there centered around the Marshall Plan to provide economic aid and the North Atlantic Treaty Organization (NATO) alliance to provide a defensive shield. Asia was only a secondary priority. In January 1950, Secretary of State Dean Acheson (1893–1971) announced that the U.S. military strategy in Asia was based, not on operating on the mainland, but instead on using bases on the island chain running from Alaska, through Japan, and down to the Philippines. This was an approach that would allow American air and sea power to operate freely and with decisive impact.

For analysts throughout the U.S. government, the key questions were the following: When and where would the next blow fall? What would it look like? A significant concern was that trying to uncover communist capabilities and intentions would be difficult because the communist countries were closed societies, with elaborate and effective security organizations that made it difficult to obtain information either openly on clandestinely.

In Asia, the Supreme Commander for the Allied Powers was General Douglas MacArthur (1880–1964), who had his headquarters in Tokyo, Japan. MacArthur had had a mixed record in World War II: getting caught by surprise in the Philippines nine hours after the attack on Pearl Harbor, but also leading the island-hopping campaign that brought American forces across thousands of miles to the doorstep of Japan. His decades of experience and many accomplishments had given him supreme confidence in his knowledge of the Orient and his own military abilities. In May 1950, MacArthur's view about the potential threat in his area of responsibility was: "I don't believe a shooting war is imminent."

MacArthur had a large intelligence staff, but, given the general's rank, ego, and experience, they saw their job mainly as confirming his assessments. In the spring of 1950, there were reports of suspicious activity on the North Korean side of the demarcation line along the 38th parallel, such as moving civilians out of the area and improving roads and bridges. There had been a pattern of incidents involving the North Koreans for months, however, and none of them had escalated to a more serious conflict. Therefore, many analysts saw continuing probes by North Korean forces as more of the same.

On June 25, North Korean troops opened fire and poured into South Korea. MacArthur's first reaction was that the attack was just "a border incident." Nonetheless, in the weeks that followed, American and South Korean troops had to abandon most of the country and fall back to a small perimeter on the southeast coast.

The United Nations (UN) named MacArthur commander of the international army that was mustered in response to the Korean attack, and he quickly recovered his footing. On September 25, 1950, an amphibious landing behind North Korean lines at Inchon, near the capital of Seoul, led to the collapse of the North Korean offensive and the restoration of MacArthur's reputation. By the second week in October, American and South Korean troops were back across the 38th parallel, and MacArthur was confident that the fighting was coming to an end and that China would remain on the sidelines.

MacArthur was not alone in his assessment that the Chinese would not intervene. The recently established CIA was aware of a buildup of Chinese forces along the border with North Korea but saw it as a defensive measure. CIA analysts believed that, having just completed a costly, decades-long struggle to take over China, surely the new communist government was not interested in taking on a new and powerful opponent. Secretary of State Acheson, for his part, believed that the Chinese were – or should be – more concerned about defending their long border with the USSR, and he thought that the Chinese government would not endanger its chances of getting a seat on the UN Security Council by getting involved in a war.

Nonetheless, there were concerns further down the chain of command. Some had noticed, for example, that when American forces recaptured the main airport outside Seoul they found that the North Korean occupiers had constructed extensive, professionally designed facilities for modern, high-performance aircraft, which they, themselves, did not have in large numbers. This degree of effort suggested that preparations had been under way for Chinese intervention. MacArthur's staff disagreed, saying that if the Chinese intended to enter the war, they would have done so immediately after the Inchon landing.

What none of the American officials and analysts understood were the views of Mao Zedong. China's new leader was determined that China would not be humiliated again by Westerners and that the power of the Chinese peasantry that had been mobilized by the communist revolution would carry the country through any military confrontation with a technologically superior United States. China would be fighting close to home, whereas America had to send soldiers and supplies over thousands of miles of ocean. Even the fearsome atomic bomb, if it were used, would have little impact on the vast territory and huge population of China. Fighting the United States would not threaten the revolution in China, but could actually consolidate the new regime's control domestically and the country's role in Asia. Part of the framework for Mao's thinking may have been that. in the Chinese written language, the character for crisis (weiji) was a combination of the characters for danger (wei) and opportunity (ji).

Although the communists' decision-making process was shrouded in secrecy, the Chinese government did send out hints about the direction in which they were going. As early as August 20, 1950, Foreign Minister Zhou Enlai (1898–1976) had informed the UN that "the Chinese people cannot but be most concerned about the solution of the Korean question."

The tone of statements out of Beijing became more ominous after the Inchon landing brought American forces much closer to China. On

September 25, the acting chief of staff of the Chinese army told the Indian ambassador in Beijing that his country will not

> ... sit back with folded hands and let the Americans come to the border... We know what we are in for, but at all costs American aggression has to be stopped. The Americans can bomb us, they can destroy our industries, but they cannot defeat us on land... They may even drop atom bombs on us. What then? They may kill a few million people. Without sacrifice a nation's independence cannot be upheld.

Five days later, Zhou stated publicly that

> The Chinese people enthusiastically love peace, but in order to defend peace, they never have been and never will be afraid to oppose aggressive war. The Chinese people absolutely will not tolerate foreign aggression, nor will they supinely tolerate seeing their neighbors being savagely invaded by the imperialists.

On October 2, Zhou told the Indian ambassador in Beijing that, if American forces crossed the 38th parallel, the Chinese government would send troops to the Korean front to defend North Korea.

On October 10 the Chinese Foreign Ministry, in a public statement, issued what would be its last warning:

> Now that the American forces are attempting to cross the thirty-eighth parallel on a large scale, the Chinese people cannot stand idly by with regard to such a serious situation created by the invasion of Korea... and to the dangerous trend towards extending the war. The American war of invasion in Korea has been a serious menace to the security of China from its very start.

A few days later, Chinese troops began slipping across the border into North Korea. Over the next few weeks, some 200,000 soldiers would move south.

Senior American officials dismissed these statements as rhetoric, blackmail, or bluff, although some working-level officials with long experience in the region thought that they should be taken seriously. The CIA's assessment during this time period was that the Chinese had the capability to intervene but did not have the intention to do so.

On October 15, 1950, General MacArthur and President Truman held a conference on Wake Island for a review of the situation in East Asia. In a summary of the situation of Korea, MacArthur claimed that, with American forces across the 38th parallel and moving north, victory was imminent. He dismissed the possibility of Chinese intervention because they had no air cover.

By late October even the press was aware of the large numbers of Chinese troops massing just over the border. There were anomalous events such as brief encounters with Chinese soldiers south of the border, and UN forces actually captured Chinese soldiers as prisoners and interrogated them. Some intelligence officers expressed concern; but MacArthur said that these indicators of a Chinese military presence were "not alarming." On November 1, a more serious clash between U.S. and Chinese troops took place, but afterward the Chinese troops faded back into the mountains. MacArthur indicated that he was becoming more worried, but he also said that he needed more time and facts to determine if the Chinese had intervened.

By November 21, American units had reached the Yalu River, the border with China. Three days later, MacArthur flew to North Korea, toured the front, proclaimed that the war was almost over, and suggested that the soldiers might be home for Christmas.

On November 25, hundreds of thousands of Chinese troops struck, catching the American government by surprise for the second time in less than six months. Looking back later, some of those who survived the initial attacks recalled how striking it was that, rather than the blows being preceded by a great deal of detectable activity by the Chinese, there was instead an eerie silence.

To put MacArthur's faulty assessment into perspective, it is worth noting that his counterparts on the other side were little better in anticipating events. Kim Il-Sung believed that, after he attacked, communist sympathizers would rise up in support, fighting would be over quickly, and the United States would not intervene. Stalin and Mao agreed that the war would be short and that Washington would find it impossible to resist a fait accompli. Later, when deciding on whether China should join the war, Mao believed that the USSR would provide significant military support, if needed. All of these scenarios turned out to be wrong.

As is so often the case, there were multiple cognitive shortcomings involved in the failure to anticipate the North Korean and Chinese attacks. These included mirror imaging and the use of the rational actor model, both of which were based on Western values and procedures. There were also examples of the confirmation bias, which involves ignoring or devaluing accurate reports that do not fit one's preconceptions, and the framing bias, which occurs when information is presented in such a way that it leads to a preferred conclusion.

From a collection perspective, there does not appear to have been clandestine access to the senior levels of North Korean or Chinese decision making, but there were multiple indicators, in both open and secret channels, that suggested what might happen. The problem was less what was collected, and more what was made – or not made – of the information that was available. There seems to have been little effort to come up with a range of alternative explanations of what was happening or more speculative possible outcomes of what could happen. Because U.S. forces were so poorly prepared in terms of numbers, training, and equipment, as well as still being in a peacetime occupation mindset, with no plans for how to respond to an attack, would a warning have made much difference?

After the disappointing performance in the Korean War, there was another major reorganization to try to make the U.S. intelligence bureaucracy more effective. The National Security Agency was founded in 1952 to provide centralized management of the interception and decryption of adversaries' communications. At the same time, there was a major reorganization of the CIA, including the establishment of a Directorate of Intelligence (DI) to focus on analysis. The DI was the first large, permanent civilian organization to be established to do all-source, multidisciplinary analysis of a wide range of foreign issues, while remaining independent of the perspectives of individual government departments. The first head of the DI's Office of National Estimates (ONE) was William Langer (1896–1977), a professor at Harvard University and former head of the OSS's Research and Analysis branch.

In 1952 Langer's deputy, Sherman Kent (1903–86), a former Yale history professor who had also served in Research and Analysis, took over as head of ONE. In grappling with some of the difficulties of analysis, Kent formulated a number of principles that became significant for the emerging profession of intelligence analysis. Among other things, he believed that analysis should be "complete, accurate, timely, and capable of serving as a basis for action." It was also his view that the authors of intelligence estimates should be

> ... masters of the subject matter, impartial in the presence of new evidence, ingenious in the development of research techniques, imaginative in their hypotheses, sharp in the analysis of their own predilections or prejudices, and skilled in the presentation of their conclusions.

Kent served as head of ONE until 1967, and over the years he further refined his views on intelligence analysis. He believed, for example, that analysts should provide objective assessments that were not linked to ongoing policy measures or proposals, carefully evaluate evidence, acknowledge that there will be uncertainty and ambiguity, articulate assumptions and identify gaps, avoid cognitive biases, be open to alternative views as long as they are soundly argued, go beyond telling leaders what they want to know (and inform them of what they need to know), and make sure presentation is clear and concise.

Questions for Further Thought

American assessments of Chinese intentions were another example of the dangers of mirror imaging, believing that others see the world as we do. How can analysts better understand the assessment of risk and threat made in other cultures?

What were some of the indicators of Chinese intervention available to analysts, and how definitive were they? Would better collection have made a difference?

How was the problem in Korea different from, or similar to, the period before the Pearl Harbor attack? How does MacArthur's record compare or contrast with Caesar's assessment of Gaul before his invasion?

What were the problems of the organizational structures in which analysts worked, in Asia and in Washington, that hindered analysis? Did reorganization address all of the problems revealed by the events of 1950?

Recommended Reading

Chen, Jian, *China's Road to the Korean War: The Making of the Sino-American Confrontation*, New York: Columbia University Press, 1994.

Goncharov, Sergei, Lewis, John, and Xue, Litai, *Uncertain Partners: Stalin, Mao, and the Korean War*, Stanford, CA: Stanford University Press, 1993.

Halberstam, David, *The Coldest Winter: America and the Korean War*, New York: Hyperion, 2007.

Manchester, William, *American Caesar: Douglas McArthur, 1880–1964*, Boston, MA: Little, Brown, 1978.

Whiting, Allen S., *China Crosses the Yalu: The Decision to Enter the Korean War*, New York: Macmillan, 1960.

Figure 17. Malaya

17

Counterinsurgency in Malaya

A NOTHER EARLY FRONT IN THE COLD WAR WAS IN SOUTHEAST ASIA. IN the late 1940s, insurgents in the British colony of Malaya hoped to follow in the footsteps of the successful communist takeover in China in 1949. Based on the Chinese model, the Malayan communists portrayed themselves as the main voice for independence and social justice, and they planned to use guerrilla tactics to drive out the British. Starting in the summer of 1948, the communist insurgents began attacking the main economic resources in Malaya – rubber plantations and tin mines – to increase the financial burden for London of holding the colony.

From the beginning of the insurgency, the British faced the difficulties of fighting a war in a complex environment far from their main sources of support. Some 80 percent of the Malayan Peninsula was covered by jungle, and British settlers, soldiers, policemen, and officials were few in number. In addition, there was a varied ethnic makeup of Malays, Chinese, and Indians, with uncertainty about their loyalties.

On the other hand, the British had some potential advantages. For example, Malaya had only a narrow land border, which could be relatively easily controlled. The only other alternative for potential external help for the insurgents was to come by sea, a route which the British could dominate. In addition, as time passed, the Korean War brought greater demand for Malayan rubber and tin, greatly increasing the financial resources available to the government.

Initially, the British tried the tactics that had been successful in the just-completed war, in which the British had engaged the Germans and Italians in the deserts of North Africa and the north European plain from France into the heart of Germany. There was an emphasis on firepower, including air strikes and heavy artillery. Mobility, another key aspect of the fighting in

World War II, was strictly limited, however, by the jungle. What the British soon found was that the elusive communist guerrillas usually managed to escape large-scale conventional operations. Moreover, the destructive fire-power's impact on buildings, bridges, and other infrastructure alienated the population. British commanders, planners, and analysts realized the need for an alternative approach, with a fresh perspective for understanding the situation.

Over time, the British developed another way to analyze and act in coun-terinsurgency. First and foremost in the revised conceptual framework was the insight that the struggle was fundamentally political, with other aspects – including military, economic, and psychological – subordinate to overall political goals and direction. To carry out such a struggle, there would have to be unity of command under a civilian, who could coordinate the various aspects.

On the broad political front the British took a number of initiatives: They sponsored independence in the foreseeable future, thus co-opting national-ist sentiment. The government also established a national savings plan for retirement pensions, which gave the population a stake in a government victory. Other political measures were more controversial. British officials used tough legal measures, including two-year detention of suspects with-out trial, mandatory death sentences for carrying weapons, and permitting searches without warrants. In addition, the officials required registration and identification cards for the entire population.

Militarily, the key principles were to win over insurgents, not kill them, and to protect villages, not destroy them. The focus of effort was on the population, which was a potential source of supplies, recruits, and intelli-gence for both sides. Therefore, the main goal was to win the "hearts and minds" (the phrase originated during this conflict) of the populace through an integrated program of political, military, economic, social, and cultural efforts that would garner support.

The British brought vulnerable parts of the population, especially eth-nic Chinese, under the authority of the government by moving them to resettlement camps, where they tried to address the population's needs and grievances. Although there were many problems with the resettlement camps, over time people had land, as well as better security, along with infrastructure, including water, power, schools, and clinics. The government also provided free seeds and farming implements. Such improvements gave the population an incentive to support a government victory, and isolated the insurgents, making them more susceptible to pressure from the security forces.

Within this political and military framework, the British developed appropriate organization and tactics. Security forces (military, police, and intelligence) were well trained and contained a substantial proportion of sympathetic Malays. The security forces were organized into small, mobile units that maintained an extensive presence in the countryside to provide a sense of security. These units controlled the movement of individuals and denied food to the insurgents through checkpoints and curfews. To complement their security forces, the British also established an armed home guard drawn from the population. British forces also conducted an extensive information/propaganda campaign through film, radio, leaflets, and even aircraft flying over the jungle, where the insurgents operated, using loudspeakers.

An important aspect of the British counterinsurgency method was an extensive intelligence system, which was integrated into the activities of the security forces in all areas and at all levels. Patrols that guarded villages were also able to collect information. Large cash awards were given in return for accurate and useful information. This system generated a vast amount of data, based largely on human sources and signals intelligence, which provided an accurate basis for planning counterinsurgency operations. Detailed and carefully managed databases also sensitized the British to the variety of local conditions, which could vary considerably, even in a small country.

Some of the British success was attributable to communist weaknesses which the insurgents were not able to overcome. The communists never expanded their base of support much beyond the ethnic Chinese minority (which was less than 40 percent of the total population). Moreover, the insurgents based themselves in the jungle, which had few resources. Finally, the insurgents never obtained significant outside support.

Effective use of intelligence, including multiple channels of information and institutional cooperation, was a substantial element of the British success in Malaya. The British were also able to develop an analytic framework to support a strategy, tactics, and intelligence for a successful counterinsurgency campaign.

Of the many lessons about counterinsurgency that the British learned in Malaya, the main one was that victory would be resource intensive, requiring large amounts of money, personnel, time, and patience.

Questions for Further Thought

How were the challenges that the British faced in Malaya similar to, or different from, those encountered when dealing with other irregular forces, past and present?

Why would intelligence analysis be a significant element of a counterinsurgency strategy?
What could be some of the potential pitfalls in analyzing a rural insurgency
  carried out among an ethnic minority?

Recommended Reading

Galula, David, *Counterinsurgency Warfare: Theory and Practice*, New York: Praeger, 1964.

Komer, R. W., *The Malayan Emergency in Retrospect: Organization of a Successful Counterinsurgency Effort*, Santa Monica, CA: Rand, 1972.

Miller, Harry, *Jungle War in Malaya: The Campaign against Communism, 1948–60*, London:
  Arthur Barker, 1972.

Nagl, John A., *Learning to Eat Soup with a Knife: Counterinsurgency Lessons from Malaya
  and Vietnam*, Chicago, IL: University of Chicago Press, 2005.

Stubbs, Richard, *Hearts and Minds in Guerrilla Warfare: The Malayan Emergency, 1948–
  1960*, Singapore: Eastern University Press, 2004.

Thompson, Robert, *Defeating Communist Insurgency: Experiences from Malaya and Vietnam*,
  London: Chatto & Windus, 1966.

Figure 18. The USSR

18

Soviet Strategic Weapons

N O ISSUE WAS MORE IMPORTANT TO WESTERN INTELLIGENCE ANALYSTS than trying to understand the capabilities of nuclear weapons and delivery systems that were being developed by the USSR. These warheads, missiles, and bombers (and in time, submarines) had unprecedented range and striking power. The USSR's strategic nuclear forces were difficult to assess in detail because they were carefully shielded by intense security measures, including denial and deception. Early efforts to anticipate developments in Soviet strategic weapons were based on limited collection and were not successful. In 1949, most U.S. intelligence agencies' views, except for the Air Force's more alarmist and more accurate estimate, were that it would take the Soviets two to five years before they had their first nuclear weapons. It came as a great shock, in September 1949, when patrol aircraft detected evidence of a successful test in the USSR.

In an effort to construct a more accurate picture of what was going on in the Soviet Union and to better anticipate developments there, analysts in the United States focused much of their efforts on what were known as National Intelligence Estimates (NIEs). These were strategic assessments of major, long-term trends in important issues, such as Soviet weapons. The estimates were based on all available reporting and were written periodically to provide updates on significant issues. Ad hoc estimates were also prepared on other issues, as needed. Estimates attempted to formulate a consensus of the various agencies that made up the American intelligence community, but agencies could register a dissent if they did not agree with their counterparts. There could also be Special National Intelligence Estimates (SNIEs) on urgent, near-term developments.

An example of the difficulties that analysts encountered when preparing their estimates occurred when they tried to gauge the Soviets' ability to deliver nuclear weapons via long-range bombers. During the display of military hardware in preparation for Moscow's 1954 May Day parade, foreign attachés and other observers saw, for the first time, a new bomber, which became known in the West as the "Bison." The following year, more Bisons were observed, and there was even more alarm when nearly thirty bombers of another new type, designated in the West as the "Bear," were spotted at the celebration of Soviet Air Force Day in July 1955. U.S. Air Force intelligence analysts expressed concern that the USSR could produce as many as 700 bombers by the end of the 1950s, which would give them more long-range aircraft than the United States had. The U.S. Congress responded by adding almost $1 billion to the Air Force budget. Analysts at Naval and Army Intelligence were much less alarmed, and they were supported by their colleagues at the Central Intelligence Agency (CIA), who were skeptical that the backward Soviet economy could support such a surge of bomber production.

This was the famous "bomber gap" that played a role in budget discussions in Congress in the late 1950s and was a source of debate in the 1960 U.S. presidential election. Much later, analysts learned that the 1955 display had been a deception operation, with just a few planes circling several times over the airfield, and that Soviet bomber production was, in fact, much lower than the Air Force had feared.

In the meantime, U.S. civilian and military analysts had detected Soviet preparations to launch a uniquely threatening weapon, an intercontinental ballistic missile (ICBM), which had a range of several thousand miles. The United States had had trouble with its own ICBM program, and even though there had been warning, there was consternation when the first successful Soviet missile test was detected in August 1957. This test was followed by a surprise to the public, in October 1957, when the USSR used an ICBM to send the first satellite, Sputnik, into orbit. An ICBM had the potential to deliver a nuclear weapon to the United States in less than thirty minutes, and there was no known way to stop it. Many in Congress and the press concluded that the Soviets were winning the space race.

Intelligence analysts shared the concern about Soviet long-range missiles, but they were also confident that they could track developments, based on dramatically better clandestine collection. The U-2 high-altitude reconnaissance aircraft had been flying over the Soviet Union since 1956, and in 1960 U.S. satellites started sending back even more photography. Over time, these satellites collected data beyond the visible spectrum of light, such as infrared and radar, and these data waere included in the broader term "imagery."

After the confrontation with the United States during the 1962 Cuban Missile Crisis, the Soviets were determined not to be caught again in a position of strategic inferiority, so during the 1960s they carried out major programs to expand their navy and long-range missile force. Initially analysts missed the magnitude of the Soviet buildup, but from the late 1960s on they had quite an accurate estimate of the number of long-range missiles. In time, the USSR's strategic rocket forces became the supreme threat, the only force ever capable of completely destroying the United States. CIA analysts tracked the growth and improvement of the strategic rocket forces by using several methods to penetrate Soviet secrecy and estimate the magnitude of the USSR's efforts. Satellites and aircraft continued to provide considerable data, both imagery and communications intercepts, that covered readily observable factors such as equipment and facilities. The data were less concrete and measurable, however, on other factors that would shape an assessment of the threat, such as research, maintenance, and any intentions to actually use the Soviets' capabilities.

Another way to approach the problem was to assess the ability of the Soviet economy to support a major expansion of the country's strategic forces. CIA economists believed that modest growth in the Soviet economy limited the number of missiles and other military equipment that could be produced. A series of NIEs therefore concluded that Moscow's goal was more or less parity with U.S. strategic forces.

In the late 1960s, analysts and decision makers became increasingly concerned that the buildup of strategic forces in the USSR was giving the Soviets equality with, or perhaps even superiority to, the United States in nuclear weapons and related systems. Satellite images and intercepted communications indicated that the Soviets were hardening their missile-housing silos, launching new submarines, and deploying better radar systems. The main worry, however, was a new Soviet missile of unusual size, the SS-9. After considering the possibility that such a large missile was intended to match the American ability to launch warheads with multiple independent re-entry vehicles (MIRVs), CIA analysts concluded, on the basis of satellite photography, that the SS-9 did not have a MIRV capability. They acknowledged that the Soviets were interested in eventually having MIRV capability, but the analysts believed that Soviet leaders realized how difficult it would be to achieve.

In contrast, Secretary of Defense Melvin Laird (1922–), backed by the Defense Intelligence Agency, believed that the Soviets were trying to exceed U.S. capabilities and that the SS-9 was intended to carry MIRVs. He believed that a hugely expensive new anti-ballistic missile (ABM) system would be necessary to counter Soviet plans. It was becoming clear that the CIA had underestimated the increase in the number of Soviet missiles and the size of the USSR's economy earlier in the 1960s, and hardliners like Laird saw the Agency's assessment of the SS-9 as another example of similar errors. Laird stopped using the NIE numbers as justification for larger U.S. defense budgets, and Congress agreed to provide funds to start development of an ABM program.

CIA analysts continued to track the Soviet MIRV program and, in 1972, warned that the Soviets were getting ready to test their version; such a test took place in 1973. The SS-9 was never used for a MIRV warhead, and a Soviet missile that could carry a MIRV, the SS-19, was not ready for deployment until 1974. Beginning in 1976 the CIA, as a result of new reporting from human sources and a revised methodology, also included higher estimates of Soviet defense spending in the NIEs. During the 1970s the USSR surpassed the United States in the significant category of number of ICBMs deployed. Many assumed that the upward trend in Soviet defense spending would continue indefinitely.

Hard-liners in the United States remained concerned that the CIA was soft on the Soviets. In 1976, the President's Foreign Intelligence Advisory Board (an oversight panel with members from academia and business, along with others, such as retired government officials and military officers) asked that an independent panel of experts be given access to the same data on Soviet strategic forces that the CIA had, to see if they would reach a different conclusion. For this exercise, the CIA's Soviet analysts were designated Team A and the outside experts Team B. Team B was composed of well-known hard-liners, rather than individuals who were neutral or open-minded on the issue. After reviewing the data, Team B generally had only minor disagreements with the Agency's analysts about Soviet capabilities but believed that their intentions were much more aggressive.

Although analytic estimates of the Soviet Union's weapons were not always acceptable to decision makers or exact in providing accurate numbers, collection and analysis during the Cold War were solid enough to make it possible for the U.S. government to sign arms control treaties with the confidence that Washington would be able to detect any significant cheating. This confidence was embodied in President Ronald Reagan's (1911–2004) maxim: "Trust but verify."

Improved technical collection and analytic methodology made it possible to have much more accurate estimates of the number of Soviet missiles from the 1970s on. These estimates helped to keep defense budgets from growing even larger, and moderated fear and suspicion, which could have led to conflict between the superpowers using weapons of mass destruction.

Imagery and intercepts, however, were not able to penetrate the denial and deception campaign that shielded what turned out to be massive chemical and biological weapons programs. For example, it was not until a senior manager from the Soviet biological weapons program defected to the West in the early 1990s that the nature and scale of that program was realized.

Questions for Further Thought

Did any collection or analytic techniques used to understand the capabilities of centralized and secretive governments, such as Philip II's Spain, prove useful against the USSR?

What was the quality of evidence on strategic weapons that was available to analysts? Were there any pitfalls or shortcomings in collection? Why might chemical and biological weapons be easier to conceal?

Why were there differences of opinion among the various individuals and organizations concerned about Soviet strategic weapons?

What are some other examples of intelligence analysis being a significant aspect of debates over policy or spending? How, for instance, was analyzing Soviet missiles similar to, or different form, trying to assess the German *Luftwaffe* in the 1930s? Did analysis help to clarify or resolve those issues?

Recommended Reading

Cahn, Anne, *Killing Détente: The Right Attacks the CIA*, University Park, PA: Pennsylvania State University Press, 1998.

Firth, Noel E., and Noren, James H., *Soviet Defense Spending: A History of CIA Estimates, 1950–1990*, College Station, TX: Texas A&M University Press, 1998.

Freedman, Lawrence, *U.S. Intelligence and the Soviet Strategic Threat*, Princeton, NJ: Princeton University Press, 1986.

Haines, Gerald K., and Leggett, Robert E., eds., *CIA Analysis of the Soviet Union, 1947–91*, Washington, DC: CIA, Center for the Study of Intelligence, 2001.

Haines, Gerald K., and Leggett, Robert E., eds. *Watching the Bear: Essays on CIA's Analysis of the Soviet Union*, Washington, DC: CIA, Center for the Study of Intelligence, 2001.

Prados, John, *The Soviet Estimate: U.S. Intelligence Analysis and Russian Military Strength*, New York: Dial Press, 1982.

Figure 19. Range of the Soviet missiles in the Cuban Missile Crisis
Source: Personal Papers of Theodore C. Sorensen Box 49 Valuables Classified Subject Files 1961–1964 \ Cuba \ Subjects \ Standing Committee – 9/62–10/62 and undated \ missile range map.

19

Cuban Missile Crisis

THE THREAT FROM SOVIET STRATEGIC WEAPONS AND THE NEED TO accurately assess Moscow's intentions and capabilities were never more important than in the 1962 Cuban Missile Crisis, the most dramatic episode in the decades-long confrontation between the United States and the USSR.

Soviet premier Nikita Khrushchev (1894–1971) was famous for his public bluster, but U.S. analysts did not appreciate the extent to which he was privately concerned that his country was at a disadvantage in the rivalry between the superpowers. For example, Khrushchev knew that, after a slow start, the United States had been able, by the early 1960s, to surpass the USSR in the production of strategic nuclear weapons and delivery systems. In addition to sites in the United States, these enormously destructive weapons were deployed on bases in Western Europe and Turkey, and thus, from Khrushchev's perspective, were able to surround the USSR. In addition, American officials had tried in 1961 to overthrow communism's only outpost in the Western Hemisphere, the regime of Fidel Castro (1926–) in Cuba.

To address these issues, Khrushchev launched a massive and daring undertaking in the spring of 1962. First, the USSR would publicly provide large amounts of conventional weapons to Cuba, including fighter aircraft, tanks, patrol boats, surface-to-air missiles (SAMs), and radar. Second, the Soviets would secretly send several dozen medium- and intermediate-range ballistic missiles (MRBMs and IRBMs) to Cuba, along with a large contingent of Soviet troops to protect them. These were weapons that could not reach the United States from bases in Russia, but could do so from Cuba. After the missiles had been installed, and it was too late for the United States to stop the process, their presence would be dramatically revealed, giving Moscow greatly enhanced stature in its dealings with Washington on issues vital to the USSR, such as Berlin.

CIA analysts were able to measure accurately the conventional weapons going to Cuba in the spring of 1962, but they did not appreciate the extent to which Khrushchev believed that the USSR was falling behind the United States, nor his willingness to take great risks in an attempt to redress the situation. The Soviets took elaborate steps to hide the shipment of the missiles through denial and deception, and their officials told their U.S. counterparts that Moscow would not provide long-range missiles as part of its package of military assistance.

Some indications of unusual activity were picked up, but for a variety of reasons analysts did not conclude that these signs meant that Soviet missiles were in Cuba.

■ During the summer there were reports from human sources in Cuba that there were Soviet missiles on the island. Analysts discounted this information, however, because such reports, which had been coming in for years, were often from Cuban exiles, who had their own motives for making Castro appear as dangerous as possible. Moreover, there were few individuals in Cuba who would have the technical expertise to distinguish between, for instance, an antiaircraft missile and an MRBM. In fact, early reports during the summer from human sources on the island were wrong, as the first missiles did not arrive until early September.

■ Reconnaissance photographs of Soviet ships going to Cuba showed that some had large hatches and were riding high in the water, suggesting cargo that was bulky but lightweight. When they arrived, some ships were unloaded at night and with tight security.

A Special National Intelligence Estimate (SNIE) on Soviet military assistance to Cuba, published on September 19, 1962, raised the possibility of missiles coming from the USSR, but then dismissed the idea as implausible. Because of its importance, Sherman Kent, the head of the Office of National Estimates, reviewed the SNIE. He concurred with the judgment that providing missiles was unlikely because it was unprecedented and too risky. Moreover, there was, as yet, no credible evidence that missiles were present.

Not everyone agreed with the SNIE's conclusions. Director of Central Intelligence (DCI) John McCone (1902–91) believed that the only reason for an extensive deployment of Soviet air defense missiles would be to protect an important asset, such as MRBMs or ICBMs. He let the SNIE prepared by his analysts go out to other Washington officials, however, while providing his personal view to the president privately. In addition, Defense Intelligence

Agency analysts noted that some of the SAM sites were laid out in a pattern similar to that used to protect long-range missiles sites in the USSR.

Although analysts did not yet believe that there were missiles in Cuba, they were concerned enough (especially about indications that missiles might be present and about the implications of the SAM sites) to request more intensive coverage by U-2 high-altitude reconnaissance aircraft. On October 14, 1962, a U-2 took photographs confirming that Soviet MRBMs were present on the island. The analysts did not believe that the missiles were operational but estimated that they could be ready to fire within approximately two weeks.

For several days after the discovery, President John Kennedy (1917–63) and his advisers made no public comments about the situation and considered their options. To assist the deliberations, CIA analysts prepared two more SNIEs. The first estimate was on the likely Soviet response to the range of options being considered by the U.S. government, and it concluded that Moscow would not go as far as war to keep the missiles in Cuba. The second estimate dealt with the capabilities of the missiles and stated that the analysts believed that some of the MRBMs, with a range of more than 1,000 miles (1,600 kilometers), were ready to fire and that the rest would be operational by the end of October. They also noted that preparations continued for sites to house IRBMS, which had a range of more than 2,000 miles (3,200 kilometers).

On October 22, 1962, Kennedy announced to the nation that the Soviets had sent long-range missiles to Cuba and that the United States, as a first step, was imposing a naval quarantine to stop any further missiles. As the crisis continued, U-2 aircraft provided imagery of continuing work on the missiles and associated activity, and intercepts of Soviet and Cuban communications helped to monitor the preparation of the SAM sites, among other things. Analysts were also able to draw on reports from an agent inside the USSR, Soviet Chief Intelligence Directorate (*Glavnoye Razvedyvatelnoye Upravleniye*; GRU) officer Oleg Penkovsky (1919–63), who provided valuable information about the capabilities and shortcomings of Soviet missiles. Penkovsky was arrested during the crisis and later executed.

On October 27, tensions reached their peak, with Khrushchev sending a tough message, a U-2 being shot down over Cuba, and a Soviet ship moving to challenge the quarantine. On that day, CIA analysts reported that all of the SAM and MRBM sites were operational and that work continued on sites for IRBMs. There was no proof that nuclear warheads were present, but it was assumed that they were. Analysts noted, however, that Soviet forces around the world did not appear to be preparing for a conflict. That evening,

Attorney General Robert Kennedy (1925–68), the president's brother, made it clear to the Soviet ambassador that the United States would use force, if necessary. The following day, Khrushchev announced publicly that the USSR would remove the missiles in return for a U.S. pledge not to invade Cuba (privately Kennedy had also agreed to dismantle U.S. missiles in Turkey).

The U.S. analysts' attention now turned to confirming that the Soviets were withdrawing the missiles. As early as November 1, they were able to verify that the dismantling of the missiles had started; a week later, it was clear that ships were taking the missiles back to the USSR.

Only decades later – after the Soviet Union collapsed, the archives were opened, and participants fell freer to speak – did it become known that the situation in Cuba in 1962 was even more dangerous than was thought at the time. An assault on the island, if it had been carried out, would have been considerably more risky than analysts or decision makers realized at the time. For example, there were numerous tactical nuclear weapons deployed on the island, and there were many more Soviet troops present than had been estimated.

The early phase of the Cuban Missile Crisis was marked by several intelligence mistakes. There were a number of cognitive distortions on the part of analysts, including mirror imaging, the rational actor model, and being too wedded to the status quo. Collection also failed to penetrate Moscow's denial and deception campaign, as well as to uncover all aspects of Soviet activity on the island.

After the missiles were discovered, an understanding of the capabilities of the Soviet missiles, based on a variety of sources, was available as part of the decision-making process. This expertise had a significant impact because analysts and senior officials kept their minds open to other possibilities and adjusted their thinking when compelling new evidence arrived. The analysts' early assessment that the missiles were not yet operational (which was accurate) gave Kennedy time to calmly consider his options. All of this happened in a decision-making environment in which President Kennedy employed restraint and good judgment. The example of the Cuban Missile Crisis also demonstrates that intelligence – good and bad – has the most impact when it is combined with other aspects of national power, such as military force and diplomacy.

Questions for Further Thought

What were some of the uncertainties during the Cuban Missile Crisis?
Was the intelligence support provided to senior American officials during the crisis a success or failure?

What, if anything, could have been done to provide better intelligence support, given the technology available at the time?

Recommended Reading

Allison, Graham T., *Essence of Decision: Explaining the Cuban Missile Crisis*, revised ed., New York: Longman, 1999.

Blight, James G., and Welch, David A., eds., *Intelligence and the Cuban Missile Crisis*, London: Frank Cass, 1998.

Brugioni, Dino, *Eyeball to Eyeball: The Inside Story of the Cuban Missile Crisis*, New York: Random House, 1990.

Dobbs, Michael, *One Minute to Midnight: Kennedy, Khrushchev, and Castro on the Brink of Nuclear War*, New York: Random House, 2008.

Fursenko, Aleksandr, and Naftali, Timothy, *"One Hell of a Gamble": Khrushchev, Castro, and Kennedy, 1958–1964*, New York: W. W. Norton, 1997.

Figure 20. Indochina

20

Aspects of the Vietnam War

THE VIETNAM WAR OF THE 1960S AND 1970S WAS A LONG AND COMPLEX conflict, with one of its key elements being the role of intelligence. In contrast to intelligence analysts' work on the massive Soviet conventional and nuclear forces, the conflict in Southeast Asia required dealing with an insurgency. There were spirited debates among analysts over whether the communist effort to take over South Vietnam was better understood as a leftist social revolution, with significant control from Moscow and Beijing, or a nationalist struggle for independence, with the key decisions being made in Hanoi. Was this a largely military conflict, in which factors such as numbers and firepower would be decisive, or was it a broader undertaking, in which the political, economic, and social aspects would be important? Intelligence analysts working on the Vietnam problem also had to be careful that their assessments were not perceived as criticism of U.S. military strategy or policy in general.

When looking at the conflict in broad, strategic terms, some analysts believed that the North Vietnamese were not likely to give up their effort to take over South Vietnam in response to the level of force that the United States was willing to apply. Many in Washington disagreed, believing that U.S. technology, numbers, and will could prevail. Analysts' assessments that Hanoi's staying power could turn out to be greater than Washington's were confirmed in the long term.

Much of the Cold War apparatus of technical means of collection was of limited use against a diffuse and low-tech enemy, such as the communist insurgents. In addition, evidence was often vague and incomplete. Therefore, analysts backed up their judgments by carefully studying data such as public statements by communist leaders, captured documents, interrogations of prisoners, and available rates of reinforcement and supply.

This careful research did not keep them from making mistakes on tactical issues. For example, analysts were caught off guard by the Tet Offensive. They had detected a buildup of communist forces in late 1967, but they believed that it was a prelude to the usual pattern of preparations for an offensive in the countryside that followed a ceasefire for the Vietnamese holiday of Tet. Although a few analysts and senior officers sensed that something unusual might be about to happen, the scale, scope, and ferocity of the attacks at the end of January 1968 came as a surprise. The communists launched their attacks before the end of the Tet holiday period, and, hoping to spark a popular revolt in the cities that would bring a victorious conclusion to the war, they shifted the focus from the rural areas to the main population centers throughout South Vietnam.

Although the communists suffered a military defeat, with heavy losses and a failure to gain their objectives, the surprise did have a significant political impact. Senior U.S. military and civilian officials' claims that victory was imminent now rang hollow, and many Americans started to doubt that victory in Vietnam could be achieved with any acceptable expenditure of troops, money, and time.

Intelligence analysis was also a significant element in devising a new counterinsurgency strategy. In the early phases of the war, from 1965 through 1968, U.S. Army tactics were narrowly focused on high-firepower "search and destroy" missions, which used body counts of insurgents as the metric of success. To support this approach, the United States also used massive bombing from the air and defoliation. Such measures often alienated the population and provided the communists with propaganda points. The insurgents' response was to either avoid large-scale battle or slip away, if confronted.

As an alternative strategy, some Army officers, along with their Marine counterparts and civilians in the Central Intelligence Agency (CIA) and elsewhere, urged a broader approach based on the lessons of the British campaign in Malaya. This alternative method would be aimed at pacification and security in the countryside, where most Vietnamese lived. Such as approach would be based on smaller units that lived in villages, had better knowledge of and sensitivity to local conditions, cooperated closely with the locals, and had more authority to make their own decisions. Moreover, they would conduct civic programs, involving political and economic development, in addition to strictly military duties, with the goal of isolating the insurgents from popular support. All of this would be done in close cooperation with, and even in subordination to, the political leadership.

After the shock of the Tet Offensive, more efforts were made to shift to the new strategy. It was too late, however; the vital support of the American population was slipping away.

Another aspect of the Vietnam War that involved analysis was the controversy over the size of communist forces. The insurgent forces in South Vietnam included many different types of personnel, including regular units (from both North and South Vietnam), guerrilla fighters, locally based militia units, and political officers. The U.S. military mission in South Vietnam, the Military Assistance Command Vietnam (MACV), was largely a regular force, and its analysts concentrated most of their attention on the opponent's regular forces, at least in part because they were easier to identify and understand. Military analysts acknowledged the existence of the irregular forces, however, and included them in their estimate of the overall strength of the enemy, which they believed was approximately 300,000.

The CIA was heavily involved in the rural pacification program, so it tended to have more contact with the irregular forces. CIA analysts concluded, on the basis of documents that were captured over time, that the total number of communist combatants had increased and that the irregular forces were much larger than originally thought. In preparing for a 1967 National Intelligence Estimate (NIE) on Vietnam, the CIA believed that the total size of the communist forces was more than 400,000.

At the time, leaders in both Washington and MACV maintained that the war was going well. The conventional wisdom was that the communists' losses were exceeding their ability to provide replacements, and it was therefore only a matter of time before the communists would have to admit defeat. The smaller the overall number of combatants, the quicker victory would come using current methods.

Casualty estimates were based on soft numbers, including the notorious "body counts." Because many of the communists did not fight in uniform, it was difficult to distinguish between the bodies of combatants and those of innocent bystanders. In addition, the communists often carried off the bodies of their casualties, to avoid revealing their losses. There was a temptation for both South Vietnamese and Americans to overestimate in reports of enemy bodies left on the field of battle. Moreover, there were many other factors besides casualties, such as logistical support and leadership, that determined the effectiveness of communist units.

In deference to their leaders, military analysts maintained that the irregular forces should not be included in the overall count because including them would mean it could take much longer to break the insurgency. MACV analysts criticized higher estimates for taking at face value the communists' propaganda about their strength. Some military analysts, however, said privately that they agreed, more or less, with the CIA's numbers.

CIA analysts, for their part, were concerned that communist strength might even be considerably higher than the 400,000 cited in the NIE. Moreover, they believed that not to include the irregulars in the total, without noting clearly that this had been done, was a distortion of the numbers and the situation. The controversy among the analysts became even more difficult when the disagreements over numbers were revealed in the press. After lengthy discussions with their military counterparts, CIA analysts reluctantly agreed to a compromise: The NIE would contain lower estimates of communist strength that were closer to the MACV numbers, and the estimate would drop local militia units from the calculation.

In 1982, after the war in Vietnam was over and it was clear that the United States had been defeated there, the CBS television network revived the story of the disagreements over the numbers and asserted that U.S. military commanders had tried to mislead the civilian leadership and the public about the size of communist forces and casualties. General William Westmoreland (1914–2005), who had been the commander of MACV in the late 1960s, promptly sued CBS and several of the individuals, including a CIA analyst, who had helped to prepare the CBS program. He claimed that they had libeled him and defamed his character. When it became clear that the resulting trial was going against him, Westmoreland dropped the charges in return for a statement from CBS that it had not intended to question his loyalty or patriotism.

As usual, cognitive issues played a significant role for both analysts and decision makers. Americans found it difficult to understand a non-Western culture and unconventional warfare. An example is the famous exchange between a U.S. military officer, who claimed – rightly – that Americans won virtually every battle, and his communist counterpart who retorted – also rightly – that, although that was true, it did not matter. On other occasions, as before Tet, analysts made a common, and occasionally disastrously wrong, assumption that the future would be more or less like the past.

More broadly, there is the issue of the perceptual framework. Was the Vietnam War a Cold War issue at all, or is it more accurate to see it in the context of the wars of colonial liberation of the 1950s and 1960s? In the short term, the outcome was a victory for communism; but over the longer term, Vietnam has peacefully moved toward a more market-oriented economy. Did the war hinder or speed up this transformation?.

Although there were many other issues in dealing with Vietnam that are familiar from other wars and crises, what is particularly striking in this instance is the difficulty of performing analysis in a heated decision-making environment. As is sometimes the case, a few analysts have a deeper or more accurate understanding of what is going on (although there is a chance that they could be wrong), and they find it difficult to convince a large, diverse, and more policy-committed government to recognize and act on their insights.

Questions for Further Thought

Were there any other sources of information or analytic techniques that would have made a difference in Vietnam?

Why did analysts disagree about the size of communist forces? Why aren't numbers alone a sufficient criteria for assessing the effectiveness of enemy forces?

How was counterinsurgency in Vietnam similar to, or different from, what took place in Malaya in the 1950s?

What role did intelligence play in the U.S. debacle in Vietnam?

Recommended Reading

Adams, Sam, *War of Numbers: An Intelligence Memoir*, South Royalton, VT: Steerforth Press, 1994.

Allen, George W., *None So Blind: A Personal Account of the Intelligence Failure in Vietnam*, Chicago, IL: Ivan R. Dee, 2001.

Halberstam, David, *The Best and the Brightest*, New York: Random House, 1972.

McNamara, Robert S., and VanDeMark, Brian, *In Retrospect: The Tragedy and Lessons of Vietnam*, New York: Times Books, 1995.

Nagl, John A., *Learning to Eat Soup with a Knife: Counterinsurgency Lessons from Malaya and Vietnam*, Chicago, IL: University of Chicago Press, 2005.

Wirtz, James J., *The Tet Offensive: Intelligence Failure in War*, Ithaca, NY: Cornell University Press, 1991.

Figure 21. Afghanistan.

21

The Soviet Invasion of Afghanistan

I N APRIL 1978, A PRO-SOVIET GOVERNMENT TOOK OVER AFGHANISTAN AFTER a coup. Afghanistan had been drifting away from a nonthreatening neutrality and Moscow used the influence it had through Soviet-trained military officers, a local communist party, and economic aid and advisors to obtain a government more in line with its interests. The new Afghan government immediately started to implement a leftist program, including land and education reforms that were anathema to much of the population, who wanted to maintain their Islamic traditions. A dramatic increase in the number of Soviet military and civilian advisers in the country also created animosity against the central government. By November 1978, tribes in the countryside were in open revolt.

Therefore, there were two questions for analysts: (1) Would Moscow allow a client state on its borders to slip out of its control? and (2) If the Soviets decided to reassert their influence, what steps would they take?

The possibility of increasing Soviet activity in Afghanistan caused concern in Washington. As early as March 1979, U.S. intelligence detected Soviet troops and equipment moving closer to the border with Afghanistan in limited numbers, apparently in response to the recent death of some Soviet advisers in the fighting. There was a debate among analysts in Washington over the meaning of these indicators, and several hypotheses were considered. Most believed that this was an exercise, but others were concerned that it was an unprecedented level of activity in a usually quiet sector. The official assessment, published toward the end of March and emphasizing what was believed to be caution in Moscow, was:

> The Soviets would be most reluctant to introduce large numbers of ground forces into Afghanistan to keep in power an Afghan government that had lost the support of virtually all segments of the population. Not only would the

Soviets find themselves in an awkward morass in Afghanistan, but their actions
could seriously damage their relations with India, and – to a lesser degree – with
Pakistan.

This line – that the Soviets recognized the potentially high costs of intervention, such as possible failure of the major Strategic Arms Limitation
Talks (SALT) II arms control treaty then under consideration and negative
sentiment in the Muslim world and the broader international community –
became the standard assessment of Moscow's thinking in the U.S. intelligence community.

Documents released publicly after the collapse of the USSR in 1991 (but
not available to analysts in 1979) made it clear that March was, in fact, when
serious discussions began in Moscow about how to handle the worsening
situation in Afghanistan. The Politburo, the senior decision-making forum,
noted the risks of sending in large forces and considered intervention as a
last resort. The leadership was in agreement, though, that they could not
"lose" Afghanistan. Beyond sending a high-ranking military team in April to
assess the effectiveness of the Afghan army (or lack thereof) and making
contingency preparations, no action was taken in the spring.

The situation of the pro-Soviet government continued to deteriorate in
the summer of 1979, with poor performance by the Afghan army, including
defeats, mutinies, and defections to the insurgency. Moscow responded
by sending more military equipment and increasing the number of civilian
and military advisers to more than 4,000 personnel. In July, the first Soviet
combat force – an airborne battalion – was sent to Bagram airfield outside
Kabul, although this battalion did not immediately engage in operations.
That same month, the East German ambassador in Kabul told his American
counterpart that he believed that the Soviets were willing to use force to
get a more effective Afghan government. U.S. analysts continued to believe,
however, that a large-scale intervention was unlikely and that the unit at
Bagram was to protect flights carrying military aid.

As the situation worsened, there were rumors that Soviet personnel were
piloting helicopters, manning tanks, and perhaps even conducting combat
operations in regiment- or battalion-sized units. In August, there was an
attempted coup in the capital by units sympathetic to the Islamic rebels.
Although it was quickly put down, it gave rise to concerns about the loyalty
of the Afghan army. U.S. analysts believed that this incident was forcing
Moscow to consider more seriously the option of a substantial intervention.
Unusual levels of activity by units on the Soviet side of the border continued, and were followed by analysts, who speculated that it might indicate
preparation for an emergency defense of Kabul. The arrival of another team

of Soviet generals a few days after the coup attempt suggested that the Soviet government was worried about the deteriorating situation. Then, a few weeks later, a less pliable Afghan leader, Hafizullah Amin, came to power, further increasing Moscow's anxiety and reducing its options. The tone of analysis coming from Washington began to shift, with a mid-September assessment saying:

> The Soviet leaders may be on the threshold of a decision to commit their own forces to prevent the collapse of the regime and to protect their sizeable stakes in Afghanistan.

This and other assessments at the time, however, also noted the high military and diplomatic costs of a major intervention. Most analysts still did not believe that large-scale invasion was the most likely scenario in the short term.

Meanwhile, Soviet preparations for a variety of contingencies continued. In October, reserves in the central republics of the USSR were mobilized. The following month a new local headquarters, with sophisticated satellite communications with Moscow, was established.

What was missing from the American analysis was an accurate understanding of how the leadership in Moscow saw the world in 1979. For a decade and a half, since the humiliation of the Cuban Missile Crisis, the USSR had been building up its armed forces. By the mid-1970s, Moscow believed it had achieved military parity with the United States, and thus much greater freedom to do what it wanted on the world stage. In the context of the Warsaw Pact, it had proclaimed the Brezhnev Doctrine – that it had the right to use force to maintain communist governments – and it had done so in Czechoslovakia in 1968. More broadly, the USSR had used substantial military aid to support leftist revolutions in Angola and Ethiopia.

Now there was an opportunity to expand Soviet power even farther, toward the oil-rich Middle East. What had been striking, from Moscow's point of view, was how little resistance had been shown by the United States, in its post-Vietnam mood of limiting foreign commitments. With all their confidence and ambition, however, the Soviet leaders were still uneasy, worried that their own Muslim populations in central Asia might be tempted by radical Islam, as well as concerned about their prestige and what people would think if they backed down or lost in Afghanistan. They considered the risks, including the difficulties of fighting in the mountains and deserts of Afghanistan and negative international reaction, but believed that these were outweighed by the need not to lose.

There were some public hints of the Soviets' evolving policy, including a chill in relations with the new government in Kabul. In November, the

Afghan foreign minister (rather than President Amin) represented the government at the celebration of the USSR's national holiday at the Soviet embassy. Then, in early December, in an exchange of messages marking the first anniversary of the Soviet–Afghan Friendship Treaty, Moscow sent greetings to the Afghan government but did not mention Amin. From Moscow's point of view, Amin's main failing may have been his reluctance to legitimize Soviet intervention by extending a formal invitation to send troops. Was Moscow signalling that it doubted Amin's long-term viability and was concerned that he might turn to the West?

Although it was not clear at the time, during late November and early December, the leadership in Moscow made the decision to send large numbers of troops to Afghanistan to take on the Muslim insurgents. Indicators of this turning point included that, in addition to increased military activity in the USSR, the Soviets were strengthening the units at Bagram airfield, prompting American analysts to note, in early December:

> ... it is also possible, although much more speculative, that the airborne and motorized rifle elements now at Bagram are merely the first increment of a much larger combat force that may be deployed to Afghanistan during the coming year ... It is not certain that Moscow has embarked on such a plan ...

A few weeks later, Soviet troops began taking control of the main roads leading from Kabul to the border. By the middle of December, U.S. analysts estimated that there were more than 5,000 Soviet troops in Afghanistan, but most of the Americans following developments in Central Asia continued to see the Soviet movements as part of a gradual buildup to prevent the collapse of a sympathetic regime.

By the third week in December, news of the Soviet buildup in and around Afghanistan, and that Washington was expressing concern to Moscow, was in the press. Published accounts also reported disagreements within the U.S. government over what it all meant. Some expressed the view that the troop movements looked a lot like what had preceded the intervention in Czechoslovakia, including participation of some of the same generals. Another indicator of possible intervention was that a special operational headquarters and large fuel depots had been set up on the USSR side of the border. In contrast, some observers characterized the activity as a gradual escalation and assessed that there were not enough troops involved to take over the struggle with the Islamists. Those who held this view maintained that there were no clear signs of the purpose of the buildup.

On December 22, 1979, the National Security Agency said that communications intercepts available to it strongly suggested that a major Soviet intervention was imminent. Then, on December 24, in the most ambitious

Figure 22. Soviet forces in Kabul, Afghanistan (U.S. Department of Defense photograph, from Wikipedia)

expansion of Moscow's power outside its borders in thirty years, large numbers of Soviet transport planes began moving troops and equipment from the western portions of the USSR to reinforce forces already in place near the border with Afghanistan. Additional aircraft went directly to the Afghan capital of Kabul and to other major cities. Within four days, several Soviet battalions had taken over the capital, killed Amin, and removed the government (see Figure 22). In addition to the airlift, more troops moved into the country by land. By the end of the year, there were an estimated 30,000 Soviet troops fanning out over Afghanistan. In time, the USSR would have more than 100,000 troops in the country and would take over the main responsibility for trying to defeat the Islamic insurgents.

Trying to anticipate what the Soviets would do in Afghanistan is full of examples of the cognitive challenges to accurate analysis. As so often in the past, mirror imaging and the rational actor model were present. There were also biases, such as anchoring, confirmation, and framing. In addition, to be fair, most of these shortcomings are realized only through generous application of the hindsight bias.

Collection was better on troop movements in the southern Soviet Union than on offices and conference rooms in Moscow. It should be noted, however, that collection of accurate information on high-level Soviet decision making in the spring and summer of 1979 would have revealed indecision and suggested reluctance to intervene.

Although senior U.S. officials later complained that their intelligence agencies did not alert them in advance of the Soviet move into Afghanistan, the record is clear that Washington was protesting Soviet ominous activity days before the Christmas Eve intervention. Given Moscow's perception of what was at stake, was there anything that officials in Washington could have said that would have stopped the invasion? Over the longer term, of course, the Soviet decision led to a disaster that played a large role in the collapse of the USSR.

Questions for Further Thought

How was trying to predict what the Soviets would do in Afghanistan similar to, or different from, the English trying to anticipate when Philip II would launch the Armada or the British trying to determine the strength of the *Luftwaffe*?

Not for the first or last time, the evidence regarding what Moscow would do was mixed. How can an analyst sort through ambiguous, contradictory, and incomplete information to determine what is likely to happen?

Is Afghanistan another case in which tactical indicators, such as the movement of soldiers and equipment, are better guides to what might happen than are strategic judgments of plans and intentions? What are some other examples?

Based on the Soviet example, what are likely to be some of the difficulties in conducting counterinsurgency operations in Afghanistan?

Recommended Reading

Arnold, Anthony, *Afghanistan: The Soviet Invasion in Perspective*, Stanford, CA: Hoover Institution Press, 1981.

Bradsher, Henry S., *Afghanistan and the Soviet Union*, Durham, NC: Duke Press Policy Studies, 1983.

MacEachin, Douglas, *Predicting the Soviet Invasion of Afghanistan: The Intelligence Community's Record*, Washington, DC: Center for the Study of Intelligence, 2002.

22

Finding Spies

Ames and Hanssen

T HE COLD WAR WAS WAGED NOT ONLY IN THE THIRD WORLD AND ON missile production lines, but also in quieter ways. During the waning months of 1985, American spies in the USSR were being arrested at an alarming rate, and by the following spring almost a dozen – virtually the entire roster of human sources operated by the Central Intelligence Agency (CIA) and the Federal Bureau of Investigation (FBI) in the Soviet Union – had been killed. Most were quickly executed; in some cases their fate was never determined. As time passed, a number of technical operations being conducted against the Soviets were also exposed. Obviously, something was terribly wrong.

In 1986, the CIA and FBI launched separate counterintelligence investigations to try to determine what had happened, so that corrective measures could be taken. The CIA's approach was to look at the records of the blown cases to see if there were common elements that might provide leads. Initially the hypotheses were: (1) that the problem was sloppy tradecraft by the Soviet agents; (2) revelations from the numerous spies arrested in 1985 (which had become known as "the year of the spy"); or (3) that U.S. secure communications with Moscow had been compromised.

It soon became clear that none of these hypotheses was a plausible explanation. That all of the American spies had made operational mistakes at the same time was unlikely. Although there had been a large number of Soviet agents exposed in 1985, they did not have access to identifying details about all of the American spies in the USSR who had been lost. A test of communications links, by sending false information that was sure to generate a Soviet response, led to nothing and indicated that electronic failure was probably not the reason for the losses of so many important human sources.

Even though a few intelligence officials were concerned that there might be a mole – in other words, an American intelligence officer working for

Moscow – this hypothesis was not given serious consideration. The assumption was that such treachery was unthinkable and that countermeasures, such as the polygraph examination, which all CIA employees were required to take, would in any case prevent a betrayal. Moreover, after the excessive suspicions when James Angleton had been the CIA's head of counterintelligence from 1954 through 1974, and many careers had been needlessly ruined by his investigations, there was a reluctance to pursue suspects too aggressively.

By 1991, with no progress in the counterintelligence investigation, the CIA decided to join forces with the FBI, with whom they had not been completely sharing information up to this point. This phase of the investigation made more use of FBI procedures, which were to try to identify suspects (rather than review case files). The joint investigation used a matrix that matched all of those who had access to the files on the Soviet assets (on one axis) against agents who had been lost (on the other axis). This procedure resulted in a list of approximately 200 names of persons who could have betrayed the American spies. Eventually the joint investigators were able, through process of elimination, to narrow the list down to twenty-nine main suspects.

In 1993, the CIA decided that the person who was most likely to be the mole was Aldrich Ames (1941–), a career operations officer. Ames had worked Soviet cases in the past, and thus had had authorized contacts with Soviet intelligence officers whom he was trying to recruit. Over time, though, he had stopped reporting all of his Soviet contacts, even those that were authorized, and his travel. Other warning indicators included that Ames had a record of mediocre performance, alcohol abuse, and spending considerably beyond his income. For years these indicators had not been recognized or taken seriously, even though his name had been on the list of twenty-nine suspects drawn up in 1991. What was most suspicious, however, was that he had made large cash deposits into his bank accounts after his known meetings with Soviet intelligence officers. Now that it was clear that this was likely to turn into a criminal case, the CIA turned it over to the FBI.

The Bureau began physical surveillance of Ames, but never caught him actually conducting spying activity, although many of his movements were suspicious. Then, in September 1993, a search of his trash revealed a torn piece of paper that, when put back together, contained a cryptic note. An alert FBI agent realized that it was directions to a clandestine meeting. This note provided the necessary probable cause to get court approval for audio surveillance of and covert entry into Ames's residence. The enhanced surveillance showed that he had suspicious material on his home computer. A search of Ames's office at CIA headquarters revealed that he had a large number of classified documents on subjects outside his area of responsibility.

On February 21, 1994, the FBI arrested Ames. During his debriefing it became clear that his main motive had been money and that the Soviets and their successors in the new Russian government had paid him some $2.7 million – and promised him even more. He also had grown cynical and dissatisfied about his CIA work and found great satisfaction in showing that he was more clever than the counterintelligence officials that he knew were trying to find the spy who had betrayed the U.S. human sources in the USSR.

Ames agreed to cooperate with investigators as part of his sentencing, but his debriefing, along with other indicators, such as reports from spies working for the United States and the betrayal of operations and assets that were not known to Ames, strongly suggested that the Russians had another high-level penetration in place. In the same way that CIA officers had assumed that the hypothesis that one of their colleagues was a traitor was not worthy of consideration, the FBI assumed that it was impossible that a second spy could be a Bureau agent. After the exposure of Ames, it was difficult for the CIA to maintain that its officers were immune to temptation. Therefore, in the late 1990s the search for a second mole focused on CIA personnel, and in 1999 one of the suspects at the Agency was subjected to intense surveillance and suspended from work, even though there was no concrete proof of his guilt.

In the meantime, the FBI had been offering a large reward for information about other traitors, and in November 2001 a defector from Russia collected the money after providing the personnel file of a spy who had been working for Moscow for years. The file did not include the agent's name, but there was a recording of a brief telephone conversation with the individual and a plastic bag that had been used to deliver stolen material. The Bureau was able to identify the voice and to recover fingerprints from the plastic bag. Both belonged to Robert Hanssen (1944–), an FBI counterintelligence agent and computer expert, who had been working off and on for various Soviet and Russian intelligence services for more than twenty years. The Bureau quickly transferred Hanssen to less sensitive work and launched an intense investigation. It was soon determined that he had a number of personal quirks that would have prompted suspicion if they had been more widely known. On February 18, 2001, FBI agents arrested Hanssen after catching him in the act of leaving classified documents to be picked up by his Russian handlers.

Like Ames, Hanssen was mainly motivated by money, as well as by sat-
isfaction in fooling the authorities and disenchantment with intelligence
work. He also betrayed the identities of Soviets and then Russians who had
worked for the United States, along with various technical operations, and
he was able to put Moscow in the enviable position of having independent
confirmation of sensitive information.

Hanssen had been much more careful than Ames, however, in managing
his contacts with foreign intelligence officers. He never gave his true name or
had face-to-face meetings; instead he provided information via dead drops,
leaving documents and picking up money and then departing, without his
handlers ever seeing him. Moscow had accepted these unusual procedures
because of the authenticity and value of what Hanssen was providing.

The counterintelligence analysts working on the Ames and Hanssen cases
found it difficult to get beyond their assumptions that it was impossible that
their colleagues could be spies for the Soviet Union. After this hypothesis
was accepted as a possibility, however, the investigation had a better chance
of success.

An investigation is a type of problem solving that has its own preconditions
and procedures. Unlike many analytic challenges, what has prompted the
inquiry is an act, or series of acts, that has already taken place. There is,
therefore, evidence (more or less) regarding what has happened and who
the perpetrator might be, and the task is to clarify those issues. Investigators
generally find it helpful to focus their work on sets of questions that have
proven to be especially helpful, such as means, motive, and opportunity, or
who, what, when, where, how, and why. Because the goal is to have the
materials for a successful prosecution (if it comes to that), the standards for
evidence must be quite high, and generally as much time as is needed is
taken to gather and assess information relevant to the case.

That said, other standard analytic procedures, such as understanding context, looking for anomalies to see if other hypotheses are needed, or asking
if the uncertain case under consideration is similar to models of cases about
which more is known, can also be helpful in counterintelligence investigations.

Questions for Further Thought

What are some of the indicators that investigators should look for when
    working on a real or suspected espionage case?
What are some of the similarities and differences between these two cases
    and the uncovering of the atomic bomb spies in the 1950s?
Why did it take so long to uncover Ames and Hanssen?

Recommended Reading

Adams, James, *Sellout: Aldrich Ames and the Corruption of the CIA*, New York: Viking, 1995.

Vise, David A., *The Bureau and the Mole: The Unmasking of Robert Philip Hanssen, the Most Dangerous Double Agent in FBI History*, New York: Atlantic Monthly Press, 2002.

Weiner, Tim, et al., *Betrayal: The Story of Aldrich Ames, an American Spy*, New York: Random House, 1995.

Wise, David, *Nightmover: How Aldrich Ames Sold the CIA to the KGB for $4.6 Million*, New York: Harper Collins, 1995.

Wise, David, *Spy: The Inside Story of How the FBI's Robert Hanssen Betrayed America*, New York: Random House, 2003.

23

Breakup of the USSR

URING THE COLD WAR, THE SOVIET UNION, AND ABOVE ALL ITS arsenal of strategic nuclear weapons, was the top priority for intelligence analysts around the world, and especially in the United States. Over the years, the Central Intelligence Agency (CIA) and the many other agencies of the U.S. intelligence community had built up a vast system of satellites, listening posts, aircraft, ships, and other means to collect information in an effort to accurately assess the Soviet threat.

CIA analysis of the USSR in the 1980s tended to focus on military issues and generally saw the country as likely to be a major threat for some time to come. An April 1981 assessment, for example, considered a number of possible scenarios for the future, but postulated that it was most likely that the Soviet defense buildup of the 1960s and 1970s would continue:

> ... we estimate – on the basis of the weapons production and development programs we have identified – that the Soviets will continue their policy of balanced force development... If the Soviets carry out the programs we have identified, their defense expenditure will continue to increase in real terms throughout the 1980s. The precise rate of increase is difficult to predict. It could be as high as 4 percent a year... A rate of 4 percent would increase the military drain on the economy and the potential for internal political problems.

In retrospect, estimates of strategic forces, based largely on signals and imagery intelligence, were sometimes exaggerated, especially in the late 1950s. As already noted, CIA analysts were changing some of their assessments of Soviet defense spending on the basis of new reporting and a different methodology. In the 1980s, this revised approach led to the more accurate judgment that growth was slowing. Nonetheless, the conclusion was that there would continue to be high levels of defense spending and that the system of domestic controls could contain any discontent on the part of the population.

A crucial aspect of measuring the Soviet threat was determining whether the USSR had the economic resources to support a large and growing arsenal of missiles, aircraft, warships, tanks, and a vast array of other equipment. Beginning in the mid-1970s, CIA analysts were reporting on deteriorating economic conditions in the USSR. In July 1977, CIA economists noted:

> Powerful remedies are either not readily available or not politically feasible . . . The slowdown in economic growth could trigger intense debate in Moscow over the future levels and pattern of military expenditures . . . These serious problems ahead seem most likely to prompt Soviet leaders to consider policies rejected in the past as too contentious or lacking in urgency.

Later, in 1983, the CIA view was that:

> Industrial growth . . . slowed unusually sharply during 1976–1982 . . . Even more dramatic was the slump in productivity . . . Prospects for turning the situation around in the rest of the 1980s are not good.

There were controversies, however, with some other economists in academia and elsewhere expressing skepticism regarding the metrics that the CIA used to measure the Soviet economy; the comparisons that were made to Western market-based systems; and the conclusions that were drawn.

Another important aspect of evaluating the Soviet threat was to consider social indicators. Unlike military hardware, "soft" issues such as social conditions were often of less interest to decision makers and harder to measure. Nonetheless, serious social problems could be readily observed by anyone who visited the Soviet Union, especially outside the major cities. Pervasive alcoholism was particularly obvious and damaging, as was corruption. Consumer goods were often of poor quality or in short supply. Indicators were also available in public statistics reporting factors such as birth rates and life expectancy. As controls loosened in the 1980s, a wider range of information about domestic conditions in the USSR became available, and U.S. analysts, who increasingly focused on the newly liberalized press, tracked growing political, economic, social, and ethnic strains on the communist system.

In 1985, the reformer, Mikhail Gorbachev (1931–), became head of the Communist Party. The early assessment was that his goal was to modify the existing system rather than transform it. A National Intelligence Estimate (NIE) published that year postulated that, although a collapse of the Soviet system was unlikely over the next five years, politics in Moscow would be dominated by the difficult choices arising from growing internal problems, and prospects for Gorbachev's success were mixed at best. In April 1986, the CIA's view was that:

> It seems unlikely, however, that Gorbachev will be able to introduce reforms significant enough to arrest long-range negative trends in Soviet society... although the regime will be able to contain societal tensions for the foreseeable future, long-range trends are producing a fundamental and growing disparity between popular aspirations and the regime's capacity to satisfy them.

In a 1987 NIE, the analytic consensus was that Gorbachev still wanted to maintain communism and expand the influence of the USSR but would do this peacefully and that reforms would keep the Soviet Union together. The estimate laid out a number of scenarios for the future, rating as most likely that Gorbachev would achieve his goals and rejuvenate the existing system. It was less likely, in the analysts' view, that the Soviet system would be completely reformed. It was possible, but even less likely, that there would be a traditionalist reaction that would threaten Gorbachev's hold on power. The chances for a market economy and democracy were seen as virtually nil. A 1988 NIE on the Soviet empire in Eastern Europe also used the scenario technique, speculating that there could be sweeping reform, popular upheaval, or a traditionalist backlash.

Estimates focused on military power continued to be skeptical of Gorbachev's rhetoric suggesting that the Cold War was over. A December 1988 NIE made it clear that most intelligence analysts believed that there had been – and in the coming decade would continue to be – little change:

> ... in terms of what the Soviets spend, what they procure, how their strategic forces are deployed, how they plan, and how they exercise, the basic elements of Soviet defense policy and practice thus far have not been changed by Gorbachev's reform campaign.

In the years that followed, Gorbachev went on to pull Soviet troops out of Afghanistan, ease repression at home, and offer to make major cuts in the USSR's nuclear arsenal.

As late as 1989, the consensus-based NIEs still extrapolated a continuation of past trends. One estimate from that year that focused on the current state of the rivalry between the USSR and the West concluded that the Soviet Union would be a serious adversary for the foreseeable future. Another NIE, done in December 1989 and focused on internal developments, stated that

> Community analysts hold the view that a continuation and intensification of the current course is most likely and believe that, despite the obvious difficulties, the

turmoil will be manageable with the need for repressive measures so pervasive that the reform process is derailed.

The CIA, however, dissented on this judgment and expressed concern that Gorbachev would lose control of events.

During 1989, analytic complacency gave way to a realization, at least on the part of some analysts, that fundamental change was under way. As Eastern Europe slipped out of Soviet control, a September 1989 analysis done by the CIA noted continued worsening of economic and social problems in the USSR and that

> ... the United States for the foreseeable future will confront a Soviet leadership that faces endemic popular unrest and that ... will have to employ emergency measures and increased use of force to retain domestic control ... Gorbachev has no easy option ... the set of problems Gorbachev has in fact fostered is likely to lead in the future to major instability in the USSR ...

Important changes that reduced tensions continued in 1990, with the Treaty on Conventional Armed Forces in Europe, the peaceful withdrawal of Soviet forces from Eastern Europe, and Moscow's acceptance of the reunification of Germany.

By 1991, tensions in the USSR had increased so much that in April of that year the CIA warned that there was a high possibility of "explosive events," which might include assassination of reformist leaders or a coup. In May 1991, the assessment was as follows:

> The essence of the current crisis is that neither the existing political system Gorbachev is attempting to preserve nor the partially emerging new system is able to cope effectively with newly mobilized popular demands and the deepening economic crisis. In short, the Soviet Union is now in a revolutionary situation ... the ingredients are now present in the USSR ... that could quickly sweep away the current system and leadership.

A June 1991 estimate noted that "The USSR is in the midst of a revolution that probably will sweep the Communist Party from power and reshape the country within the five-year time frame of this Estimate." This time, the scenarios were continued instability, peaceful evolution to a more democratic system, a violent breakup of the USSR, and an effort by hard-liners to restore the old order.

On August 17, 1991, the CIA warned in the President's Daily Brief that the planned August 20 signature of a new union treaty was likely to trigger action by Gorbachev's opponents, although the analysts had no specific details. In fact, on August 19, hard-liners launched a coup. After a tense few days, the coup failed, but in the weeks that followed many of the constituent republics of the USSR began to declare independence. By the end of the year, the USSR had dissolved and the Cold War was over.

As is often the case with complex issues, the analysts' record on the breakup of the Soviet Union is mixed. On the basis of observations of military hardware and operations, they wrongly speculated that the security threat from the USSR would be serious and long-lasting. They were alert to the internal dangers from social and economic problems, but did not realize how quickly they would have an impact. After tensions accelerated, they did quite well in helping decision makers to understand the possibilities.

A major challenges for CIA analysts working on the Soviet Union in the 1980s was to cope with the temptation of status quo thinking – that is, the view that what has been the case for so long will continue to be the case. To complicate matters further in trying to anticipate and understand what was happening in the USSR, there were two processes occurring more or less simultaneously: the discrediting of an ideology and the disintegration of an empire. Difficulty in anticipating a major discontinuity such as the breakup of the USSR also involved the paradox of expertise: Analysts who had worked on the problem, sometimes for decades, found it difficult to envision that a radically different set of circumstances was possible. Finally, there could be a serious potential for misunderstanding what was going on by focusing on the more serious and observable security-related factors while paying less attention to factors that were more subtle and hard to discern from a distance, such as social and ethnic problems.

Analysts also need to be careful about emphasizing leaders' intentions as an accurate guide to the future. Gorbachev did not intend to end communism and break up the USSR, but his policies gave a decisive push in that direction.

One way that CIA analysts sought to deal with uncertainty associated with rapid and important change was through scenarios, or multiple possible outcomes. They correctly identified that the main drivers would be the Soviet leadership's desire for higher defense spending, the inability of a communist-inspired economy to support this desire, and the population's increasing disenchantment with the resulting poor living standards and repression of nationalist sentiment among non-Russians.

From the wider perspective of the other components of the U.S. government concerned with national security that were the consumers of intelligence analysis, such as Congress, the Pentagon, and the State Department, the main focus – justifiably – was the Soviet military, the only force that had the potential to destroy the United States. Senior decision makers were no more willing than were intelligence analysts to believe that the breakup of the USSR was imminent. Although much of the Reagan administration's approach was based on an assumption of Soviet vulnerabilities, it was believed that a long effort to achieve victory in the Cold War was still ahead. The administration of President George H. W. Bush (1924–), for its part, was initially skeptical about Gorbachev's expressed willingness to move beyond the Cold War.

In addition, it should be noted that the NIEs were judgments based on consensus, and there was a vigorous debate among analysts over the future of the USSR that did not make it into the final product. Nonetheless, few (if any) analysts believed that the Soviet empire would collapse quickly, completely, and peacefully.

Questions for Further Thought

What kind of data would have revealed the impending collapse of the Soviet Union? How available were they to analysts?

Are there other complex contemporary issues – such as terrorism, climate change, or China's growth and integration into the global economic and political system – that are not being correctly understood by analysts because of a focus on a particular aspect of the issue? Is a partial or distorted perspective influencing the information that is being collected on these issues?

How did looking at both capabilities and intentions help analysts to understand – or misunderstand – the breakup of the Soviet Union?

Recommended Reading

Beschloss, Michael R., and Talbott, Strobe, *At the Highest Levels: The Inside Story of the End of the Cold War*, Boston: Little, Brown, 1993.

Bush, George, and Scowcroft, Brent, *A World Transformed*, New York: Knopf, 1998.

Fischer, Benjamin B., ed., *At Cold War's End: U.S. Intelligence on the Soviet Union and Eastern Europe, 1989–1991*, Washington, DC: CIA Center for the Study of Intelligence, 1999.

Gates, Robert M., *From the Shadows: The Ultimate Insider's Story of Five Presidents and How They Won the Cold War*, New York: Simon & Schuster, 1996.

Haines, Gerald K., and Leggett, Robert E., eds., *CIA Analysis of the Soviet Union, 1947–91*, Washington, DC: CIA, Center for the Study of Intelligence, 2001.

Part V

Other International Security Issues, Other Places

THE RIVALRY BETWEEN THE UNITED STATES AND THE USSR DOMINATED THE last half of the twentieth century, but there were other problems. The rest of the world had its own difficulties in dealing with issues such as modernization, as well as age-old disputes over land. Seeing such issues through a Cold War prism could sometimes lead to seriously misunderstanding them.

Many of these problems involved classic military issues of surprise and deception and the impact of new technology. Intelligence analysts also were grappling, however, with newer predicaments, such as limiting the proliferation of nuclear weapons and assuring the flow of energy to industrialized economies.

There was also a sense that history was speeding up – events were unfolding at an accelerating pace. The gap between developed countries and the rest of the world was widening, as was the potential for major revolutions, discontinuities, and changes in traditional trends and patterns. Islamic fundamentalists responded to these changes and were willing to use terrorism to promote their agenda.

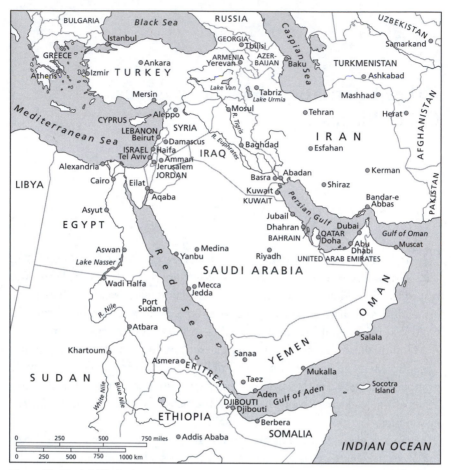

Figure 23. The Middle East.

24

The Yom Kippur War

THE MIDDLE EAST IS A REGION OF INTENSE GLOBAL INTEREST BECAUSE IT is a source of much of the world's oil, as well as the home of three of the world's major religions. Israel sits in the heart of this important and volatile region. Because it is small and is surrounded by hostile, much larger, and more populous Arab neighbors, Israel puts a high priority on having effective intelligence collection and analysis. In June 1967, when intelligence suggested that Israel faced imminent attack, it launched a preemptive strike against three of those neighbors: Egypt, Jordan, and Syria. Using their excellent knowledge of where enemy forces were located, the Israeli Defense Forces (IDF) wiped out most of the Egyptian air force in just three hours and went on to defeat all three of the rival armies in six days. This feat made Israel the dominant military power in the region. As a result, Israeli civilian and military leaders assumed that they had little to fear from their Arab neighbors and that they would be able to detect and deal with any future threat.

This assessment did not change after Anwar al-Sadat (1918–81) became president of Egypt in 1970. Israeli analysts saw Sadat's threats to retake the Sinai Peninsula (which had been lost in 1967) and to proclaim 1971 the "Year of Decision" as empty rhetoric, especially when nothing happened.

Israel's reluctance to react, unless necessary, was shaped by the fact that it had only a limited number of its military personnel on duty in peacetime. Mobilizing its reserves was expensive and disruptive to civilian life. The main responsibility for providing a threat assessment that might trigger a mobilization fell to the Directorate of Military Intelligence (AMAN), which had promised to provide at least several days' warning of any attack.

The head of AMAN since October 1972, General Eli Zeira (1928–), believed that the Arabs would not start a war unless they were sure that they would win. This analysis was supported by reporting from a well-placed human source, who said that President Sadat would not attack until he had missiles and bombers that would improve Egypt's chances of gaining air superiority. Zeira also assumed that Syria would not fight until Egypt did. Israel's other neighbors, Jordan and Lebanon, were unlikely to join such a war, for a variety of reasons. AMAN also envisioned a number of scenarios of what an Egyptian attack across the Suez Canal might look like, ranging from scattered raids to an all-out attempt to recapture the Sinai Peninsula. In December 1972, however, Zeira announced that the chances of Egypt crossing the canal were "close to zero," and he continued to hold that view in the months that followed. This analytic framework became known as "The Concept" or "The Conception." Behind The Concept was self-confidence, even arrogance, mixed with racial and ethnic stereotypes that Arabs were incapable of sophisticated organization and warfare in a technological age. As late as October 5, 1973, Zeira was still saying that "the probability for a war initiated by Egypt and Syria is still very low."

Most senior Israeli officials agreed with Zeira's assessment that the chances of war were low. In September 1973, for example, with elections looming, Defense Minister Moshe Dayan (1915–81) from the ruling Labor Party was most worried about the possibility of limited Syrian strikes on Israeli settlements near the border and said, "I do not forecast a war for the coming ten years." At the same time, former general Ariel Sharon (1928–), now a leader of the opposition Likud Party, stated, "Israel stands now before quiet years, from the security perspective . . . we actually have no security problems." A few analysts at the working level were more worried, but their concerns had little impact on Israel's leaders.

U.S. analysts, for their part, picked up some indications that a war was coming but assumed that, because the Israelis had such good information and had more at stake, they would have a more accurate assessment. If the Israelis were not worried, the U.S. analysts saw no reason why they should be.

The Israelis were confident that their varied and multilayered collection would provide both strategic and tactical warning. Pride of place went to an extremely sensitive human intelligence source. For several years, Ashraf Marwan (1944–2007), former president Gamal Abdel Nasser's son-in-law and a senior member of Sadat's staff, had been providing material, including even the Egyptian war plan, to Israel's external intelligence service, the Mossad. Israel also had aerial surveillance and communications intercepts that could give warning several days in advance if an attack was being prepared. Finally, troops on the ground could directly observe both Egyptian and Syrian forces that were only a few hundred yards away. Zeira was so confident in this collection system that he had told the Israeli parliament that AMAN could provide accurate and timely warning and that the country could not be surprised.

The mind-set brought about by belief in The Concept became the mental filter through which the Israelis interpreted reports that they received. For example, they detected that Egypt had acquired more air defense missiles and antitank weapons, but they saw them as defensive measures because of the assessment that war was not likely. When there were large-scale Egyptian military exercises in the spring of 1973, Zeira told the Israeli leadership not to worry. When there was, in fact, no attack, the leaders saw it as confirmation of Zeira's judgment and The Concept. Bellicose speeches by Sadat were dismissed as empty rhetoric. A few clandestine reports gave the exact timing and goals of the attack, but these were not taken seriously. A dissenting assessment from a midlevel analyst was buried in the files. Even a personal warning from Jordan's King Hussein to Prime Minister Golda Meir (1898–1978) in late September was dismissed.

The Israelis missed, however, that Sadat had a different idea of what the next steps should be. In the fall of 1972, Sadat had decided not to wait for the missiles and bombers. Instead, he envisioned a limited war that would seek only to seize a small amount of territory and to inflict significant casualties on the Israelis. Sadat did not intend to try to defeat the IDF or destroy the State of Israel, which he well knew was beyond Egypt's capabilities. For Sadat, the driver was a search for a political victory, which would come through a limited military success that would restore Arab pride and prompt superpower pressure for a settlement. None of this was picked up by Israeli intelligence.

The Egyptians and, to a lesser extent, the Syrians carefully masked their plans, including high-level talks between Egyptian and Syrian officers to coordinate war planning. (These talks were not detected by the Israelis.) Only an extremely small number of senior Egyptian and Syrian military and civilian officials knew that an attack would be launched in early October 1973; many officers knew what was going to happen only a few hours in advance. The Egyptians made many of their preparations look like part of the usual cycle of maneuvers and exercises. In addition, public announcements on security and diplomatic matters were carefully engineered not to indicate a crisis. Senior commanders involved in the preparations tried to maintain the appearance of a normal schedule, and, in some cases, word was spread that Egypt was concerned about a possible Israeli attack. The Egyptians (with the possible exception of Marwan) made little effort, however, to reinforce the deception by sending false information through channels that would be picked up by Israeli clandestine collection.

From August on there were indictors, such as the Syrians canceling leaves, calling up reserves, and reinforcing their units along the border. In late September the Egyptians postponed officer promotion examinations, started removing mines on their side of the canal, and closed Cairo International Airport. Then, on October 1, the long anticipated fall exercise along the canal began. The Israeli commanders believed that all of these developments were defensive in nature.

Several last-minute indicators were misunderstood. Further Egyptian military activity, including the movement forward of large quantities of ammunition and a sharp drop in the level of wireless communications, was seen as part of the exercise. As the Egyptian maneuvers continued, senior Israeli civilian and military officials considered the possibility of an attack but continued to believe that it was improbable. On October 4, the Israelis noticed that families of Soviet personnel (who, unknown to the Israelis, realized that a war was coming) started hastily leaving Egypt and Syria. In addition, Soviet ships began leaving Egyptian ports. Israeli analysts were mystified by what it might mean. Had there been a break in diplomatic relations? Did the Russians fear an Israeli attack? Did they know an Arab attack was imminent and want their people on the sidelines? The same day, aerial reconnaissance showed unprecedented levels of Egyptian troops and vehicles, including bridging equipment, along their side of the Suez Canal. This information was confirmed by observers on the ground, but the alarming details were diluted as summarized reports were passed up the chain of command. Uncertain but worried, the armed forces command ordered an increased level of alert on October 5.

Saturday, October 6, was the holiest day on the Jewish religious calendar, and as a result many active-duty members of the military were on leave. Early that morning, the Mossad disseminated a report from Marwan that war would start toward nightfall that evening. The setting sun would be in the eyes of the Israeli defenders and enable the opening phase to take place in darkness when it was hoped that Israeli air power would be less effective; this was in accordance with the plans Marwan had already passed to the Israelis. Army Chief of Staff General David Elazar (1925–76) was becoming increasingly concerned and recommended preemptive air strikes and a full mobilization of the reserves. Defense Minister Dayan rejected the air strikes, however, and would allow only partial mobilization. Although Zeira admitted that there was ambiguity in the situation because of increasing tactical indicators of Egyptian movements along the canal, he still believed that strategically it did not make sense for Egypt to start a war that it could not win. Therefore, war was not yet certain. Zeira's views, as well as concern about the risks and expense of actions that might turn out to be pointless, influenced Defense Minister Dayan, who continued to oppose a full mobilization or a preemptive air strike. Prime Minister Meir, however, overruled the doubters and approved mobilization of the reserves.

It was too late. At 2:00 P.M., Egyptian troops stormed across the Suez Canal. This attack represented a late change of the time that had been planned only a few days earlier in a compromise with the Syrians, who wanted to attack in the morning. There were only approximately 450 Israeli troops (many of them poorly trained reserves) present on their side of the canal, and 75 tanks, to face an attack by five Egyptian divisions, including more than 80,000 soldiers and nearly 1,000 tanks. Simultaneously, three Syrian divisions, with more than one thousand tanks, attacked in the north.

The war that followed put the very existence of Israel at risk for a few days before Israeli forces were able to halt the Egyptian and Syrian attacks and then advance into Egypt. It also prompted the Arabs to use oil as a weapon and began an era of high and volatile energy prices. Another consequence was the most serious superpower confrontation since the Cuban Missile Crisis, when the Soviets threatened to intervene militarily to avoid an Egyptian defeat, and the United States had to act vigorously to convince Moscow to reconsider. In response to an investigation and recommendations from a parliamentary commission, Israeli intelligence instituted a number of reforms, including institutionalizing a devil's advocate to challenge conventional wisdom.

The period leading up to the outbreak of the Yom Kippur War is an exceptionally rich example of the many challenges in intelligence analysis. The most sobering aspect of these challenges is that smart, experienced, informed, and dedicated analysts and decision makers anywhere in the world can make serious mistakes.

From a psychological perspective, the failure again showed the power of familiar cognitive biases, such as confirmation and framing. It was also an example of what is known as the "cry wolf syndrome," previously seen in the months before Pearl Harbor, in which repeated warnings that turn out not to be true reduce the credibility of warnings that may be true.

Denial and deception were also factors, as well as the typical circumstance that those who are deceived are often complicit in their own errors. The Egyptian deception effort was not a particularly sophisticated one, as it was not conducted through multiple channels over a sustained period. Some Israeli analysts saw through it, but the seeds sown by the Egyptians fell on fertile ground, and, in combination with other factors, such as complacency and overconfidence in Israel, even the modest deception had a powerful impact.

The success of even a simple deception operation in 1973 points to several useful lessons for intelligence analysts. For example, factual observations, such as the numbers of troops and equipment, can help in assessing capabilities, but they should be used with caution when trying to determine intentions. In addition, fact-based tactical observations should be given equal, or even superior, weight, compared to strategic judgments of an adversary, which may be based on vague or out-of-date information. At the strategic level, the Israeli military assumed that war was not possible, so, although there were some accurate tactical indicators, these were distorted and unappreciated and did not find their way up the hierarchy. Finally, keep in mind the importance of anomalies – valid information that does not fit existing hypotheses and suggests that new hypotheses are probably necessary.

All of this naturally had an impact on the collection effort. The Israelis did not collect some crucial information, such as the degree of cooperation between the Egyptian and Syrian military high commands, at least in part because they were not looking for it. Moreover, they put too much faith in a high-ranking human source – Marwan – whose role, in retrospect, is ambiguous, and who some believe may have been a skillfully planted and maintained double agent.

Bureaucratically, some working-level officers in AMAN, as well as some outside the formal assessment process, such as the Mossad, were more concerned about the possibility of war, but their views had little impact. Groupthink (a situation in which, because of solidarity and loyalty, a small group pays insufficient attention to accurate information that contradicts their view of a situation) was also a significant factor. These incorrect assumptions were reinforced by arrogance and complacency, both personal and institutional.

Questions for Further Thought

In 1973 the Israelis did many things right, including seeking information from a variety of sources. What did they do wrong?

Sometimes, such as before the attack on Pearl Harbor, it is unfair to have expected the analysts to have made a correct evaluation, given the information that they had at the time. Did the Israelis have enough information to have reasonably enabled them to anticipate an attack, if they had their minds open to other possibilities?

Given what was known at the time, what were some reasonable alternative
  hypotheses that could have explained what the Israelis observed in Egypt
  and Syria before October 6?
Would looking at the problem from a wider political point of view, instead of
  a narrow military perspective, have helped in better understanding Sadat's
  thinking?

Recommended Reading

Bar-Jospeh, Uri, *The Watchman Fell Asleep: The Surprise of Yom Kippur and Its Sources*,
  Albany, NY: State University of New York Press, 2005.
Blum, Howard, *The Eve of Destruction: The Untold Story of the Yom Kippur War*, New York:
  HarperCollins, 2003.
Herzog, Chaim, *The War of Atonement: The Inside Story of the Yom Kippur War*, Boston:
  Little, Brown, 1975.
Rabinovich, Abraham, *The Yom Kippur War: The Epic Encounter that Transformed the Middle
  East*, New York: Schocken Books, 2004.

Figure 24. Iran

25

The Fall of the Shah

I N 1978, THE AMERICAN GOVERNMENT WAS PREOCCUPIED WITH TRYING TO arrange peace in the Middle East, to negotiate an arms control agreement with the USSR, and to normalize relations with communist China, among other things. Washington was not concerned about Iran under Mohammad Reza Shah Pahlavi (1919–80), who had been on the throne since 1941, at least in part because of a Central Intelligence Agency (CIA)-sponsored coup in 1953. At a time when the British were withdrawing their military and naval forces "east of Suez" and the United States was reluctant to take on more international commitments, Iran emerged as an important military ally of the United States. Among other things, a strong Iran would help to block Soviet expansion toward the oil-rich Middle East.

Energy was also an important issue, as prices had fluctuated widely, but usually in an upward direction, in the wake of the Arab oil embargo imposed after the Yom Kippur War. Iran exported approximately 5,000,000 barrels of oil a day (the second largest source in the world) at a time when U.S. demand for oil was outpacing domestic supply. The shah had pressed for higher prices, but he did not support Arab-inspired boycotts of exports to the West to punish support for Israel. Moreover, Iran spent much of its profits from oil on weapons from the United States. Arms sales went from just over $500 million in 1972 to almost $4 billion in 1974.

Therefore, Washington's main interest in the country was maintaining close ties and stability. In January 1978, while on a trip to Tehran, President Jimmy Carter had stated that "Iran, because of the great leadership of the Shah, is an island of stability in one of the most troubled areas of the world."

As a result, the priorities for intelligence collection were the following: any Soviet efforts to undermine the Shah, including the activities of Iran's communists, the Tudeh Party; Iran's foreign policy; the status of the oil industry; and the strength of its armed forces.

In deference to the shah, the State Department and the CIA collected little on domestic issues, and U.S. diplomats had few contacts outside official circles. The U.S. embassy noted in August 1976 that it

> had difficulty in developing information about dissidence . . . because of Iranian sensitivities and the Government of Iran's disapproval of foreign contacts with these groups.

Information about internal politics came from the shah himself or from officials loyal to him, including the brutal internal security force, the State Organization for Intelligence and Security, or SAVAK.

American intelligence, which might have produced an objective – or at least different – point of view, suffered from similar problems. The CIA had cooperative relations with SAVAK, which it saw as an ally against Soviet subversion. Moreover, listening posts in Iran were an important source of communication intercepts from the USSR, including data on Soviet missile activity. An assessment in August 1977 forecast that "the shah will be an active participant in Iranian life well into the 1980s."

As a result, Washington had little knowledge about or understanding of what was actually happening in Iran. Significant domestic opposition to the shah began to grow in 1977, with riots as early as January 1978 against the shah's modernization programs. The shah and those around him had their own blinders and refused to believe that there could be any sincere opposition to their well-meaning policies. Opposition, in their view, had to be the result of a foreign-inspired conspiracy, most likely from the USSR but perhaps from the CIA. In fact, the Soviet Union had occupied parts of Iran at the end of World War II and been reluctant to depart, there had been subversion from Moscow, and there had been assassination attempts on the shah. In response, the shah launched a campaign of repression, which further alienated many of his people, especially merchants and conservative Muslim clerics.

Because of this situation, the United States had no contacts in the slums of the major cities or out in the countryside, where there were numerous tensions and problems. New wealth meant increasing prices, and a growing population meant food shortages. The government found that it could not provide enough housing, jobs, health care, and other social services to the huge numbers who were moving to the cities. Schools were producing thousands of graduates who could find nowhere to use their education or skills.

In response to change and uncertainty, many Iranians looked to traditional Islamic values of piety and modesty. Movie theaters, liquor stores, banks, and other aspects of Western modernity were deeply offensive to many. The clerics, or *mullahs*, were also well-organized and had an important stake in any plans to redistribute land, which would affect their incomes and the endowments that supported their work. They also provided significant social services, such as settling local disputes. Traditional merchants, or *bazaaris*, provided goods, but also loans. In the public at large, there was resentment against the perceived arrogance, corruption, and brutality of the Shah's regime and the programs of Western-oriented modernization.

The leading figure in the opposition was Ayatollah Ruhollah Khomeini (1902–89). Khomeini's goals had been clearly stated in a variety of lectures and books. He had developed his own idiosyncratic interpretation of Islam, and wanted rule by the *mullahs* in accordance with Islamic law. He was also intensely anti-Semitic. Khomeini had been able to use modern technology, such as cassette tapes and direct-dial telephones, to spread his message. Few, however, had taken the trouble to consider his views, or, if they did, to take them seriously. U.S. analysts, who mostly came from a secular, Western environment, had little understanding of Khomeini's appeal.

In Washington, the assumption was that the shah had the experience, funds, and political and military support to prevail over the poorly organized and backward-looking minority that opposed his rule. Intelligence assessments assumed that the shah would remain in power for years to come and any transition to another ruler would be smooth. In August 1978, for example, the CIA asserted "Iran is not in a revolutionary or even a 'prerevolutionary' situation." A month later, the Defense Intelligence Agency (DIA) forecast that the shah "is expected to remain actively in power over the next ten years." As late as November, a psychological assessment concluded that the shah was "not paralyzed with indecision ... in accurate touch with reality ... continuing to cope with the problems of his regime." High-ranking political, military, and business figures who met the shah at the time told a different story, though. What U.S. analysts did not know (it was a closely held secret) was that the shah was dying of cancer, which made him indecisive, preoccupied, and fatalistic.

When it became clear in early November that the opposition was gaining momentum, U.S. leaders requested better information about what was going on, such as the views of the military and the goals of the opposition. At a meeting in Washington, Director of Central Intelligence Stansfield Turner (1923–) acknowledged that there were gaps in collection, and reminded the meeting attendees of the longstanding reluctance to offend the shah by having official contact with the opposition. Secretary of State Cyrus Vance (1917–2002) concurred that any effort to gather more information should not be done in a way that undercut the shah. The only decision made was to install more satellite communications equipment in the American embassy in Tehran to improve voice communications. A few days later President Carter also expressed dissatisfaction with the quality of political intelligence coming from Iran. The response from the intelligence community was that it would take time to rebuild robust reporting structures.

In January 1979, with crowds in the streets, soldiers deserting, and oil exports decreasing, the shah fled the country. Two weeks later, Ayatollah Khomeini, who had been living in exile in France, returned to the country. Many in Washington believed that a likely scenario for the future was that an aging cleric could not run a government, liberal moderates would probably take power, and stability would return.

After a brief interval, a government dominated by Muslim extremists took power. Alienated not only by cultural and policy differences, but also by resentment of the longstanding support of the shah by the United States, the new regime adopted a hostile attitude toward the West, in general, and toward Washington, in particular. Among other things, this attitude led to Iranian sponsorship of terrorist attacks against American targets as well as a desire, at least on the part of some Iranian officials, to obtain nuclear weapons to enhance their prestige and deter future outside interference.

There were many reasons why intelligence analysts and U.S. officials misunderstood what was happening in Iran in the late 1970s. Most saw Iran through the prism of the Cold War and thought that the main threat was Soviet expansion. The shah had had difficulties in the past, but he had always overcome them; so status quo thinking was also present. In addition, U.S. analysts, living in a secular culture, underestimated the appeal of religion in the Muslim world as well as the potential of issues of faith to have a political impact.

Cognitive biases, as usual, also played an important role. Especially noteworthy in this case was the paradox of expertise. Many analysts and officials in Washington had been observing and working with the shah for decades. As a result, it was difficult for them to perceive the gradual changes that were taking place in Iran or to imagine a world without the shah. In addition, their long familiarity with the situation in Iran gave them unwarranted confidence in the accuracy of their judgments and their ability to predict the future.

In retrospect, what happened in Iran in 1978 and 1979 – and was happening in Afghanistan at exactly the same time – was one of the great turning points in history. The much feared Soviet Union was actually in decline, and would break up in little more than a decade. At the same time, the Muslim religion, which few in the Western world knew or cared about, was on the verge of a major transformation, in some quarters, into a dangerous force that would bring destruction and fear. It is possible, after all, to pay too much attention to history and trends. It would have taken an exceptional analyst, perhaps impossibly so, to realize what was going on and then convince senior officials in Washington that they had to stop spending so much time worrying about Soviet missiles and focus instead on an angry old man in a villa outside Paris fulminating against a long-time American ally.

Even more than the typical cognitive problems, missing the fall of the shah of Iran was a matter of inadequate collection of accurate and relevant information. The analysts simply did not have large amounts of useful data about what was happening in the urban slums and the countryside. Such data could have alerted them to the high degree of popular dissatisfaction with the shah's regime and the attractiveness of the appeal of Islamic fundamentalism. Even if someone had been insisting on information on Iranian public sentiment, Cold War era collection systems that stressed satellite imagery and communications intercepts would have been of little help. Shortcomings in U.S. collection were exacerbated by overdependence on information from the Iranian government, and especially SAVAK, In the shah's Iran, courtiers, officials, generals, and intelligence officers were all reluctant to take bad news to an authoritarian ruler.

As is typically the case, any deficiencies in intelligence collection or analysis were part of a broader pattern in the government of preoccupation with other problems and reluctance to consider unpalatable alternatives. Moreover, there were divisions among senior decision makers: Some supported the shah, whereas others warned him not to use force and criticized his record on human rights; some wanted to intervene, whereas others were inclined to stand aside.

Questions for Further Thought

Trying to understand the inner workings of authoritarian governments has been a challenge for analysts for centuries. What analytic tools might have helped analysts in 1978 to understand that there were problems beneath the surface of the shah's regime in Iran?

What kind of data would have helped, and how difficult would they have been to obtain?

What are some developments that could be happening right now and could have a significant impact in coming years, but are not being thought about because analysts and decision makers are not asking the right questions or looking in the right places?

Recommended Reading

Ledeen, Michael, and Lewis, William, *Debacle: American Failure in Iran*, New York: Alfred A. Knopf, 1981.

Pollack, Kenneth, *The Persian Puzzle: The Conflict Between Iran and America*, New York: Random House, 2004.

Seliktar, Ofira, *Failing the Crystal Ball Test: The Carter Administration and the Fundamentalist Revolution in Iran*, Westport, CT: Praeger, 2000.

Sick, Gary, *All Fall Down: America's Tragic Encounter with Iran*, Bloomington, IN: iUniverse, 2001.

26

Nuclear Weapons Tests

I N THE 1970S, THE SITUATION THAT HAD PREVAILED FOR SEVERAL DECADES, during which only the members of the United Nations (UN) Security Council – Britain, China, France, the United States, and the USSR – had nuclear weapons was beginning to erode. India tested a device in 1974; a number of other countries, including Israel, South Africa, and Taiwan, were suspected of having active programs; and even more countries were interested in eventually having this ultimate power to destroy or deter. A world in which many countries had nuclear weapons would be a markedly more dangerous one. As a result, there was intense interest at the senior levels of the American government in monitoring nuclear weapons programs so that, if a country showed signs of making serious progress toward having nuclear weapons, efforts could be made to stop it.

At 3:00 A.M., Washington time, on September 22, 1979, a U.S. satellite detected an intense double flash of light in the southern hemisphere. Such a double flash was characteristic of a nuclear explosion, so there were immediately questions to intelligence analysts about whether there had been a nuclear explosion and, if so, who had been responsible. The satellite, however, had been launched more than a decade before, and its capabilities had deteriorated. Not enough data were generated by the satellite to confirm that the flash actually had been a nuclear explosion. Worse, because of the lack of precision in the data, the suspected area in which the incident had taken place was estimated to be anywhere within a 3,000 mile (4,800 kilometer) swath across South Africa and Antarctica, as well as the southern portions of the Atlantic or Indian oceans. All of this information meant that it was impossible to identify immediately what country might have been responsible.

No hostile action followed, so clearly there had not been an attack. What had happened? Given the initial shortage of data, there were several hypotheses to explain what had taken place: a test of a nuclear weapon, an accidental detonation of a nuclear weapon, a malfunction of the satellite, or lightning or some other natural phenomenon, such as a meteor striking the satellite.

To try to solve the mystery, analysts in several U.S. government agencies began by consulting other clandestine means of collection. Unfortunately, no other satellite had been covering the area in question. Spies and communications intercepts also produced nothing relevant. Data from U.S. Navy hydrophones used to track Soviet submarines suggested, however, that there had been a loud sound at approximately the same time as the unusually bright flash of light.

Because clandestine collection could not resolve the issue, analysts, appreciating the value of considering as wide a range of sources as possible, also checked with a number of outside experts and open sources. U.S. officials sent aircraft to collect air samples, but no radioactive debris was found. Neither seismic recordings, nor civilian weather satellites, nor air traffic control tapes could settle the issue.

The initial analysis, completed in December 1979, found reasons to eliminate most hypotheses about what had happened and stated that there probably had been a nuclear explosion, although that was not certain. Who the sponsor had been was even less clear.

Given the location, South Africa was high on the list of suspects. A South African naval base at Simon's Town, near Cape Town, had been on alert for a day or so before and after the incident, and the authorities at another naval base at Saldanha had put a maritime search and rescue unit on alert during that period; but of course, there could have been other reasons for this activity. The Central Intelligence Agency sent operatives to look for signs of unusually high radiation on land, but they found nothing. Although South African officials made coy remarks in public about secret weapons programs, their response to the specific questions and accusations surrounding a possible nuclear test in 1979 was to deny that their country had been responsible.

The situation in other countries was even less clear. Another leading suspect was Israel – either alone, or in partnership with South Africa – but, like their South African counterparts, officials in Israel denied that they had been involved in a weapons test. Washington had important issues at stake with both countries and could not confront them unless the evidence was beyond challenge. U.S. analysts believed that other nations, including Argentina, Brazil, Iraq, Pakistan, and Taiwan, did not have the necessary material or technology to build a nuclear weapon.

With no definitive answer, U.S. officials consulted several panels of scientists, and collection was widened to include less conventional sources. Analysts looked at radar data and readings from a radio telescope that tracked changes in the ionosphere. There were other checks of factors such as magnetic field data, very low frequency sound, and other technical measurements from around the world. In an especially creative inquiry, analysts examined the level of iodine in the thyroid glands of Australian sheep (which absorb radiation). Most of these exotic methods were inconclusive, and the scientists could not agree; but the sheep, along with a few other methods, generated some readings that were consistent with a nuclear explosion. To this day, the issue of what happened in the southern hemisphere in September 1979 remains unresolved.

Nuclear programs around the world, including those in Iran, Iraq, Libya, and North Korea, continued to be troublesome for intelligence analysts. The United States was especially concerned about proliferation in the volatile region of South Asia. In response to China's development of nuclear capability, India had already conducted one test in 1974 but had then suspended its program, in part because of pressure from Washington. The authorities in New Delhi were also worried about Pakistan, a country with which they fought several wars. Would the Indians resume work on a nuclear bomb as its rival Pakistan moved ahead toward acquiring nuclear capability?

The U.S. intelligence community had many assets for monitoring the nuclear weapons program in India. It was an open country with many diplomatic and commercial ties to the United States and other countries. Moreover, Washington had the full panoply of satellites, communications intercept facilities, and human intelligence on which it could draw. Using its many collection assets, the United States closely watched activity at the Indian test site. Over the years, U.S. officials had shown their Indian counterparts satellite photography of Indian test sites to demonstrate the ability of the United States to monitor the status of the nuclear weapons program. An unintended consequence of this was that Indian officials had a fairly good idea of the capabilities of American satellites, and thus the basis for coming up with ways to thwart surveillance from space.

U.S. intelligence found, however, that there were also many reasons for the Indian nuclear program to be a difficult target. For example, the Indian research had been conducted indigenously, and outsiders did not have detailed knowledge of it, so Russian and Chinese precedents did not necessarily apply. Moreover, only a few Indian officials were aware that there had been enough progress in the nuclear program to make it possible to detonate a test device.

Nonetheless, there were indicators that India might conduct a nuclear test. For example, on several occasions in early 1998 the government of Pakistan warned that an Indian test was imminent, but this warning was discounted in Washington as a sign of Pakistani insecurity and fear, and not of a possible test. Pakistan had issued such warnings many times before, and there had been no test.

More seriously, the Indian People's Party (Bharatiya Janata Party; BJP), Hindu nationalists who had just been returned to power as head of a coalition after elections in March 1998, had openly promised during the election campaign that they would conduct a nuclear test. Their goal was to deter China and Pakistan, as well as to demonstrate India's status as a global power worthy of respect. When Pakistan tested a new long-range missile only a few weeks after the election, the new government decided to act on the BJP's campaign pledge and reactivate the nuclear program.

U.S. analysts assumed that, as in the United States, campaign rhetoric does not necessarily mean that action will follow. The analysts also assumed that India would not take an action that would provoke Pakistan and risk sanctions from Washington. This assessment appeared to be confirmed by a public BJP announcement that the new government would delay a decision on whether to test and by private assurances from Indian diplomats that no test was imminent.

In fact, the BJP government was determined to have a nuclear weapon, and it carried out an elaborate campaign of denial and deception to head off any U.S. efforts to block a test. As a result of the earlier revelations from American diplomats seeking to convince the Indians that American intelligence could track Indian activities, officials in New Delhi knew when the satellites would pass over; also, the Soviets may have provided data on U.S. satellite capabilities as a sign of friendship.

Therefore, the Indians carefully timed their preparations and took other denial and deception measures. For example, technicians covered or replaced large electric cables that could be spotted from space and placed camouflage over the shafts that would hold the devices. Much work was purposely done at night. In addition, officials increased activity at another, distant test site to distract attention from where the test would be conducted. At the actual test site, the Indians raised activity to a high level a considerable time before the planned test, and then kept at that level, so that increased activity would not be an indicator of an imminent test. The Indians chose May to conduct the test because there are seasonal sandstorms that would obscure satellite photography and quickly blow away tire tracks that would indicate increased vehicular activity. Moreover, the high temperatures that month also would make heat-measuring sensors less effective.

As a result of these careful preparations, U.S. analysts were not able to determine that a test was imminent, and the Indians conducted a series of underground nuclear tests on May 11, 1998.

Less than three weeks later, Pakistan conducted its own tests to demonstrate that it, too, now had nuclear capability. This time, U.S. intelligence spotted the preparations. The American government asked Pakistan not to increase tensions by testing, but officials in Islamabad proceeded anyway. Within less than a month, the world had two new nuclear powers to worry about, with a heritage of conflict and distrust between them.

In failing to anticipate that India would become a nuclear power, there were certainly cognitive problems. Because of mirror imaging, officials in Washington did not understand other countries' priorities when it came to nuclear weapons. Moreover, analysts assumed that politics in other countries worked more or less the way they did in the United States. There were also faulty assumptions about the ability of less advanced countries to conduct denial and deception operations that could thwart sophisticated collection methods.

Both of these cases are useful examples of the limitations of intelligence collection technology. By the 1970s the indicators of nuclear weapons programs were fairly well known in intelligence agencies, so this was more a problem of collection rather than trying to understand a new technology. What analysts and officials found out was that, despite the billions of dollars that are spent on them, satellites can break down or be fooled. Overdependence on only one or two channels of collection makes it easier to conduct successful denial and deception campaigns.

Decision makers in Washington complained that the intelligence analysts had not given them sufficient warning so that U.S. officials could try to stop the tests. In the end, was there anything Washington could have done to keep these two countries from fulfilling their ambitions to become nuclear powers? Admiral David Jeremiah, who conducted the postmortem, said, "No, I don't think you were going to turn them around."

Questions for Further Thought

The response to the double flash in 1979 was an example of creativity and persistence in trying to find useful data. What are some current collection problems, and what would be some imaginative ways to deal with them?

Denial and deception were present in both 1979 and 1998. What were the
significant differences between the ways that analysts handled these two
different incidents?

What other kinds of problems might not be susceptible to solution solely
through technical means of collection?

Recommended Reading

Chengappa, Raj, *Weapons of Peace: The Secret Story of India's Quest to Be a Nuclear Power*,
New Delhi: HarperCollins India, 2000.

Perkovich, George, *India's Nuclear Bomb: The Impact on Global Proliferation*, Berkeley, CA:
University of California Press, 1999.

Richelson, Jeffrey T., *Spying on the Bomb: American Nuclear Intelligence from Nazi Germany
to Iran and North Korea*, New York: W. W. Norton & Co., 2006; chapters 7 and 11.

27

A. Q. Khan

STOPPING PROLIFERATION OF NUCLEAR WEAPONS, ESPECIALLY TO UNSTA-
ble countries or terrorist groups, has been a major concern of governments. Because of their extreme danger, it is illegal under international
treaties to sell or transport materials associated with nuclear weapons. However small the chance of misusing nuclear weapons, the potential damage is
so great that the risk cannot be ignored. Therefore, how to understand and
thwart anyone who would try to evade the restrictions on nuclear technology
is a high priority for intelligence analysts.

In the early 1970s, Abdul Qadeer Khan (1936–), a metallurgist from
Pakistan, was working in the Netherlands when the Pakistani government
announced that it was determined to acquire nuclear weapons in an effort
to achieve deterrence and strategic equality when dealing with its giant
rival, India. Pakistan had just lost another war with India, which had led to
the dismemberment of the country and the founding of the independent
state of Bangladesh. As it turned out, the company for which Khan worked
enriched uranium into fuel for reactors, a technology that could also be used
to produce nuclear weapons.

In September 1974, Khan wrote a letter to the Pakistani government
offering to help in the development of a nuclear weapon. Islamabad accepted
his proposal, and before departing for home Khan stole or copied a large
number of blueprints for equipment that could be used to enrich uranium.
He returned to Pakistan in 1975, and a year later became head of one of
Pakistan's two nuclear laboratories, with a large budget provided by the
government.

In the years that followed, Khan used his knowledge of the nuclear business to quietly acquire the components for a weapon in defiance of international controls. Khan found that by buying a few items here, waiting,
and then buying a few more items there, he could stay below the radar of

western intelligence services and regulatory bodies such as the International Atomic Energy Agency (IAEA). As long as there was money to be made, there were companies that were willing to do business without asking too many questions. In addition, many suppliers were not overly concerned, as they doubted that a poor and backward country like Pakistan could ever master the technology to produce a nuclear weapon.

Within a few years of Khan's return to Pakistan, analysts at the Central Intelligence Agency (CIA) who were watching the pattern of Pakistani imports and drawing on a variety of clandestine sources, expressed concern that Pakistan might be able to build a nuclear bomb. In 1979, the U.S. Congress passed legislation banning aid to countries that imported nuclear materials outside the IAEA framework. After the Soviets invaded Afghanistan, however, Pakistan became essential as a route for supplies to the anti-Soviet resistance, and American pressure on the nuclear issue eased. By the late 1980s, Pakistan had the means to construct a bomb, but did not actually test it. Senior Pakistani officials, in deference to Washington and the IAEA, often claimed that they did not intend to complete the process. Over time, relations between Washington and Islamabad improved and worsened, as did concern about trying to stop Pakistan's nuclear program. In the 1990s, with the Soviets out of Afghanistan, interest in applying pressure on Pakistan revived in Washington. Then, after the 9/11 attacks, Pakistan was again an essential pathway to Afghanistan.

All this time, analysts continued to follow Khan, who was a prominent public figure in Pakistan. They used the usual array of human sources, satellite images, and communications intercepts. Khan liked the limelight, so there was also often material in the press, including Khan's very public claims that his nuclear program was the guarantor of Pakistan's sovereignty and security. In 1998, Pakistan finally tested a nuclear device, confirming Khan's status as a national hero – the man who had given his country strategic equality with India.

CIA analysts initially had seen Khan as a bureaucrat carrying out the orders of his government. They kept an open mind, however, and noted that he was accumulating considerable personal wealth, although he was ostensibly only a civil servant. This alerted them to the possibility that he had another source of significant income. Khan also traveled more extensively than his official responsibilities would have required. For years, analysts had been following imports of nuclear materials into Pakistan, but as their suspicions about Khan grew they realized that much more nuclear-related equipment was being imported than Pakistan could use. Therefore, the analysts also started looking at exports.

What they found was that Khan had used his knowledge of nuclear technology and international business to establish a huge clandestine network to resell components for making nuclear weapons for personal profit. This private clandestine network was much more ominous because it suggested that Khan would provide nuclear materials to anyone who could pay the price. In 1987, Khan began selling nuclear equipment to Iran. Eight years later, Libya became a customer. Then in 1996 he agreed to provide nuclear technology to North Korea in return for long-range missile technology. There were also offers to Iraq, which never panned out, and rumors of another big deal that was in the works.

By 2003, the global scope of Khan's activities had become clear, as well as the need for international cooperation, and the British and American intelligence services were conducting a joint operation against Khan. The political environment was also changing, with doubts growing about the value and sincerity of Pakistan as an ally in the struggle to defeat terrorists. Now officials were worried that at least some people in Pakistan might be involved in selling nuclear components that might get into the hands of terrorists. As a result, officials in Washington were more willing to act than they had been in decades, but they still would need solid evidence.

Then, in September 2003, the joint British and American team following Khan's network received the Holy Grail in the intelligence business: accurate information received in time to take decisive action. A report indicated that a German-owned ship, the *BBC China*, then in Dubai, had loaded proliferation-related cargo provided by Khan and was on its way to Libya. U.S. and British officials quickly decided to ask the German owners to divert the ship to Italy so that the suspect cargo could be inspected. In early October, the *BBC China* arrived in Taranto, Italy, and an expert team of analysts verified that some of the containers on board contained parts for a centrifuge that could be used to refine uranium into a nuclear bomb. This information enabled Britain and the United States to convince Libya that they knew all about the country's nuclear program and that there was no point in lying about it. The recent defeat of Saddam Hussein, and a desire to normalize relations with Washington and London, was enough to convince Libyan leader Muammar Qaddafi (1942–) to abandon his plans to obtain nuclear weapons.

At the same time that the diversion of the *BBC China* was being prepared, President George W. Bush (1946–) was meeting with Pakistani President Pervez Musharraf (1943–) on the margins of the UN General Assembly meeting in New York City. After a review of other issues, Bush asked Musharraf to pay strict attention to another visitor. Bush left, and in walked

Director of Central Intelligence George Tenet (1953–), who presented a detailed dossier on Khan's activities, including banking, travel, meetings, shipments, contracts, facilities, and other details that had been prepared by U.S. and British analysts. It was so convincing that Musharraf had no counterargument and simply agreed to take care of the problem.

As it became clear that there was a chance that the government of Pakistan would begin legal proceedings against him, Khan publicly admitted to wrongdoing and accepted full personal responsibility in a February 2004 apology to the Pakistani nation. In his statement, Khan referred elliptically to the "disturbing disclosures and evidence by some countries" that had prompted his confession. He also claimed that the government of Pakistan had not authorized his personal proliferation efforts. Within days, Musharraf pardoned Khan, but placed him under house arrest, which prompted speculation that there had been some kind of deal.

In the years that followed, the Pakistani government refused to allow the Americans, British, or representatives of the IAEA to question Khan. The government of Pakistan eased the conditions of Khan's house arrest in February 2009. It remains unclear what various parts of the government knew, or did not know, about his activities.

The A. Q. Khan case is an excellent example of how to deal with potential cognitive problems that could undermine analyses. Analysts following Khan's activities had to escape the mindset that, because of its expense and potential danger, the proliferation of nuclear weapons could be carried out only by governments. That a private individual could greatly expand nuclear proliferation for personal profit was difficult to envision in the 1980s. The analysts dealt with these issues by being open to other possibilities, and they understood the value of anomalies, such as Khan's personal wealth, as a spur to generate more hypotheses. Persistence also paid off, not only in making it possible to gather more information, but to move effectively when the right reporting arrived and the policy environment became more receptive to action.

Questions for Further Thought

What were the key elements of the overall strategy that proved to be successful in breaking up the Khan proliferation network?

How could such a strategy be used against other proliferators? What would change if the target were a government rather than a private individual?

What are the lessons for working on other targets, such as terrorism and organized crime? Would anything else be needed against other targets?

Recommended Reading

Armstrong, David, and Trento, Joseph, *America and the Islamic Bomb: The Deadly Compromise*, Hanover, NH: Steerforth Press, 2007.

Corera, Gordon, *Shopping for Bombs: Nuclear Proliferation, Global Insecurity, and the Rise and Fall of the A. Q. Khan Network*, Oxford, UK: Oxford University Press, 2006.

Frantz, Douglas, and Collins, Catherine, *The Nuclear Jihadist: The True Story of the Man Who Sold the World's Most Dangerous Secrets . . . and How We Could Have Stopped Him*, New York: Twelve, 2007.

Levy, Adrian, and Scott-Clark, Catherine, *Deception: Pakistan, the United States, and the Secret Trade in Nuclear Weapons*, New York: Walker and Company, 2007.

Richelson, Jeffrey T., *Spying on the Bomb: American Nuclear Intelligence from Nazi Germany to Iran and North Korea*, New York: W. W. Norton & Co., 2006; chapter 8.

Tenet, George, *At the Center of the Storm: My Years at the CIA*, New York: HarperCollins, 2007, chapter 15.

28

Iraqi Weapons of Mass Destruction

PRESIDENT SADDAM HUSSEIN OF IRAQ (1937–2006) WAS A BRUTAL AND aggressive tyrant in a volatile part of the world. After the terrorist attacks of September 11, 2001, decision makers in Washington and London were especially concerned that Saddam had weapons of mass destruction, which he might use himself or give to terrorists. Saddam's record showed that there was cause for concern. In 1981, Israel had bombed the Osirak reactor at Tuwaitha out of concern that it could be used to produce materials for nuclear weapons. It was well documented that the Iraqi government had chemical weapons and that it had used them against the Kurdish minority in March 1988 and on numerous occasions during the war with Iran in the 1980s. Moreover, after the First Gulf War in 1991, investigators found that, because of successful denial and deception operations, Iraq had been able to conduct biological weapons programs of which the U.S. intelligence agencies had not been aware and to push forward a nuclear weapons program that was much further advanced than had been suspected. In the years that followed, United Nations (UN) teams caught Iraqi officials in the act of moving sensitive equipment, personnel, and documents around to avoid inspections.

In the wake of the 9/11 attacks, there was widespread concern that economic sanctions and UN inspections might not be enough to keep Iraq from pushing ahead with its weapons-of-mass-destruction programs. Therefore, decision makers around the world asked intelligence analysts to assess the current status of Iraq's arsenal of biological, chemical, and nuclear weapons as well as whether it had the means to deliver them to distant targets via ballistic missiles. Both human and technical sources produced a large volume and wide variety of reports on Iraqi weapons of mass destruction.

In 1995, Hussein Kamel, Saddam's son-in-law and head of the Military Industrialization Corporation, which controlled, among other things, the country's weapons-of-mass-destruction programs, defected to Jordan. He appeared to be an authoritative source on biological, chemical, and nuclear issues. Kamel's debriefing produced a mixed bag of distorted and self-serving information, as might be expected, but he did acknowledge that Iraq had had a significant biological weapons program.

As part of sanctions-enforcement operations, a shipment of high-quality aluminum tubes was seized. Some analysts at the Central Intelligence Agency (CIA) and the Defense Intelligence Agency (DIA) believed that such tubes could be used in centrifuges to refine uranium to weapons grade. Given Saddam Hussein's record of ambition, aggression, and brutality, it seemed only prudent to assume the worst, but other analysts at the State Department's Bureau of Intelligence and Research and the Department of Energy, in addition to other experts, believed it was more likely that the tubes were for rockets.

It was clear that Iraq was smuggling in sizable amounts of materials that could be used for weapons of mass destruction. Moreover, Iraqi officials adamantly refused to allow international investigators into Saddam's many palaces. Why would the Iraqis act so suspiciously, unless they had something important to conceal?

There were other reports that Iraq had tried to purchase from Niger material known as "yellowcake," which could be processed into uranium for a reactor and was regulated by the International Atomic Energy Administration (IAEA). The CIA looked into the issue and concluded that there probably was not an unauthorized purchase of yellowcake from Niger.

The German external intelligence service had an Iraqi defector with the code name "Curveball" who claimed that he had visited secret biological weapons facilities. Curveball's handlers considered his behavior to be erratic, but his descriptions contained a great deal of detail about locations and personalities, some of which could be verified by other sources. Therefore, the DIA went ahead and disseminated the reports. When American intelligence officers asked to debrief Curveball to pose their own questions and draw their own conclusions, the Germans refused, saying that the Iraqi refused to talk to Americans.

Meanwhile, data from other sources increased concern. Satellite images showed sites in Iraq with elaborate security measures, including bunkers, guards, and fences; other images showed tanker trucks that had been used to carry decontaminants in case there was a chemical weapons accident. Communications intercepts caught Iraqi officers saying, "We evacuated everything. We don't have anything left" and "Make sure there is nothing there" when UN inspectors were scheduled to arrive.

With military action against Iraq becoming increasingly likely in the fall of 2002, analysts in Washington and London were uncertain about the status of Saddam's weapons of mass destruction, given the mixed reporting, but believed that the responsible approach was to lay out the worst case, so that military commanders could institute countermeasures. Better safe than sorry.

When American and coalition troops took over Iraq in the spring of 2003, however, they found no weapons of mass destruction.

After the United States and its allies had captured the Iraqi leadership, they interrogated them to find out what the real story had been. These lengthy interrogations revealed that Iraq under Saddam had been a bizarre environment, virtually impenetrable to Western intelligence analysts who were outsiders largely dependent on indirect methods of collection, such as satellite imagery or communications intercepts. In Saddam's Iraq, persons who dared to tell harsh truths could lose their jobs – and perhaps their lives. Therefore, lies and flattery pervaded Iraq's security forces, the main mission of which was to defend Saddam rather than to protect the country. Loyalty was more important than competence, experience, or initiative. For example, outsiders were baffled by the appointment of Major General Barzan Abd al-Ghafur to head the Special Republican Guard. Why did a man with such obviously limited experience and ability hold one of the most sensitive positions in Iraq, responsible for the security of Baghdad? The reason, in Saddam's world, was that anyone who held such a position was in an excellent position to launch a coup, and so had to be incompetent and a coward.

Another example of how bizarre Saddam's world was, and how hard it was for outsiders to understand it, was the mystery of the concrete warhead. During the First Gulf War, the Iraqis had launched at Israel some SCUD missiles that had warheads containing concrete. What, analysts wondered, did that mean? Were they mistakes, tests, deception, or an effort to penetrate bunkers? In fact, Saddam had been much impressed with the Palestinians' bravery during the intifada, when unarmed demonstrators threw stones at the much better equipped Israeli army. Saddam wanted, symbolically, to demonstrate solidarity with these brave fellow Arabs and "throw stones" at Israel.

As the 1990s unfolded, Saddam Hussein felt that he was confronting contradictory pressures. On the one hand, it was extremely valuable to him to have weapons of mass destruction to deter attacks from Israel and Iran. On the other hand, Iraq was suffering from sanctions imposed as a result of the discovery of the extent of its illegal weapons programs after the 1991

Gulf War, and Saddam needed to convince UN inspectors that Iraq no longer had any biological, chemical, or nuclear weapons. Saddam wanted to maintain the capability – such as scientists, facilities, and technology – to eventually resume production of weapons of mass destruction, but first he had to end the damaging UN sanctions. His solution – perfectly logical to him – was to bluff and lie at the same time, trying to convince the inspectors that the weapons were dismantled, while doing nothing to disabuse the Israelis and Iranians of their suspicions that he still had them. The stocks of actual weapons had been destroyed shortly after the 1991 Gulf War.

Over time, Saddam came to the conclusion – backed by an implacable Washington – that there was no concession that would satisfy the UN inspectors and thus bring an end to sanctions. He saw the vigorous UN inspections, which included demands to search his own palaces, as at least an effort to humiliate him, and more likely an attempt to undermine his authority and eventually overthrow him. As he put it, the choice was between sanctions with inspections or sanctions without them, so he preferred the latter. He certainly had the intention to have weapons of mass destruction, especially over the longer term, but in 2002 he lacked the capability.

Many streams of reporting on what was going on in Iraq had serious flaws. Iraqi senior officials and generals acknowledged that they never saw or had control of weapons of mass destruction, but they assumed that some of their colleagues did. If they had been asked, or their phones had been tapped, information received would have indicated that they sincerely believed there were biological, chemical, or nuclear weapons somewhere in Iraq.

In fact, there had also been a colossal intelligence failure in Baghdad, where Saddam believed he could bluff his way through without having to fight. In addition, he had no idea that he was starting a process that would eventually bring his fall from power and, eventually, his death.

Analysts outside Iraq who had been trying to uncover biological, chemical, and nuclear weapons had fallen into a number of cognitive traps. If someone is looking for weapons of mass destruction, and the evidence is ambiguous, he or she is likely to conclude that there is a high probability that such weapons exist. The pattern bias can lead to believing that there is organization or a central cause behind events, when in fact they are coincidental. The confirmation bias means that the mind pays more attention to data that support judgments already made and devalues contradictory evidence. Mirror imaging and the rational actor model make it hard to accurately grasp how people in another culture deal with problems. For example, Iraq smuggled materials because, with UN sanctions in place, it was the only way to obtain them; moreover, corrupt senior officials got a cut of the high fees in return for allowing illegal shipments to proceed.

It turned out that there had been serious flaws in virtually all of the reporting from human sources. Curveball was a fabricator who was mainly interested in getting permission to live in Europe. Many of the other human reports had come through the Iraqi National Congress, an exile opposition group that wanted to get the United States to overthrow Saddam.

Other reporting was equally flawed, and often there was a less sinister explanation that was not related to weapons of mass destruction. The documents on uranium from Niger were forgeries. The high-quality aluminum tubes were for rockets. Iraqi officials had been reluctant to allow Saddam's palaces to be searched because they were trying to protect his personal security – not hide weapons of mass destruction.

There had also been accurate reports that had not been taken seriously. Kamel had claimed, for example, that Iraq had destroyed any biological, chemical, or nuclear weapons it had had shortly after its defeat in the 1991 Gulf War. Moreover, the Iraqi foreign minister had been a spy for French intelligence, and the minster had also told his French handlers that Iraq no longer had any weapons of mass destruction. Finally, when UN inspectors returned briefly to Iraq in the autumn of 2002, they were not able to find anything.

Even the much vaunted "technical means" of collection – satellite images and communications intercepts – were far from perfect indicators. Starting in 2001, for example, there was a dramatic increase in the number of satellite images of suspected sites where weapons of mass destruction were produced or stored because priorities had been shifted away from airfields and air defense sites that had threatened U.S. and British pilots monitoring the no-fly zones in northern and southern Iraq. There was more reporting, not more activity. Other data from technical collection turned out to be far less suspicious than originally believed. The heavily guarded bunkers contained things such as supplies and records – not chemical weapons – and the tanker trucks were being used for water – not decontaminant. Intercepted communications between Iraqi officers saying, "We evacuated everything" and "Make sure there is nothing there" were actually attempts by the officers to demonstrate compliance with UN inspections. The "facts" – images and intercepts – had been accurate, but the context was misunderstood.

Analysts wondered why there was virtually no direct evidence of weapons of mass destruction. They attributed this to a continuation of Iraq's well known and successful campaigns of denial and deception, but it turned out that there was little evidence because there was nothing there, or what was observed was misinterpreted.

After no weapons of mass destruction were found in Iraq, various commissions and legislative committees in the United States, Britain, and elsewhere issued scathing reports on the intelligence analysis of the issue. The reports concluded that analysts had fallen victim to various mindsets and biases. As a result, there were mistakes, such as attributing the most sinister implications to dual-use items like the aluminum tubes. There were also numerous assumptions that may have been true at one time but did not remain accurate, such as that old weapons programs or old patterns of denial and deception were continuing. Analysts had focused on a narrow range of hypotheses – that Iraq had multiple threatening programs – and did not use analytic tools such as Red Teams or Devil's Advocacy to explore the likelihood of other hypotheses. Although some analysts had doubts and concerns, these were not given sufficient weight or communicated clearly.

All of these flaws were exacerbated in a decision-making environment in which many leaders had well-established priorities and goals, were in a hurry to act, and saw different points of view as disloyalty.

Questions for Further Thought

Again, trying to fathom what was going on in the mind of a powerful and secretive leader was a challenge for intelligence analysts working on the Iraq problem. Have the techniques for dealing with this problem improved over the centuries?

What were some of the assumptions that were made in dealing with Iraqi weapons of mass destruction? How would an analyst go about determining if those assumptions were valid?

What was the quality of the evidence available to analysts looking for Iraqi weapons of mass destruction? How could it have been improved?

What would be the key elements of an effort to accurately gauge weapons-of-mass-destruction programs in other countries, such as Iran or North Korea?

Recommended Reading

Commission on the Intelligence Capabilities of the United States Regarding Weapons of Mass Destruction, report available online at: http://www.gpoaccess.gov/wmd/indes .html.

Duelfer, Charles, *Hide and Seek: The Search for Truth in Iraq*, New York: Public Affairs, 2009.

Richelson, Jeffrey T., *Spying on the Bomb: American Nuclear Intelligence from Nazi Germany to Iran and North Korea*, New York: W. W. Norton & Co., 2006, chapters 12 and 13.

Ricks, Thomas E., *Fiasco: The American Military Adventure in Iraq*, New York: Penguin, 2006.

Tenet, George, *At the Center of the Storm: My Years at the CIA*, New York: HarperCollins, 2007, chapters 16–24.

Whitney, Craig R., ed., *The WMD Mirage: Iraq's Decade of Deception and America's False Premise for War*, New York: Public Affairs, 2005.

Woods, Kevin, et al., *The Iraqi Perspectives Report: Saddam's Senior Leadership on Operation Iraqi Freedom from the Official U.S. Joint Forces Command Report*, Annapolis, MD: Naval Institute Press, 2006.

Woodward, Bob, *Plan of Attack*, New York: Simon & Schuster, 2004.

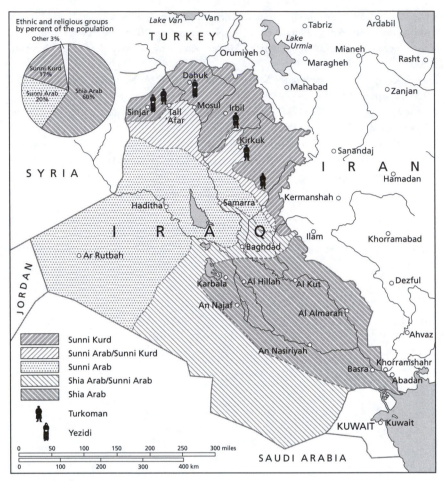

Figure 25. Ethnic groups in Iraq

29

Violence in Iraq

FROM MARCH THROUGH APRIL 2003, A U.S.-LED COALITION WAS INVOLVED in a large-scale conventional conflict with organized units of the Iraqi army, plus some irregular units. American military officers and civilian planners had been envisioning this kind of campaign for decades. Huge amounts of equipment, on land and in the air, would maneuver quickly over vast spaces. Forces would employ high volumes of accurate firepower using "smart" weapons that could be guided with precision directly to their targets. All of the vehicles, aircraft, artillery, and other machinery, as well as the people, would be tied together electronically by using the Internet and computers. Massive amounts of accurate information, constantly updated, would be made available to all levels of the chain of command, making it possible to respond rapidly to a fast-changing situation. This battle, and the intelligence that supported it, was at an entirely different level than what had been known previously.

Such an application of high-tech warfare quickly brought down Saddam Hussein's regime, but peace did not follow. Almost immediately, there was domestic resistance and terrorism, some of it supported by outsiders. During the spring and summer that followed the conventional military victory, some irregular pro-Saddam elements conducted direct attacks on coalition forces, especially in the Sunni areas of the country. They used a residual organizational structure based on Saddam's Baath Party, as well as weapons and funds that had been set aside in advance. There was little popular support for a restoration of Saddam, however, and the attackers were quickly overcome by superior coalition firepower, which still did not bring an end to the violence.

From the summer of 2003 to the end of 2005, various forces moved to fill the vacuum left by the collapse of the Saddam regime and pursued their own agendas. The level of violence increased, and Iraqis of all persuasions blamed the lack of security and economic recovery on the United States.

- The Sunni minority, which had dominated the country under Saddam, launched an insurgency, based mainly in the western part of the country, to try to force out what they regarded as a foreign army of occupation (but not necessarily to restore Saddam or the Baath Party), as well as to regain at least some of the privileges that they had under Saddam. Their weapon of choice was the roadside improvised explosive device (IED).
- Foreign jihadists, inspired by al-Qaeda, started a campaign of suicide bombings aimed at aggravating religious tensions. They remained a small percentage, perhaps 5–10 percent, of the fighters.
- The Shiite majority began to organize militias to defend their position as the majority. After a brief series of uprisings by Muqtada al-Sadr's Mahdi Army, the Shiites quieted down and concentrated on organizing rather than fighting.
- In addition, organized crime took advantage of the disorder to profit through smuggling, kidnapping, and robbery.
- The northern Kurdish area was largely quiet as the Kurds consolidated their autonomous region. The Kurds had their own armed forces, flag, social services, and other attributes of a government.

Most of the weapons and explosives used in the violence came from huge stores accumulated under Saddam that had not been destroyed or brought under control after the end of conventional fighting in the spring of 2003. Outside support existed, but was not significant; so sealing the borders, even if possible, would not have ended the violence. The targets of the attacks were varied and, in addition to U.S. troops, included the new Iraqi army and police, civilian Iraqi leadership, foreign aid workers, and the infrastructure, including electrical generation and the oil industry. U.S. commanders adjusted their tactics to reduce the amount of property damage and civilian casualties caused by American forces, but the overall level of violence continued to grow.

The change in the nature of the violence, from conventional fighting to insurgency, meant that support from intelligence collection and analysis also had to change. As the British had learned in Malaya, as well as the Americans in Vietnam, this change would entail a different way to think about problems.

During the first few months of the insurgency there were some important successes. For example, intelligence analysts used network analysis to track down former Iraqi president Saddam Hussein in 2003. An interagency team of analysts and operators from the Defense Intelligence Agency, the Central Intelligence Agency, the special operations community, and the regular army worked for months to uncover Saddam's support network after the fall of the regime. Analysts found out that, in 1959, after a failed coup attempt, Saddam had hidden in his hometown of Tikrit, so they believed that was probably an area where he felt comfortable. This information helped them to narrow the scope of their search.

With the old military, political, and police structures gone, it was also likely that Saddam had reverted to a different support network of more traditional personal and tribal ties. Using a creative alternative to the main lines of investigation at the time, which focused on trying to capture the former leaders of the regime (the famous "deck of cards"), some analysts worked on unraveling Saddam's support network from the bottom up, investigating persons who provided Saddam with transportation, lodging, food, and money. The vast amounts of data that were gathered from a wide variety of sources were incorporated into link charts that showed relationships but also gaps in the chains, and thus where more collection would be needed.

Using this method, the U.S. team eventually filled out the chart and in the process identified Saddam's key protector, who then provided a location near Tikrit where he claimed the fallen dictator was hiding. Initially the agricultural laborer's hut at the site did not appear promising, but when the soldiers found a trunk containing $750,000 in cash they suspected they were on the right track and kept looking. Shortly afterward, as their detailed inspection continued, they found Saddam in a cramped underground hiding place.

Despite such successes, as time passed the situation in Iraq deteriorated. U.S. tactics of massive firepower, nighttime raids on homes, and widespread arrests brought a temporary decrease in violence, but also caused many civilian casualties and violated local cultural norms. As a result, much of the population became alienated and increasingly viewed American soldiers as occupiers.

By the beginning of 2006 the nature of the violence was changing yet again, and increasingly it was spurred by rivalries among the main religious groups. Shiites were seeking revenge for decades of oppression, whereas Sunnis were concerned that the Shiites were being manipulated by Iran. In addition, there were intense rivalries within the Shiite community, as well as the beginning of fighting between Shiites and Sunnis (on the one hand) and Kurds (on the other) for control over the oil-rich north of the country.

During 2006 the level of violence continued to increase, with the sectarian rivalries causing most of the casualties, and the various ethnic communities increasingly looking to their own militias to provide security. At the same time, criminal activity and attacks by foreign Islamists accelerated. Efforts to construct a central army and police force proceeded at a slow pace, with especially the police proving to be ineffective because of corruption or infiltration by the sectarian militias. In response to the lack of security and economic opportunities, millions of Iraqi fled mixed areas and either sought safety with their coreligionists or left the country.

In 2007, the United States implemented a new strategy for working with a host government as partners to deal with the various dimensions of the insurgency. Its key principles, many of which depended on effective intelligence, were the following: manage information and expectations, use the appropriate level of force, learn and adopt, empower the lowest level, and support the host nation. The new strategy also included some ideas that were paradoxes for soldiers and analysts used to conventional warfare:

- Sometimes, the more you protect your force, the less secure you may be.
- Sometimes, the more force is used, the less effective it is.
- The more successful the counterinsurgency is, the less force can be used and the more risk must be accepted.
- Sometimes doing nothing is the best reaction.
- Some of the best weapons for counterinsurgents do not shoot.
- The host nation doing something tolerably is normally better than us doing it well.
- If a tactic works this week, it might not work next week; if it works in this province, it might not work in the next.
- Tactical success guarantees nothing.
- Many important decisions are not made by generals.

This new strategy was based on the experience in Malaya and other counterinsurgency campaigns but was adopted to fit different times and changed conditions. Some of the British methods could be used to great effect in Iraq. For example, a key goal was to win the sympathies of the population rather than to kill insurgents. In addition to providing protection, U.S. forces also supported economic development and political reform. They also were alert to differing conditions in various parts of the country, because of ethnic diversity, and sought local allies where possible. Better information made it possible to detect indicators of hostile activity and to counter them. Other elements of the British strategy, such as lengthy detentions, were found to be problematic. Finally, some things that the British had done, such as establishing resettlement camps and using food as a weapon, were not adopted.

One of the benefits of getting out into neighborhoods and villages to provide better protection, as well as to collect information on local tribal and family networks, was that this strategy made it possible to deal with the problem of IEDs. The various insurgents and militias used the vast numbers of artillery shells, mines, and other explosives still available throughout Iraq to improvise bombs that were placed along the roadside and detonated when U.S. forces approached. Over time, this became by far the largest single source of U.S. casualties. As American forces developed countermeasures, such as detection devices and stronger armor on vehicles, the insurgents responded with their own more advanced methods, such as wireless detonators and more powerful devices. Insurgents were learning and adapting – and they were doing it faster than the American military and civilian bureaucracies were. This insufficient response time changed after multidimensional (military, civic, intelligence, even anthropological) teams moved off bases and got a better grasp of a diversified and fast-changing situation. More extensive patrols made it possible to uncover and deal with the networks of planners, suppliers, financiers, and operatives who arranged the IED attacks. These networks were often based on family and tribal relationships that were difficult for outsiders to penetrate.

The new counterinsurgency strategy brought a dramatic reduction in military and civilian casualties in Iraq. It also made possible the drawdown in U.S. forces, and gave the Iraqi government more time to make political reforms, reconcile the various ethnic communities, and perhaps even to make progress against crime and corruption. Whether there will be a prosperous, stable, and democratic Iraq over the long term, however, depends on far more than just the tenets of a counterinsurgency strategy.

Traditional cognitive problems took on a different meaning in Iraq. A continuing problem in dealing with insurgents there is gaining deep understanding of the local culture. Most soldiers, even analysts whose job it is to have a deeper insight into what is going on, do not speak the local language, nor are they likely to have a profound knowledge of the factors such as the history of the country or the social structure. As soon as they pick up a few basics, such a Islamic sensitivities about alcohol and women, or start establishing the all-important personal ties, they are transferred.

Modern technology has brought vast collection capabilities from multiple sources, but much of what is collected is inaccurate, irrelevant, or quickly out of date. Technology has also provided means, such as computers, to attempt to master this flow of information. The Pentagon uses phrases like "information dominance" and "information preparation of the battle-field" to describe this situation. There has been considerable success using electronic means, especially against readily observable, capabilities-related targets, such as buildings and equipment.

As the first years of the U.S. engagements in Iraq demonstrated, however, there were serious shortcomings in this high-tech, high-firepower approach. It could defeat a conventional army, but there was still the challenge to understand more abstract issues, such as intentions. Moreover, mistakes through friendly fire – where one error is one too many – still happen.

Therefore, it was also important to develop other ways to think about military decision making. Counterinsurgency strategy encourages flexibility and open-mindedness to counter status quo thinking. Tools such as network analysis focus on relationships. Scenarios make analysts and planners sensitive to multiple possible outcomes and help to avoid surprise. There could be even more and different strategies and techniques for intelligence analysts to use in the future.

Questions for Further Thought

How were the coalition forces in Iraq's problems of trying to understand their area of operations similar to, or different from, those faced by Caesar in Gaul? Which of Sun Tzu's recommendations would help?

What assumptions underlie the principles of counterinsurgency strategy? Are they valid? What if some of them are wrong or out of date?

What risks and opportunities are available in counterinsurgency operations? Are counterinsurgency methods appropriate for every problem?

What are some scenarios for the future of Iraq and for other areas, such as Afghanistan, where counterinsurgency operations are being conducted?

Recommended Reading

Hammes, Thomas X., *The Sling and The Stone: On War in the 21st Century*, St. Paul, MN: Zenith Press, 2004.

Hashim, Ahmed S., *Insurgency and Counterinsurgency in Iraq*, Ithaca, NY: Cornell University Press, 2006.

Kilcullen, David, *The Accidental Guerrilla: Fighting Small Wars in the Midst of a Big One*, New York: Oxford University Press, 2009.

Maddox, Eric, with Seay, David, *Mission: Black List #1: The Inside Story of the Search for Saddam Hussein – as Told by the Soldier Who Masterminded the Capture*, New York: HarperCollins, 2008.

Moore, Robin, *Hunting Down Saddam: The Inside Story of the Search and Capture*, New York: St. Martin's Press, 2004.

Ricks, Thomas E., *The Gamble: General David Petraeus and the American Military Adventure in Iraq, 2006–2008*, New York: Penguin Press, 2009.

Shultz, Richard H., and Dew, Andrea J., *Insurgents, Terrorists, and Militias: The Warriors of Contemporary Combat*, New York: Columbia University Press, 2006.

The U.S. Army – Marine Corps Counterinsurgency Field Manual, Chicago, IL: University of Chicago Press, 2006; available online at: http://www.usgcoin.org/library/doctrine/COIN-FM3-24.pdf. http://usaac.army.mil/CAC/Repository/Materials/COIN-FM3-24.pdf.

Part VI

Domestic Law Enforcement

M ANY OF THE SAME ANALYTIC FRAMEWORKS AND PROCEDURES USED IN national security (e.g., hypotheses, trends, relationships, and indicators) are also useful in law enforcement. In fact, some widely used analytic techniques, such as network analysis, were pioneered in law enforcement. There are also some similarities in collection based on multiple kinds of sources. Both national security and law enforcement use imagery (surveillance photos and video in police work), reports from human sources (witness statements, confidential informants), and communications intercepts (telephone taps), for example.

There are also significant differences, however. Instead of trying to anticipate and plan for developments, law enforcement generally does not act until after a crime has taken place. Given the high stakes and the pressure of time, military and political leaders often have to make decisions before the facts are clear. The judicial system can take more time, and has higher standards of proof: for a case, "preponderance of evidence" in civil cases and "beyond a reasonable doubt" in criminal ones. Court procedures, such as maintaining a clear and unadulterated chain of custody for evidence, are much more stringent than the way "evidence" is handled in the national security agencies. The consumers of intelligence are also different in law enforcement. They often include local political and police officials who need to carefully apportion scarce resources to pursue investigations and prosecutions that will succeed and have an impact. Consumers can also include operators, who use analysis to target key suspects for arrest.

It used to be the case that there were sharp distinctions between the foreign and domestic realms, as well as between intelligence (especially clandestine collection) and the open court procedures of law enforcement. Since the 9/11 attacks, however, those differences have become much less important, and the pressure for better cooperation between law enforcement and intelligence has brought a blending of perspectives, although there is still much to be done in this regard.

30

The Lindbergh Kidnapping

I N 1932, WITH MEMORIES OF HIS 1927 SOLO FLIGHT ACROSS THE ATLANTIC Ocean still fresh, Charles Lindbergh was one of the best known and most highly respected people in the world. His wife, Anne, was the daughter of a partner in the J. P. Morgan bank who had also served as ambassador to Mexico. At approximately 7:00 P.M., on the evening of Tuesday, March 1, 1932, the Lindberghs put their 20-month-old son, Charles, to bed in his upstairs room at their country estate near Hopewell, New Jersey. Construction was not quite completed on the house, and usually the family only stayed there on weekends. Because Charles had had a cold, however, they had stayed longer. Also in the house that evening were three servants: a butler, a cook, and a nursemaid. At approximately 10:00 P.M., the nursemaid checked on the baby and found the crib empty. One of the bedroom windows was open, and there was a small, white envelope on the sill. A quick search inside and outside the house turned up no sign of the child. The local police responded quickly to a call, and a further search revealed a custom-made collapsible ladder and a chisel in the yard.

One of the early casualties in the investigation was the crime scene. The first detectives to arrive did not take accurate measurements or make plaster casts of footprints and tire tracks that they found. In addition, as more police, reporters, and sightseers arrived, these prints and tracks were obliterated. Police dusted the baby's room, the ladder, and the chisel for fingerprints, but no usable ones were found. The investigators did take some photographs.

When the envelope was opened, there was a ransom note inside, which read:

Dear Sir!
    Have 50,000$ redy in 20$ bills 1 5000$ in 10$ bills and 10000$ in 5$ bills.
After 2–4 days we will inform you were to deliver the Mony.

We warn you for making anyding public or for the polise the child is in gut care. Indication for all letters are signature and 3 holes.

In the lower right-hand corner was a symbol made up of two interlocking circles with a red mark in the center and three holes punched through the paper in the center and sides of the symbol.

On March 4 and March 5, further messages from the kidnappers arrived, saying that the child was in good health, they would keep him longer because the police had been brought into the case, and the ransom would be increased to $70,000. The notes included the symbol of the interlocking circles.

From the beginning there were different conceptions of the problem, and thus what analytic support would, or would not, be needed in making decisions. Lindbergh wanted something – anything – that would get his son back, and he was inclined to accept the kidnappers' demand that the police be kept on the sidelines. Law enforcement officials, however, wanted to identify, apprehend, and prosecute the perpetrator. Because of Lindbergh's celebrity status, the police tended to defer to him and abide by his wishes in conducting the investigation.

The kidnapping touched off a sensational circus of greed, ambition, and media hype. There was a nationwide search, along with the usual large number of false tips generated by a highly publicized case. Even the recently convicted Al Capone expressed his outrage and offered to help – if he were released. President Herbert Hoover offered the assistance of the federal government, including the Federal Bureau of Investigation (FBI).

Despite the offers of help from law enforcement officials, Lindbergh kept them at arm's length. He allowed the police to use his house as a temporary communications center, but he was wary of further law enforcement involvement, given the warnings in the letters. Instead, he turned to the unofficial offers of help and was determined to act as his own intelligence analyst.

From the many offers of help from gangsters, swindlers, spiritualists, and a host of others, the desperate Lindbergh picked several to pursue. The careful preparations, such as the ladder and lack of fingerprints, seemed to indicate that professionals had been involved, so Lindbergh asked a shady bootlegger to use his connections in the underworld to see if contact could be established with the kidnappers. He also agreed to let the wife of the publisher of *The Washington Post* hand over $100,000 in cash to another dubious individual who claimed to be in contact with gangsters who had taken the child. In Norfolk, Virginia, a retired Navy officer, who had commanded the warship that had brought Lindbergh back after his 1927 flight, said a local man there knew the kidnappers. Nothing came of any of these leads, but much time, money, and emotion was expended in following up on them.

On March 8, a retired teacher in the Bronx, John Condon, put a notice in the local paper offering to act as an intermediary with the kidnappers of the Lindbergh baby. A reply, which had been mailed in the Bronx, came the next day. That response enclosed a note to Lindbergh with further details on how to deliver the ransom money as well as the correct identifying symbol of the interlocking rings. These details seemed to prove that this lead was more legitimate than the others. Lindbergh decided to follow up and to keep the effort secret from the press and the police.

During the evening of March 11, a man with a German accent telephoned Condon at home and told him to stand by for further instructions. The following evening a cab driver delivered another message with detailed directions to a meeting. The ransom money was not ready yet, but Condon decided to go anyway. At the meeting, Condon and the representative of the kidnappers, who said his name was "John," had a lengthy conversation during which Condon explained that he would have to see the baby before delivering any money. John said that he would send the sleeping suit the baby had been in as proof that he and his confederates had the child.

Negotiations via coded newspaper notices continued for the next several weeks. Condon put an announcement in the March 14 newspaper saying that the money was ready and there would be no police. A few days later, the sleeping suit arrived in the mail, along with further instructions and the familiar authenticating symbol. A subsequent newspaper notice from Condon on March 17 confirmed that the money was ready.

As the ransom money was being prepared, Elmer Irey, the Internal Revenue Service agent who had helped to trap Capone for tax evasion, joined the case. Irey suggested that they take advantage of the fact that gold-backed currency was being withdrawn from circulation and pay the ransom in gold certificates, which would make them easy to spot as time went by. He also urged that a list be compiled of the serial numbers on the bills. Lindbergh wanted to avoid the possibility of provoking the kidnappers, but eventually agreed. By early April, all negotiations and arrangements had been completed.

On the evening of April 2, Condon and Lindbergh, who had insisted on participating personally, received instructions and proceeded to an assigned meeting place in the Bronx. John provided a note specifying the child's location, on a boat off the coast of Massachusetts near Martha's Vineyard, in return for $50,000. An extensive search over the next several days, aided by the Navy and the Coast Guard, yielded nothing. At this point, news of the negotiations, which had been secret up to this point, surfaced in the newspapers, along with the information that the serial numbers on the random payment had been recorded. There was another round of false leads as various people tried to gain notoriety or money from involvement in the case.

Then, on May 12, the baby's body was found in the woods a few miles from Hopewell; he had obviously been dead for some time. The various helpers claiming to have knowledge of the child's location, sincere or otherwise, were now exposed as useless or fake. Because murder had clearly been committed, the New Jersey State Police now took a more prominent role.

In the months and years that followed, the trails of the various investigative leads went cold, making it difficult to develop hypotheses. Handwriting experts concluded that all of the ransom notes with the symbol had been written by one person, who was probably a native German speaker, but they had no specific suspect. The ladder suggested familiarity with carpentry. A government expert in wood spent a year and a half checking with 1,600 lumber mills and traced the material used in the ladder to a retail outlet in the Bronx, but no further. There was much speculation that the kidnapping might have been an inside job. A maid at the estate of Mrs. Morrow, Lindbergh's mother-in-law, and who was one of the few people who knew that the Lindberghs were not on their regular schedule the night of the kidnapping, was evasive and contradictory during questioning. In June, the maid committed suicide, apparently for personal reasons rather than guilt over involvement in the kidnapping. A few of the distinctive gold certificates used in the ransom payment had surfaced in New York City but had not produced any viable leads.

Then, on September 15, 1934, two and a half years after the kidnapping, the manager of a gas station in upper Manhattan accepted a ten-dollar gold certificate from a customer. Worried that it might be counterfeit, the manager wrote the customer's license plate number on the bill. When the bill was deposited at the bank three days later, a teller found that it was on the list of the ransom money. The languishing investigation in New York City was now being run by a team made up of investigators from the FBI, the New Jersey State Police, and the New York Police Department. The team verified who had made the deposit and then talked to the gas station manager, who remembered that the customer who paid with the gold certificate spoke with a German accent. When they traced the license plate number on the bill, they found that it belonged to a Bruno Hauptmann (1899–1936), a German-born carpenter living in the Bronx.

An expanded joint team brought Hauptmann in for questioning on September 19 and found that he had another one of the gold certificates in his wallet. As the reinvigorated investigation continued, several witnesses from the Hopewell area said that they had seen Hauptmann there the day of the crime. In addition, the cab driver who had delivered a note to Condon identified Hauptmann as the man who had paid for the delivery, but Condon himself did not confirm the identification after confronting Hauptmann. When investigators searched Hauptmann's garage, they found more than $14,000 of the Lindbergh ransom money hidden there, and in his house was a notebook with a design for a collapsible ladder like the one used in the crime and a tool chest with a wide range of implements except for a chisel. Subsequently, they found Condon's address and phone number written on the door trim of a closet, as well as a gap in the flooring of the attic where a piece of the ladder fit.

For his part, Hauptmann denied any knowledge of the kidnapping except for what he had read in the newspapers, and claimed that he had been working in New York the day of the crime. At first, Hauptmann had denied that he had any more of the gold certificates. When confronted with the results of the search, however, he changed his story and said the money was not his and he was holding it for a business partner. He acknowledged that Condon's address and phone number in his closet was in his handwriting, but he claimed he had just been interested in the case like everyone else. Hauptmann also confirmed that he had quit work as a carpenter in the spring of 1932 and had spent money freely after that, but he claimed that the funds had come from successful investments in the stock market. The New York authorities were not convinced, and turned him over to their counterparts in New Jersey for trial.

The Lindbergh kidnapping trial, in January 1935, was another media circus. The testimony mainly covered familiar ground, except that Condon now was sure that it was Hauptmann who had received the ransom money. Hauptmann's wife testified that he had been with her the night of the crime and when the ransom was handed over to Condon. The prosecution was unable to produce any witnesses that saw Hauptmann take or kill the Lindbergh child, but it did present a powerful circumstantial case. During the six-week trial, the defense was unable to produce credible witnesses that could undermine the prosecution's case or prove alternative theory. After eleven hours of deliberation, the jury delivered a guilty verdict. Hauptmann went to the electric chair in April 1936 still refusing to admit that he was the kidnapper.

The early phases of the Lindbergh case revealed the shortcomings of the investigative methods of the time. Leads were followed before being ranked on the basis of plausibility. Forensics was admittedly in its early stages, but was still poorly done even by the contemporary standards. There appears to have been little thought about what gaps there might be in crucial factors, such as evidence and the list of suspects. Databases of personal or financial information that would have helped were rare or difficult to search at the time.

When the break in the case came in 1934, it was largely a matter of luck and, as is often the case, was the result of assistance from a citizen rather than of an investigation by the police. That said, law enforcement officials were able to exploit the recovery of one of the ransom notes because of effective planning and research.

Among the most serious difficulties was the environment in which the case took place. Lindbergh's celebrity meant that massive resources were available, but it also brought attention from a range of ambitious and dubious characters. Moreover, Lindbergh's status gave him an inappropriate role in shaping the nature of the investigation. Finally, the publicity made it difficult for the authorities to deal with the case, but the media was also of some help as a channel of communications with the suspected kidnapper.

Questions for Further Thought

Were any cognitive biases or assumptions at work in the investigation? What else was right or wrong with the various phases of the investigation, from an analytic perspective?

The case against Hauptmann was admittedly circumstantial. What was the quality of the evidence, and how convincing was it?

Are there other possible explanations for the facts presented at the trial?

Recommended Reading

Berg, A. Scott, *Lindbergh*, New York: G. P. Putnam's Sons, 1998.

Fisher, Jim, *The Lindbergh Case*, New Brunswick, NJ: Rutgers University Press, 1987.

Kennedy, Ludovic, *The Airman and the Carpenter: The Lindbergh Kidnapping and Framing of Richard Hauptmann*, New York: Viking, 1985.

31

Breaking the Mafia

VIRTUALLY EVERY MODERN SOCIETY, NO MATTER HOW PROSPEROUS, structured, or even authoritarian, has organized crime. This is true in countries such as Britain and France, but also in Russia and China. There always seems to be individuals who for whatever reason – poverty, discrimination, lack of skills, or perhaps just a shortage of patience – cannot fit into normal organizations, relationships, and careers. They turn to crime. These individuals get money and power from the formal society, along with acceptance and respect from their criminal colleagues. The key to their success is to provide what is missing or forbidden, such as drugs, prostitutes, or gambling. They then protect themselves through corruption, deception, intimidation, and murder and become even more successful by organizing on a large scale.

In the Western world, one way that organized crime came about began in rural Sicily in the nineteenth century. With the Italian government distant, ineffective, and unresponsive, private organizations grew up to provide protection and settle disputes. A parallel, unofficial society emerged, which came to be known as the mafia. Mafia organizations were reinforced by family ties, and they provided honor and respect for their members. They also protected themselves through secrecy and violence. Over time, it was natural for the mafias to become involved in organized crime, which became extremely lucrative.

In twentieth-century United States the atmosphere was better, but immigrants were still subject to discrimination and often found it hard to achieve the American Dream through legitimate channels. Drawing on the traditions of their homeland, immigrants from Italy, along with outsiders from other ethnic groups, organized themselves into profitable criminal groups, which became known as the mafia. Then the mafia expanded into transportation,

construction, the unions, and other areas. By the 1970s, the mafia was international in scope and bringing in tens of billions of dollars a year, which
was more than most large corporations. They were also moving increasing
amounts of their money into legitimate businesses in Las Vegas, Havana,
and elsewhere. Secrecy and violence continued to be crucial elements of the
mafia's success.

To cope with these developments, law enforcement officials realized that
they would need tools beyond traditional measures such as the cop on the
beat. For example, wiretaps had long been used for covert collection in
national security cases, but the results were not admissible as evidence
in court. Then, under Title III of the 1968 Omnibus Crime Control and
Safe Streets Act, a judge could authorize tapping a telephone line if law
enforcement provided "probable cause," that is, reasonable suspicion of
criminal activity. Such evidence, having been obtained in a legal manner,
could then be used in trials. Another significant change in the legal context
was the passage of the Racketeer Influenced and Corrupt Organizations
(RICO) Act in 1970. Under this act, individuals could be prosecuted and
harsh sentences imposed for a pattern of illegal activity, rather than just
a single act. The RICO Act made it possible to prosecute groups as well
as leaders who had not been directly involved in criminal acts. The act
could only be effective, however, as a result of long, and often multifaceted,
investigations to uncover many of the details of how a criminal enterprise
functioned.

Within this new legal framework, law enforcement officials found it useful
to adopt some techniques used in national security intelligence gathering.
For example, they made more use of clandestine methods of collection,
including wiretaps, undercover officers, and confidential informants within
criminal organizations. Given the complexity and deception involved in the
problem, analysis would also be valuable. In their management of the large
amounts of data generated by investigations, law enforcement analysts used
tools such as link analysis, flow charts, and timelines.

All of these developments were the background for the breaking of the
mafia's "pizza connection" in the 1980s. This case gave an important boost
to the careers of a number of the prosecutors involved, including Michael
Chertoff, who later became Secretary of Homeland Security, Louis Freeh,
who became director of the Federal Bureau of Investigation (FBI), and
Rudolph ("Rudy") Giuliani, who became mayor of New York City.

In the early phases of the pizza connection case, investigators tracked
suspects and collected evidence in a variety of ways, but initially had trouble
making sense of it all. Video surveillance produced pictures of packages

being moved from one vehicle to another. Suspects who were being tailed were seen carrying briefcases and going in and out of banks. There were cryptic telephone conversations using obvious code names. Then there were the bodies. What did it all mean?

Over time, investigators and analysts uncovered an alliance between the American mafia, or as they called themselves *La Cosa Nostra* ("our thing"), and the Sicilian mafia. The Sicilians had replaced "the French connection" as the main shippers and refiners of illegal drugs, turning opium from Asia into heroin, and then smuggling it across the Atlantic Ocean. After reaching the United States, the drugs would be distributed through pizza parlors. The profits would then be turned into legitimate funds, or "laundered," through other international channels. Between the mid-1970s and the mid-1980s, the pizza connection produced more than $1.5 billion in net income.

Analysts working on the case had to master a variety of issues that were generally not part of traditional law enforcement investigations. They had to learn about international finance, as well as obscure Sicilian dialects spoken by the suspects. The analysts also had to use frameworks of understanding that were quite different from the hierarchical organizations in which most analysts worked. The mafia was made up of small cliques based on personal loyalty that both cooperated with, but also conducted murderous turf wars with, other cliques on a broader regional (and sometimes national) basis. The mobsters who had put together the pizza connection extended this system to an international stage. The agents who would actually carry out the arrests, as well as the prosecutors, also had to change their mindsets and move beyond a focus on just individuals accused of a single crime. They also had to learn to deal with charges of ethnic profiling.

Another key element of the case was unprecedented institutional cooperation. Nationally, the agencies involved included the Drug Enforcement Administration, the FBI, the Immigration and Naturalization Service, the Internal Revenue Service, as well as the police departments of the state of New York and New York City. Internationally, productive links were established with Italian police and prosecutors.

Based on the work of the investigators and analysts, prosecutors were confident that they had a strong case and proceeded with one of the largest and most complex trials in U.S. criminal history. In September 1985, the pizza connection trial opened in New York City with twenty-two defendants in the dock. During the next year and a half, the results of collection and analysis were presented, including 15,000 exhibits and more than 40,000 pages of wiretap transcripts. In March 1987, eighteen individuals were convicted on all counts, and three more on most accounts. Only one was acquitted.

At roughly the same time, techniques similar to those used in the pizza connection case were also employed against the "Commission," the leaders of the five mafia families in New York City, and later against John Gotti, among others. More prosecutions took place in Philadelphia, Detroit, and other cities. A total of approximately 2,500 mafia members ended up in prison. The Italian–American mafia was not eliminated, but it was dealt a crippling blow.

The pizza connection and other mafia cases demonstrated how far investigative and analytic techniques in law enforcement had come in the half century since the Lindbergh kidnapping. Analysts developed a variety of resources, both nationally and internationally, and integrated them into a compelling presentation that could stand up to the stringent requirements of court proceedings.

Questions for Further Thought

Understanding organized crime requires knowing the context. What factors in the context of Italian–American organized crime would provide useful questions that could be asked in an investigation of organized crime linked to other ethnic groups?

What kinds of information would an investigator need for a network analysis of a criminal organization such as the mafia? Does the atomic bomb spies case provide a useful model?

How do techniques used to penetrate deception and secrecy in national security cases compare and contrast with what is – or could be – used in law enforcement?

Recommended Reading

Blumenthal, Ralph, *Last Days of the Sicilians: At War with the Mafia, the FBI Assault on the Pizza Connection*, New York: Times Books, 1988.

Bonavolanta, Jules, and Duffy, Brian, *The Good Guys: How We Turned the FBI 'Round and Finally Broke the Mob*, New York: Simon & Schuster, 1997.

Freeh, Louis, *My FBI: Bringing Down the Mafia, Investigating Bill Clinton, and Fighting the War on Terror*, New York: St. Martins, 2005.

Griffin, Joe, *Mob Nemesis: How the FBI Crippled Organized Crime*, Amherst, NY: Prometheus Books, 2002.

Repetto, Thomas A., *Bringing Down the Mob: The War Against the American Mafia*, New York: H. Holt, 2006.

32

Airline Tragedies

Pan Am Flight 103 and TWA Flight 800

AIRLINE TRAGEDIES, WITH THEIR SUDDEN LOSS OF A CONSIDERABLE NUM-
ber of lives, are a great concern to a public that travels a great deal,
and these incidents garner a great deal of attention from the media. People
quickly ask: What could cause such a shocking event? Typically, proving
the cause is a demanding procedure, because witnesses rarely survive. In
addition, there are usually a number of possible answers, as the aircraft are
complex mechanisms and, sadly, there are any number of people who could
wish them harm.

On December 21, 1988, Pan Am Flight 103, a Boeing 747 jet traveling
from London to New York, exploded thirty-seven minutes after takeoff at
31,000 feet, as it passed over the village of Lockerbie, Scotland. A total of
270 people died as a result of the crash, including 189 passengers from the
United States, and 11 British subjects on the ground. The Federal Bureau of
Investigation (FBI) immediately sent a team to work with British authorities
to collect the approximately 10,000 pieces of debris scattered over almost
900 square miles (2,340 square kilometers) so that they could reconstruct
the aircraft and try to uncover how it had been destroyed.

It quickly became obvious that a bomb had destroyed the plane. There
had been no distress call, nor any indications of mechanical trouble; and
many pieces of wreckage had the tell-tale warping that indicated that an
explosion had taken place. Moreover, there were virtually no large pieces
from the forward cargo hold, suggesting that a bomb there had almost
totally destroyed that part of the aircraft.

Determining who might have planted the bomb was much more difficult. There were many who had grudges against the United States at the
time, including the Palestinians, the Libyans, and the Iranians. As examination of the recovered debris continued, investigators focused on traces that
had been found of Semtex, a powerful plastic explosive sometimes used by

terrorists. There was also great interest in the tiny pieces of a portable audio cassette player that had apparently been destroyed by an explosion, as these recorders had been used by Palestinian terrorists to conceal bombs. Indicators such as fibers and explosive residue linked the cassette recorder with the contents of a single suitcase that had been checked onto the flight in Malta. One of the items that had been in that suitcase was a piece of clothing with a label showing that it had come from a shop in Malta. When the owner of the Maltese shop was interviewed, he recalled a strange visit by an Arab man, who had hurriedly selected and purchased a random collection of items. FBI investigators, assisted by Central Intelligence Agency (CIA) technicians, determined that another tiny item recovered from the wreckage was from a type of electronic timer used by the Libyan military.

British and American authorities eventually charged two Libyans of involvement in a plot to destroy the aircraft. After much delay, the Libyan government allowed the two to appear before a Scottish court, which was held in the Netherlands (mutually agreed as a neutral location). One of the two individuals, a Libyan intelligence officer who had made the purchases in the shop in Malta, was convicted in 2001, based largely on the compelling forensic evidence, and sentenced to life imprisonment. In addition, the Libyan government agreed to pay up to $2.7 billion in compensation to the families of the victims.

Eight years after the bombing of Pan Am Flight 103, the FBI and CIA again cooperated to solve another loss of an airliner. On July 17, 1996, TWA Flight 800 exploded only a few minutes after taking off from New York, with wreckage and 230 victims falling into the sea just south of Long Island. The main initial hypotheses were that (1) a bomb had exploded on the plane, (2) a missile had brought the plan down, or (3) there had been a mechanical failure.

Terrorism was strongly suspected because a number of airliners, such as Pan Am Flight 103, had been destroyed by terrorist bombs. Moreover, the trials resulting in convictions of the persons involved in the 1993 World Trade Center bombing were in progress in New York, and the Atlanta Olympics were due to start in less than two weeks. In addition, some of the eyewitnesses had described seeing streaks of light and smoke that looked like flares or fireworks rising into the sky. The flares or fireworks, according to the witnesses, were seen just before a bright fireball in the sky, which was immediately followed by the sound of a loud explosion, which was seen and heard by many more witnesses.

Even though a terrorist attack was initially the leading hypothesis, FBI investigators kept an open mind, as there were still loose ends. As is often the case, there were numerous claims of responsibility by a variety of terrorist groups, but none of them were particularly convincing. Divers brought up more than 90 percent of the wreckage, making it possible to reconstruct the plane. The wreckage showed none of the telltale signs of damage caused by explosives from either a missile or bomb, however.

As time went by and there was no clear explanation, the FBI called on CIA analysts for assistance. The CIA analysts were provided with data from a wide variety of sources typical of those used in investigating airline crashes, including the aircraft's flight data and cockpit voice recorders, eye witness accounts, the pattern of the wreckage on the ocean floor, and air traffic control tapes. The CIA also brought something unusual to bear: data from a reconnaissance satellite that had picked up an intense heat source, which helped to confirm the exact time and location of the explosion.

To organize the data so that they could uncover meaningful patterns, the analysts used tools such as a timeline and a matrix. The timeline organized the exact sequence of events, based on the onboard recorders, air traffic control data, and the satellite. The matrix, in contrast, was used to compare and contrast the statements of the several hundred witnesses, on one axis, with the various sights and sounds associated with the breakup of the aircraft, on the other.

After months of work, the insight that light and sound traveled at different speeds put witness statements about a simultaneous explosion and loud sound into perspective. The fact that the sight and sound of the explosion were seen and heard at almost the same time did not mean that they had happened at the same time; instead, the explosion had taken place almost a minute earlier. CIA analysts concluded that the explosion that started the breakup of the plane (which either had not caused a flash, or the flash had not been seen by witnesses) had, in fact, taken place before the streaks of light noted by the eye witnesses. The pattern of the wreckage on the bottom of the ocean showed that the nose of the aircraft had dropped off first, then the rest of the plane kept moving for approximately 40 seconds, trailing burning fuel, which was probably the streak of light that many witnesses said they saw. The large fireball that witnesses described was the spectacular display caused when the remaining fuel caught fire as the plane broke up and plunged into the ocean.

After the right framework was applied, the data, which had previously been inconclusive, fit together, demonstrating that the bomb and missile hypotheses were impossible, and therefore a mechanical failure was the most likely cause. As a result, the FBI dropped its criminal investigation.

Questions for Further Thought

Often it is a useful analytic procedure to look at several similar examples, as lines of inquiry that helped in one case might be useful in another. What were some of the similarities in and differences between these two past airline tragedies, and might they help in better understanding similar incidents in the future?

What were the strengths and weaknesses of the evidence supporting the various hypotheses regarding perpetrators in the Pan Am Flight 103 case?

What were the key elements of success in the TWA Flight 800 case?

Recommended Reading

Emerson, Steven, and Duffy, Brian, *The Fall of Pan Am 103: Inside the Lockerbie Investigation*, New York: Putnam, 1990.

Milton, Pat, *In the Blink of an Eye: The FBI Investigation of TWA Flight 800*, New York: Random House, 1999.

33

Aum Shinrikyo

FORTUNATELY, THERE HAVE BEEN ONLY A FEW EXAMPLES OF CHEMICAL and biological agents being used by terrorists. The impact after an attack using such agents could be readily envisioned and would be horrific. What indicators would analysts and law enforcement officials be looking for to provide warning before an incident took place? This problem would be especially difficult the first time an assault using weapons of mass destruction was carried out, when there were no precedents. Although they did not realize it at first, this was the challenge that Japanese police faced in the mid-1990s.

Shoko Asahara (1955–) was an ambitious, poor boy from rural Japan who was frustrated that society did not recognize his abilities. He became a practitioner of alternative medicine in Tokyo and, in 1984, founded *Aum Shinrikyo*. The first part of the name derived from the Sanskrit word that Hindu mystics used in meditation, and the second part is Japanese for "supreme truth." Asahara spliced together fragments from Buddhism, Hinduism, Christianity, and even the sixteenth-century French prophet Nostradamus into a new age doctrine that promised enlightenment and supernatural powers. *Aum Shinrikyo* quickly became a cult that found some resonance as an alternative to the prevailing Japanese culture and lifestyle. Within a decade, the group had approximately 10,000 members, including many well-educated professionals such as lawyers, engineers, and scientists, as well as government officials and members of the armed forces and police. Branches of *Aum Shinrikyo* also opened overseas, in Western Europe, Russia, Australia, and the United States. The group's tax-free status enhanced its ability to accumulate considerable assets through donations and business activities, which included restaurants, book shops, and computer stores.

Over time, Asahara increasingly focused in his sermons on prophecies that a nuclear war was coming between Japan and the United States. Asahara and his disciples became fascinated with high-tech weaponry, such as ray guns and poison gas, as means to prevail in this apocalyptic struggle. They maintained that only members of *Aum Shinrikyo* would survive the cataclysm and then thrive in the age of spiritual renewal that would follow.

Aum Shinrikyo had a dark side that included fraud, narcotics, and ties to organized crime. As with some other cults, there were accusations that discipline and loyalty were maintained, at least in part, through psychological manipulation, as well as abductions and violence. Over the years, for example, a number of critics of the group had disappeared mysteriously. In addition, neighbors also complained of strong smells coming from buildings owned by the group. The group's aggressive and unconventional behavior led to a series of lawsuits.

As a result of his group's dark side, Asahara had come to the attention of the Japanese police. Japan was a famously orderly society, with one of the lowest rates of violent crime in the world. In dealing with *Aum Shinrikyo*, or any other problem, Japanese law enforcement officials depended more on tips from citizens and confessions obtained through interrogation than on forensic science or lengthy investigations. In reaction to the excesses of the police in the years before World War II, the authorities did not use techniques such as undercover operations or telephone taps, and they were wary of violating religious freedom. Therefore, when complaints or suspicions arose, the Japanese police viewed Asahara and *Aum Shinrikyo* as eccentrics and possible criminals, but were reluctant to conclude that there was a serious threat or to launch a vigorous investigation. To put the police's shortcomings into perspective, it should be noted that the broader government, the public, and the media in Japan had a similar view of the cult.

What neither the government nor the media had grasped was that Asahara was determined to demonstrate the correctness of his doomsday prophecies by working secretly to bring them about, using the scientific skills of some of the cult's members. In 1993, *Aum Shinrikyo* tested an anthrax-based weapon. The attack was a failure, however, without any of the desired casualties, because the group's scientists had unknowingly picked a harmless strain of anthrax for the experiment. Therefore, Asahara turned his attention to chemical weapons. By 1994, the group's scientists had produced sarin, a nerve agent that produces vomiting, shortness of breath, impaired vision, convulsions, and then quick death. Sarin had originally been developed in Nazi Germany and later was banned by international agreement.

In 1994, there were several suspicious incidents throughout Japan. The first, in June, took place in the town of Matsumoto, northwest of Tokyo, where *Aum Shinrikyo* was being sued for obtaining local land under false pretences. Cult members drove a truck with a crude storage and release mechanism to the neighborhood where several of the judges involved in the case lived, released sarin, and then left the scene. The wind changed direction, however, and spread the poisonous mist elsewhere in the neighborhood. Seven people died, and more than 150 became sick. The police investigation uncovered a local man who had some chemicals in his residence and whom they believed had botched an effort to produce a homemade weed killer. The man maintained that he was innocent, and further investigation revealed that the cause of the deaths was sarin, which could not have been produced by the chemicals in his possession. The man with the stock of chemicals in his house was eventually released, and no other suspects were identified. Court action on the land fraud case was postponed indefinitely, so Asahara regarded the attack as a success.

A month later, in July, people living around the cult's compound near Mount Fuji complained about nausea and shortness of breath, but none died. In November, there were more complaints about odd smells and dead plants. The police found samples of chemicals that were associated with sarin and that matched residue found earlier in the year at Matsumoto. They also discovered that one of *Aum Shinrikyo*'s businesses had purchased large amounts of chemicals that could be used to produce sarin. Again, because they had only circumstantial evidence, the police did not investigate the cult aggressively. Instead, they preferred to attribute the mysterious deaths and odors to leftover munitions from World War II or to a strike by the North Koreans, hypotheses which conveniently could not be pursued with any reasonable hope of resolution.

In light of the problems with producing and using sarin, Asahara ordered his scientists to undertake an alternate program: produce VX, a nerve agent that had been discovered by British scientists in the 1950s and subsequently banned. Cult members used VX to try to kill several of the cult's enemies, but were successful in only one case, in Osaka in December 1994, when a former member of the group died mysteriously. Police were again unable to make any strong connection to *Aum Shinrikyo*, and added the death to their file of unsolved cases.

As these events were taking place, Asahara was developing a plan for *Aum Shinrikyo* members to release sarin in an attack in downtown Tokyo that he hoped would bring down the Japanese government. He believed that this would promote the chaos that would bring his group to power and enlightenment. In March 1995, *Aum Shinrikyo* learned from its members in the police department that the authorities, concerned about allegations that the group was engaged in criminal activity, were finally planning a raid on the group's facilities. To forestall the raids, Asahara ordered that sarin be immediately used to attack the Tokyo subway. Because of the tight deadline, only a small amount of low-quality toxin could be prepared.

On March 20, 1995, five members of the group got onto different trains on the subway that were converging on a station that was located near police headquarters and several government ministries. At approximately 8:00 A.M., they punctured plastic bags containing liquid sarin, which quickly turned into a gas that spread throughout the crowded subway tunnels. It was not a suicide attack; the members then fled the scene. Immediately hundreds, and then thousands, of commuters began complaining about nausea, impaired vision, and shortness of breath.

Again, the authorities, faced with an unfamiliar situation, did not realize for several hours that a chemical attack was underway. They first responded slowly or inappropriately. Initially commuters and officials believed that there had been an explosion in one of the subway tunnels. Uncertain about what was going on, subway officials kept the trains running, which further spread the poisonous vapors. First responders, emergency communications, and hospitals, which had never planned on dealing with a chemical attack, were overwhelmed. Some first responders themselves became victims. Television crews concentrated on transmitting pictures, and refused to allow their vehicles to be used to evacuate the wounded and dying.

It was several hours before sarin was identified as the cause, and it became clear that the incident was not an accident. Military units were the only people who had decontamination equipment. By early afternoon, based on the similarity of symptoms, some in the press were linking this incident to the 1994 attacks. On March 22, Japanese police began raiding *Aum Shinrikyo* facilities around the country and arresting members, although it was months before they actually formulated charges and started trials. Asahara was sentenced to death in 2004.

Tokyo was lucky; because of the poor quality of the sarin and the crude method of dispersal, only twelve people died. Several hundred others were injured to varying degrees. Thousands more were traumatized by stress and fear.

Although the Japanese police had had some clues, they did not have an accurate framework of analysis, either of *Aum Shinrikyo* or of a chemical attack. Biases such as anchoring, in which it is difficult to escape the limitations of existing judgments, and framing, in which information is dealt with in ways that lead to preferred or conventional conclusions, meant that it was difficult to understand what was happening. It appears that law enforcement officials made no effort to come up with a wide enough range of hypotheses to grasp what was actually being planned in the cult. To be fair to the police, Asahara's goals were so bizarre that it would have been difficult to clearly understand him and to use the conclusions to justify action, especially harsh action.

Conventional thinking also affected what information was collected, and thus the facts on which to base assessments and action. The police were focused primarily on fraud, and, to a lesser extent, on missing individuals. Because they were not looking for evidence of a chemical attack, they disregarded the few clues that they encountered.

Because there had never been a large-scale attack in an urban area, in Tokyo or anywhere else, there had been no justification for government officials to decide to make the sizable expenditure that would have been necessary to have medicines, trained personnel, facilities, and equipment ready to deal with such an emergency.

Questions for Further Thought

Why were traditional Japanese police methods not more effective in uncovering what *Aum Shinrikyo* was up to in Japan?

Has law enforcement gotten any better in assessing the threat from cults? Do analysts dealing with other unconventional situations, such as North Korea, have similar problems?

What would senior officials in any country need from analysts to be better prepared for a chemical attack?

Recommended Reading

Kaplan, David E., and Marshall, Andrew, *The Cult at the End of the World: The Terrifying Story of the Aum Doomsday Cult, from the Subways of Tokyo to the Nuclear Arsenals of Russia*, New York: Random House, 1996.

Lifton, Robert Jay, *Destroying the World to Save It: Aum Shinrikyo, Apocalyptic Violence, and the New Global Terrorism*, New York: Henry Holt, 1999.

Murakami, Haruki, *Underground: The Tokyo Gas Attack and the Japanese Psyche*, New York: Alfred A. Knopf, 2001.

Reader, Ian, *Religious Violence in Contemporary Japan: The Case of Aum Shinrikyo*, Richmond, Surrey, UK: Curzon Press, 2000.

Figure 26. The Caribbean Sea

34

Colombian Drug Cartels

I N THE 1980S, ANALYSTS OBSERVING TRENDS IN THE INTERNATIONAL DRUG trade began to see that cocaine from South America was replacing heroin from Europe (the famous French Connection) as the main type of narcotic imported into the United States. Coca plants, the source of cocaine, could grow in a variety of areas, but the climate and geography of Bolivia, Colombia, and Peru provided the perfect conditions. The political and economic climate in this region, with weak, often corrupt governments and poor, small-scale farmers with few viable options for making a living, are also amenable to the coca plant. These circumstances have given rise to a trade in narcotics that, by the 1990s, was worth tens of billions of dollars a year, making it the largest, and most profitable, sector of global organized crime.

Taking on the formidable international trade in illegal drugs is a huge challenge for law enforcement. In addition to the resources of personnel, money, and equipment, effective countermeasures depend on an accurate and detailed understanding of not only the strengths, but also the vulnerabilities, of the process of producing and shipping drugs.

Colombia, which produces more than 75 percent of the world's cocaine, was one of the main centers of the illegal drug trade. Poor farmers in Colombia became interested in expanding the cultivation of coca in the 1980s and 1990s, after a decline in the price of coffee, which had previously been the country's largest export. The fact that Colombia has large areas of land that were remote from law enforcement made it perfect for growing coca, especially because the plants could flourish in marginal soil and did not require large amounts of skilled labor. The cocaine trade, however, also required international connections and skilled labor for processing. Colombian drug lords imported large additional amounts of coca by air from other growing areas in Bolivia and Peru, and became the center of turning coca leaves into cocaine. First, the leaves were turned into a paste by crushing the leaves and then boiling them in a mixture of limewater and kerosene. The next step, in which the paste is turned into powder, required considerable skill. It also required more elaborate supplies of imported chemicals, including sulfuric acid, potassium permanganate, sulfur dioxide, and ammonium hydroxide.

The end product of cocaine in powder form was attractive as contraband because it had both a high value per unit of volume and high profit margins: a kilo in Colombia worth $15,000 could be sold on the streets of major cities in the United States for $50,000 or more. The main problem for the drug lords was that the area where the drug was produced, in Colombia, was so far from the main markets, which were in the United States. Therefore, the cocaine smugglers built up transportation networks that spanned the Caribbean. The huge profits of the cocaine trade meant that there were vast amounts of money to cloak the shipments in elaborate denial and deception operations, including constantly shifting physical locations (laboratories, warehouses, apartments), false documents, concealment devices for shipments, and extensive use of airline travel – even their own airplanes. Over time, two Colombian cartels, based in Medellin and Cali, dominated this extensive system for producing and shipping cocaine.

In addition to the social harm done by increasing drug use, the cartels became notorious for corruption and violence. The huge profits meant that there was plenty of money to bribe police and politicians, as well as to tempt respectable bankers and lawyers to cooperate. By the 1980s, Colombia had one of the highest murder rates in the world, nine times that of the United States.

The most successful of the drug lords was Pablo Escobar (1949–1993), head of the Medellin cartel. Escobar created a hierarchical, vertically integrated enterprise running from the coca fields of Colombia to sales on the streets of major cities in the United States, with elaborate support mechanisms for money laundering and protection from law enforcement. In the process, he became one of the richest men in the world, and he did not hesitate to flaunt his wealth through lavish personal spending and charity, which garnered considerable popular sympathy. Escobar was notorious for his brutality, using bombing, murder, intimidation, and corruption to protect his operations. His approach was captured in the phrase "silver or lead" (*plata o plomo*), meaning that those who opposed him had the choice of taking a bribe or receiving a bullet.

Besides the system of production and shipment, another key issue for analysts was to determine the extent to which the drug cartels were linked with the most dangerous Colombian insurgent group, the Revolutionary Armed Forces of Colombia (*Fuerzas Armadas Revolucionarias de Colombia,* or FARC), which had started a left-oriented insurgency in the countryside in the 1960s. The FARC provided rudimentary social and judicial services in poor rural areas in return for "taxes." Originally the FARC was critical of the drug trade, which it disapproved of for ideological reasons, and the guerrillas concentrated on attacking military units to get supplies and hostages. As it expanded, the FARC found that the drug trade could become a significant source of funds for recruitment and weapons, so it began providing protection to growers in return for a share in the profits. By the 1980s, the FARC had forged alliances with both the Medellin and Cali cartels, and it had tens of thousands of uniformed insurgents in the field.

In response to the FARC, landowners, politicians, and army officers set up illegal private paramilitary units, which came to be known as the United Self-Defense Forces of Colombia (*Autodefensas Unidas de Colombia*, or AUC). Over time, the AUC established its own ties to the drug trade, drawn by the same magnet of cash.

To the north, in the United States, the deleterious effects of drugs prompted President Ronald Reagan, in 1986, to declare the illegal international trade in narcotics to be a threat to American national security. President Reagan's invocation of national security committed the resources of the federal government against a problem that had previously been handled by local law enforcement. A higher priority for counternarcotics also encouraged the various federal agencies, such as the Central Intelligence Agency (CIA), the Drug Enforcement Administration (DEA), the Federal Bureau of Investigation (FBI), and various component of the Department of Defense, to cooperate more closely.

Over time, law enforcement authorities realized that just making more and more busts of drug peddlers on the street was not enough; they would have to have a strategy that took into account the cartels as a whole and used multiple sources of information. When the information on the drug trade was gathered and analyzed, it became clear that cartels had compartmented units for key functions such as obtaining raw materials, processing, shipping, and distribution. Any individual or group that was involved knew only those with whom they were in direct contact and had little idea of the overall structure. Only a few at the top understood how the whole system worked, and this knowledge was what analysts would have to put together. After studying the drug-smuggling system as a whole, from the coca fields to the street peddlers, analysts concluded that communications and transportation were the main vulnerabilities.

Communications were important targets for collection and disruption because the cartels made extensive use of a variety of communications means. They preferred beepers and pagers rather than private lines that could be tapped. At first, the drug lords believed that law enforcement could not tap pay phones; when they realized that that was possible, they shifted to fax and cell phones. Therefore, law enforcement had to get permission from the courts to tap those new technologies.

Analysts also concluded that transportation provided many opportunities to disrupt the flow of drugs. In addition to interdicting shipments of the drugs themselves as they entered the United States, the DEA, assisted by the Navy and the Coast Guard, tried to block shipments of the chemicals that were necessary for processing and could not be obtained in large quantities in Colombia. Efforts were also made further back in the supply chain to reduce the supply of raw coca from neighboring countries.

Another aspect of the struggle against the drug cartels was to reconsider the focus on kingpins. Traditionally law enforcement had given a high priority to arresting the leaders of criminal enterprises, hoping that this would be followed by the disintegration of the whole organization. This approach had been used against many leaders of organized crime, including Al Capone. Similar efforts focusing on Escobar proved to be ineffective, so the authorities were open to an alternative approach. What they decided on was to work from the bottom up, rather than the top down – a method that would require accurate and timely analysis.

The turning point came in 1993, when the Colombian government concluded that Escobar was out of control and requested increased assistance from the United States. Washington agreed to provide personnel and equipment. Law enforcement and military personnel from both countries worked together to systematically locate and pursue the various components of the Medellin cartel's support network, including lawyers, bankers, gunmen, corrupt politicians and policemen, and Escobar family members. Signals intelligence was particularly useful, and the results of reports from a variety of sources were used. Analysts and operators also constructed elaborate link charts to lay out the relationships between the many aspects of Escobar's criminal empire.

Another key element of the assault on the Medellin cartel was the emergence early in 1993 of a mysterious vigilante group, People Persecuted by Pablo Escobar (*Perseguidos por Pablo Escobar*, or *Los Pepes*), which preferred killing individuals rather than trying to capture them for trial. Many details are still unknown, but *Los Pepes* was apparently supported unofficially by the Colombian police, along with the factions within the Medellin cartel as well as the Cali cartel, which – as a business undertaking – provided human intelligence on the activities of the members of their rivals in the Medellin cartel.

Los Pepes took credit for the murders that began to spread among Escobar's associates, as well as the bombing of facilities such as drug labs, air strips, and residences. As a result of these various pressures, key Escobar supporters were killed, imprisoned, or forced to leave the country.

Escobar himself became increasing isolated, and by the fall of 1993 his once elaborate support network was reduce to a single bodyguard. On December 2, 1993, the Colombian police, using direction-finding equipment, located Escobar in Medellin while he was making a phone call to his son. He was shot and killed in the firefight that followed, and the dissolution of the already seriously weakened Medellin cartel quickly followed.

After Escobar was dead, law enforcement officials turned their attention to uncovering the way the drug lords in Cali did business. It turned out that, after the death of Escobar, the Cali cartel, which had played a role in the destruction of its rivals in Medellin, took over most of the trade and changed the business model. It was less flamboyant, believing that such excesses only drew the attention of law enforcement and made the cartel more vulnerable. Violence continued to be an essential element, however. In addition, the Cali cartel offered a purer product at a lower price. With supplies of raw coca from Peru and Ecuador being disrupted, the Cali drug lords expanded coca cultivation in Colombia and also diversified into growing opium poppies, the source of heroin. In addition, the Cali cartel shifted shipment routes to pass through Central America and Mexico, and expanded their markets into Europe and Asia.

To counter the new threat of the Cali cartel, analysts needed to refine their assessments of vulnerabilities and countermeasures. In addition, the U.S. government provided large amounts of equipment to the Colombian army to increase the resources that would be needed against a more widespread and diversified target. More effort was also put into eradicating the coca crop, with information on the size and location of the crop often based on satellite imagery. Analysts worked out patterns of shipments, making it possible to seize drugs and arrest key personnel. A few of those arrested agreed to work with the government, providing valuable human intelligence on the organizational context of the shadowy network. Some of these confidential informants later appeared as witnesses in court.

In June 1995, Colombian authorities, with assistance from U.S. agencies, arrested Gilberto Rodriguez Orejuela (1939–), who was one of cofounders of the Cali cartel and served as its strategic planner. Two months later, his brother Miguel (1943–), who was the operations manager, was arrested. The two brothers, along with several other leaders of the cartel, were put on trial and received stiff sentences.

After the defeat of the Cali cartel, the nature of the drug trade in Colombia evolved further. Their successors have decentralized their networks even further, making them more flexible and resilient. Instead of large cartels, hundreds of small groups now make up a decentralized network that handles the main functions. These small, specialized groups come together quickly to carry out one operation, then they break up and recombine later into a different grouping to carry out another. Rather than use the telephone, they prefer to use disposable cell phones, the Internet, and commercial encryption. All of this decentralization has made it much more difficult to monitor the drug smugglers' activities. The traditional strategy based on kingpins is of little use in this environment, so the analytic focus is on supporting the bottom-up network analysis that had been so productive against Escobar's Medellin cartel.

Law enforcement intelligence analysts also found it important to use many of the techniques that would be applied to understand legitimate international business. Although the cartels have become less structured over time, they still have a careful division of labor, with individuals and small groups having specific functions, such as production, transport, distribution, sales, financing, and security. Like any business, they pay close attention to the efficiency of each function as well as to the system as a whole.

Analysts also found that they had to get beyond mirror imaging and try to see the world as the drug lords do. Law enforcement views the world in terms of jurisdictions (local, national, and, to a limited extent, international) in which it has authority. In contrast, international criminals, such as drug lords, see the world holistically, with their main focus on where and how to make money. They are not concerned with borders and different jurisdictions, except to the extent that they offer them opportunities.

As in so many cases, in law enforcement and elsewhere, it was crucial to collect and integrate information from a wide variety of sources. Reports from confidential informants, for example, could confirm and illuminate data from wiretaps, which often lacked context.

For all of the elaborate collection and analysis, in these examples (as in many others) there was an element of luck, such as in finally locating Escobar as a result of his ill-advised call to his son.

The defeat of the Colombian cartels also depended on overcoming bureaucratic barriers. Despite the usual distrust and rivalry, there was interagency cooperation. Having plenty of financial and personnel resources was also important.

Questions for Further Thought

How would either using various methodologies, such as financial and network analysis, or looking at the political impact of corruption be helpful in investigating other cases of organized crime, including white collar crimes, such as embezzlement, fraud, money laundering, theft of technology, and computer crimes? Are there any other perspectives that could also contribute?

Much of the take-down of the Medellin cartel was done outside of the courtroom, whereas the Cali cases went to trial. From an analytic perspective, what accounts for the different ways in which the authorities handled these cases?

How might some of the methods used against the drug cartels be applied to counterterrorism?

Recommended Reading

Bowden, Mark, *Killing Pablo: The Hunt for the World's Greatest Outlaw*, New York: Atlantic Monthly Press, 2001.

Chepesiuk, Ronald, *The Bullet and the Bribe: Taking Down Colombia's Cali Drug Cartel*, Westport, CT: Praeger, 2003.

Livingstone, Grace, *Inside Colombia: Drugs, Democracy, and War*, New Brunswick, NJ: Rutgers University Press, 2004.

Rabasa, Angel, and Chalk, Peter, *Colombian Labyrinth: The Synergy of Drugs and Insurgency and Its Implications for Regional Stability*, Santa Monica, CA: RAND, 2001.

35

Wen Ho Lee

O N SEPTEMBER 25, 1992, CHINA TESTED A NEW TYPE OF NUCLEAR BOMB. For the next several years, analysts and scientists in the United States studied data on the test; in time, scientists at the Los Alamos nuclear labs, where the first U.S. nuclear weapons had been developed, became worried that the test showed that the Chinese were developing dramatically smaller warheads. If true, this represented a dramatic potential increase in China's nuclear capabilities. Miniaturized warheads could go on mobile missiles that would be harder to detect, and eventually they could be used as multiple warheads on strategic intercontinental missiles. The scientists were concerned that the Chinese could only have made such progress if they had based their warhead designs, in part, on nuclear weapons technology stolen from the United States. These fears appeared to be confirmed by a 1995 Central Intelligence Agency (CIA) report, based on 1988 documents, stating that the new Chinese bomb was similar to American technology.

Counterespionage investigations are among the most daunting challenges for intelligence analysts. It can be difficult to determine for certain, especially over the short term, whether espionage has even taken place. Spies are often experienced professionals who know how to cover their tracks. Even if there are well-founded suspicions, coming up with evidence that can hold up in court can be demanding. In any case, the investigation is almost certain to require considerable amounts of time, money, and expertise, with an uncertain outcome.

Nonetheless, given the possibility that there could be a spy – or spies – inside some of the most sensitive installations of the United States, the Department of Energy (DOE), which runs the U.S. nuclear labs and is responsible for security at them, asked the Federal Bureau of Investigation (FBI) to investigate. After a brief inquiry, the FBI replied that there was not enough evidence that a crime had been committed. Therefore, the DOE launched its own investigation.

DOE investigators soon focused on one hypothesis: suspicion of Wen Ho Lee, a software technician at Los Alamos who had been born in Taiwan. The investigators uncovered that in 1982 Lee had offered to help a fellow Taiwanese American being investigated in another case of possible nuclear espionage. Initially Lee had denied his involvement in the case. When confronted, however, he admitted his offer to assist. In 1986 and 1988, he had attended conferences in China, where officials had asked him about his work. These contacts had resembled recruitment pitches by intelligence services, with appeals to helping the homeland and strokes to his ego. He had also given unclassified information to Taiwanese officials, when asked, and had done consulting work for a Taiwanese institute. Lee had delayed fully reporting all of these contacts with foreign nuclear scientists, as he was required to do. Lee and his wife hosted Chinese delegations when they visited Los Alamos, and, during a 1994 visit, the head of China's nuclear program had recognized Lee among a group of other scientists and thanked him for his help. Lee had also been informed that he would be laid off if personnel cuts were made at the labs, so he may have been resentful.

The case had its ambiguities, however. Lee and his wife had been working with the CIA and FBI when they hosted the Chinese delegations. There was no proof that he had revealed any classified information on his trips abroad. More broadly, scientists were used to exchange information internationally as a normal part of their work, and the U.S. government, in an effort to improve relations with Beijing, was sharing a wide range of technology with the Chinese. In 1996, the DOE turned the results of its investigation of Lee over to the FBI, but the Bureau did not think it was important enough to make it a high priority.

Over the next several years there were a number of inquiries into the issue of Chinese espionage in the United States. In 1997, the CIA assessed that the new Chinese bomb was not a duplicate of an American weapon. This assessment raised the possibility that the Chinese could have developed miniaturization largely on their own. The following year a Congressional investigation concluded that there had been large-scale Chinese espionage, but it did not give Lee as an example. Then, in 1999, there were two studies by U.S. intelligence officials. The first concurred that Chinese espionage had occurred but noted that the contribution of spying to the new Chinese miniaturized bomb was uncertain. The second determined that security at nuclear labs was terrible and that the miniaturization technology was widely available.

While these investigations were going on, another scientist – not Wen Ho Lee – admitted to passing nuclear secrets to China, suggesting that there might be an unknown number of spies that could be passing American technology to the Chinese. In fact, the typical way in which the Chinese intelligence service operated was to stay below the counterespionage radar by having many unprofessional assets (such as students, journalists, tourists, businessmen, and scientists) make small and single acquisitions and then return to China before they aroused suspicion.

Meanwhile the low-priority FBI investigation continued, and it did uncover some suspicious activity. It turned out that for years Lee had moved huge amounts of sensitive – but very little of it actually classified – data on the design of nuclear weapons to unclassified computers at Los Alamos. Once there, it could be accessed by unauthorized outsiders. When asked about the downloads, Lee said he was backing up his files. When it became clear that he was under investigation, he downloaded the information on to tapes, most of which were never found, and then deleted the files. After he was denied access to his office in a sensitive area of Los Alamos because he was under investigation, he snuck back into his work space.

There continued to be ambiguities, however. In a 1998 sting operation, an FBI agent, pretending to be a Chinese official, called Lee and tried to get him to come to a meeting; Lee refused. He was given several polygraph examinations, with mixed results. Investigators never found any proof that Lee passed classified information to a foreign government. Finally, the CIA said that, after a review, it was unsure about the accuracy of the 1995 report than the new Chinese bomb was based on U.S. technology.

Nonetheless, in March 1999 Los Alamos labs fired Lee for mishandling classified information. Later in the year he was arrested and denied bail because of the seriousness of the concerns. Prosecutors started work on more than fifty charges related to espionage.

Lee spent nine months in prison. During this time it became clear that the U.S. government had not been able to put together a case that would hold up in court. Experts claimed that the material that Lee had downloaded was not classified or essential for warhead miniaturization. Moreover, his lawyers had skillfully shifted the issue from espionage to ethnic profiling by claiming that Lee had been singled out for investigation largely because he was Chinese. In September 2000, Lee pleaded guilty to one charge of mishandling classified information, was sentenced to time served, and was then released. The judge handling the case apologized to him for being wrongly persecuted based largely on his ethnicity.

Questions for Further Thought

What is the strength of the evidence for the hypothesis embodied in the outcome of the court case: that Lee was innocent of the accusations that he was a spy? For the hypothesis that he was a spy? That there was espionage, but it was conducted by someone else? That there was no spy at all?

What were some of the analytic errors that investigators made?

What would a clever spy look like to an outside observer?

Recommended Reading

Lee, Wen Ho, *My Country Versus Me: The First-Hand Account by the Los Alamos Scientist Who Was Falsely Accused of Being a Spy*, New York: Hyperion, 2001.

Strober, Dan, and Hoffman, Ian, *A Convenient Spy: Wen Ho Lee and the Politics of Nuclear Espionage*, New York: Simon & Schuster, 2001.

Trulock, Notra, *Code Name Kindred Spirit: Inside the Chinese Nuclear Espionage Scandal*, San Francisco, CA: Encounter Books, 2003.

36

9/11

I N THE SPRING OF 1999, OSAMA BIN LADEN (1957–), the head of the al-Qaeda terrorist group, agreed to support a plan submitted by Khalid Sheikh Mohammed (1964–) to use airplanes as weapons to crash into buildings, or what they came to call the "planes operation." In the months that followed, they selected targets, including the World Trade Center in New York City and the White House, the Capitol, and the Pentagon in Washington. As the plans matured, bin Laden picked a group of young men who had attended al-Qaeda training camps in Afghanistan – Mohamed Atta, Nawaf al-Hazmi, Ziad Jarrah, Khalid al-Mihdhar, and Marwan al-Shehhi – to pilot the aircraft. The planning was done in extreme secrecy. None of these individuals knew how to pilot an aircraft, however, so two essential steps for the operation to succeed were to get them into the United States and to get them trained as pilots. Could U.S. intelligence analysts detect what was going on in time to prevent an attack in the United States?

Two of the intended pilots, Hazmi and Mihdhar, had fought with their fellow Muslims in Bosnia earlier in the decade, in addition to having traveled to Afghanistan for training. Therefore, intelligence analysts were likely to see them as suspicious. Nonetheless, they were granted visas by the State Department. The other potential hijackers had no derogatory information on file, and thus were indistinguishable (from the point of view of being potential threats) from thousands of other Middle Eastern men traveling internationally; they too had no trouble getting visas.

In late December 1999, the National Security Agency, which monitors international communications, detected that Mihdhar, along with a group of other men (one of whom as identified only by his first name, "Nawaf"), would be traveling to Kuala Lumpur, Malaysia. The Central Intelligence Agency (CIA) tracked Mihdhar as he proceeded to Kuala Lumpur and, working with liaison services, determined that he attended a January 2000 meeting there hosted by an al-Qaeda affiliated group, Jemaah Islamiya. Photos were taken of Mihdhar and the other attendees, but there was no audio surveillance, so the analysts could not be sure about the purpose of the meeting. They assumed that the gathering was suspicious but, given the record of terrorist activities to date, they also assumed that any attack that might result would be overseas, not in the United States.

After the Kuala Lumpur meeting, the CIA lost track of Mihdhar. Because neither Mihdhar nor Hazmi was on the watch list, they were permitted to enter the United States in January 2000. By March 2000, CIA analysts had figured out that "Nawaf" was Hazmi and that both Mihdhar and Hazmi had visas and tickets for the United States. Moreover, Saudi Arabian liaison identified Mihdhar and Hazmi as al-Qaeda members. A Federal Bureau of Investigation (FBI) agent working on terrorism in the Counterterrorism Center at CIA headquarters drafted a memo that would have passed to other parts of the government the CIA's information on Hazmi and Mihdhar's membership in al-Qaeda and that they might be traveling to the United States, but it was never approved.

After arriving in the United States, Mihdhar and Hazmi settled in San Diego, where they actually had contact with an FBI informant. Again, because the FBI had no reason to be suspicious of them, it took no action. Neither of the two ever learned much English, and thus could not complete their assignment to learn how to pilot large airliners. Therefore, their job was changed to providing "muscle" to assist in taking over the aircraft, and al-Qaeda had to look for other pilots.

In May and June 2000, Atta, Jarrah, and Shehhi entered the United States. As they had no records of criminal or terrorist activity, they were not stopped by immigration authorities. They soon enrolled in flight schools in Florida. Hani Hanjour, who already knew the basics of being a pilot, arrived in December and went to Arizona for refresher training.

In July 2000, an agent in the FBI's Phoenix field office notified his headquarters and the CIA about his concerns regarding the unusual number of Middle Eastern men in local flight schools and his worry that bin Laden might be behind it. The agent in Phoenix recommended a national effort to compile information about such students. FBI headquarters found no information on the names that Phoenix provided and believed that a huge effort to check all of the flight schools in the United States, which might only result in similar dead ends, would be a waste of resources. Therefore, no further action was taken.

Between April and June of 2001, another eight operatives arrived; their job was to assist in using force to take over the airplanes. Again, none of them had difficulty getting a visa or being cleared by immigration. In August, however, a twentieth operative tried to enter; he was turned back by immigration authorities because he had no apparent business or ties in the United States – not because he was suspected of terrorism. While in the United States, the al-Qaeda operatives received wire transfers of money from Mohammed and other al-Qaeda operatives, and they opened bank accounts and used ATM cards. Some travelled extensively, apparently to observe airline procedures; many of the others made fewer trips, including some trips abroad. Apparently under instruction to avoid attention from law enforcement, they maintained a low profile, committing no crimes and taking no overt hostile action. Except for an occasional traffic stop by the police, they succeeded. There was virtually nothing to distinguish them from thousands of other foreign tourists and students. Between August 25 and September 5, the al-Qaeda teams purchased tickets for flights on September 11.

Meanwhile, during the spring and summer of 2001, indicators surged suggesting that a major al-Qaeda operation was being prepared. There were reports of threats in Boston, Genoa (where there was going to be a G-8 summit), London, New York, Rome, and other cities; further reports mentioned Bahrain, Israel, Italy, Jordan, Kuwait, Saudi Arabia, Yemen, and other countries. Reports said that the method of attack would be high explosives, aircraft hijacking, or further attacks on embassies, among others. Many said that something spectacular was in the works. When talking with visitors, Bin Laden sometimes made vague references to a big attack against U.S. targets that would happen in the near future. Analysts believed that all of this reporting suggested that something major was going on, but there was not enough specific detail in any of the reporting to make the warning a higher priority on the crowded agenda of senior decision makers.

In response, though, some actions were taken. U.S. Navy ships were moved, an exercise in Jordan was canceled, and an embassy was temporarily closed. Preventative arrests of suspects were made in several countries. Some of the threat information was passed to law enforcement officials in the United States, but the officials were not sure what they were supposed to do with it.

In early August, President Bush, concerned about the drumbeat of threat reporting, asked his CIA briefer for a summary of what was known. The result was an item that was included in the August 6, 2001, President's Daily Brief, one of the few pieces of analysis on terrorism for senior consumers from 2001 that has been released (see Figure 27).

Declassified and Approved
for Release, 10 April 2004

Bin Ladin Determined To Strike in US

Clandestine, foreign government, and media reports indicate Bin Ladin since 1997 has wanted to conduct terrorist attacks in the US. Bin Ladin implied in US television interviews in 1997 and 1998 that his followers would follow the example of World Trade Center bomber Ramzi Yousef and "bring the fighting to America."

After US missile strikes on his base in Afghanistan in 1998, Bin Ladin told followers he wanted to retaliate in Washington, according to a ████████████ service.

An Egyptian Islamic Jihad (EIJ) operative told an ███████ service at the same time that Bin Ladin was planning to exploit the operative's access to the US to mount a terrorist strike.

The millennium plotting in Canada in 1999 may have been part of Bin Ladin's first serious attempt to implement a terrorist strike in the US. Convicted plotter Ahmed Ressam has told the FBI that he conceived the idea to attack Los Angeles International Airport himself, but that Bin Ladin lieutenant Abu Zubaydah encouraged him and helped facilitate the operation. Ressam also said that in 1998 Abu Zubaydah was planning his own US attack.

Ressam says Bin Ladin was aware of the Los Angeles operation.

Although Bin Ladin has not succeeded, his attacks against the US Embassies in Kenya and Tanzania in 1998 demonstrate that he prepares operations years in advance and is not deterred by setbacks. Bin Ladin associates surveilled our Embassies in Nairobi and Dar es Salaam as early as 1993, and some members of the Nairobi cell planning the bombings were arrested and deported in 1997.

Al-Qa'ida members—including some who are US citizens—have resided in or traveled to the US for years, and the group apparently maintains a support structure that could aid attacks. Two al-Qa'ida members found guilty in the conspiracy to bomb our Embassies in East Africa were US citizens, and a senior EIJ member lived in California in the mid-1990s.

A clandestine source said in 1998 that a Bin Ladin cell in New York was recruiting Muslim-American youth for attacks.

We have not been able to corroborate some of the more sensational threat reporting, such as that from a ██████████████ *service in 1998 saying that Bin Ladin wanted to hijack a US aircraft to gain the release of "Blind Shaykh" 'Umar 'Abd al-Rahman and other US-held extremists.*

continued

For the President Only   ███████████   Declassified and Approved
6 August 2001   for Release, 10 April 2004

Figure 27. The August 6, 2001, President's Daily Brief Item on al-Qaeda (courtesy of the CIA)

— Nevertheless, FBI information since that time indicates patterns of suspicious activity in this country consistent with preparations for hijackings or other types of attacks, including recent surveillance of federal buildings in New York.

The FBI is conducting approximately 70 full field investigations throughout the US that it considers Bin Ladin–related. CIA and the FBI are investigating a call to our Embassy in the UAE in May saying that a group of Bin Ladin supporters was in the US planning attacks with explosives.

For the President Only
6 August 2001

Figure 27 (*continued*)

Meanwhile FBI and CIA personnel continued to investigate. In June 2001, there was a meeting of CIA analysts and agents from the FBI field office in New York City. The CIA officers produced surveillance photos of the Kuala Lumpur meeting and asked if the agents knew anyone in the photos. The Bureau personnel asked for more details; but, except for Mihdhar's name, the CIA analysts declined to provide any more information.

Other FBI agents investigating the October 12, 2000, attempt to sink the *USS Cole* in Aden, Yemen, were convinced that al-Qaeda was responsible for that attack. They believed that the Aden plot, along with the August 7, 1998, attacks on two U.S. embassies in Kenya and Tanzania, showed that al-Qaeda was an organization with significant resources and a global reach. When they asked for information on al-Qaeda suspects from the CIA, however, they got little assistance.

Both agencies operated within what they believed to be strict barriers, known informally as "the wall," between intelligence gathering and court-room prosecution. Justice Department lawyers had determined that intelligence gathering and criminal prosecution had to be kept separate to keep clandestinely gathered information, which might not meet constitutional standards, from potentially preventing a successful trial. Agencies involved in clandestine collection, such as the CIA and the National Security Agency, for their part, were legally obligated to protect methods and sources.

In August 2001, agents from the FBI's Minneapolis field office detained a French national, Zacarias Moussaoui, because of his suspicious activity at a local flight school. A quick investigation uncovered that he had traveled to Pakistan (the usual transit point to terrorist training camps in Afghanistan), was reluctant to talk about his religious beliefs, and had large amounts of cash that he could not explain. They also contacted the French government, which said that Moussaoui had contacts with Muslim extremists. Unknown to them at the time, he was yet another al-Qaeda operative in the United States as a back-up for the planes operation or a follow-on wave of attacks. The agents asked FBI headquarters in Washington for permission to search Moussaoui's laptop, but their request was denied by officials in Washington who believed they did not have sufficient probable cause.

During July and August, FBI agents in CIA's Counterterrorism Center were reviewing old material and came across the records on Mihdhar and Hazmi. They found enough information in various databases to arouse alarm, and on August 24 they put the two names on the watch list. It was too late, of course, as the two were already in the United States. The FBI agents also started the procedures for a domestic investigation to find and question the suspects. As had been the case in the past, concerns about "the wall" slowed down procedures, and on September 10 the investigation was only getting started. On the morning of September 11, nineteen al-Qaeda operatives passed through airport security without being stopped and boarded four airliners.

A special commission later reviewed the records leading up to the attacks of September 11, 2001. The 9/11 Commission criticized analysts for not having Red Teams that tried to think like the adversary or imagine how an airplane could be used as a weapon, as well as what preparations for such an attack might look like and what relevant reporting requirements collectors should have. More broadly, the Commission took the intelligence community to task for not gathering into one place the diverse data that were available and not conducting a comprehensive review of the terrorist threat. Those familiar with the history of intelligence will recall that similar concerns after the attack on Pearl Harbor were among the reasons for founding the CIA.

A fundamental problem not addressed in detail by the 9/11 Commission was that the analysts were not asking the right questions. They were focused on threats abroad, which was not unreasonable, given that there had not been serious attacks by foreigners in the United States. Analysts were also worried predominantly about the danger from terrorists gaining possession of weapons of mass destruction, not only because of high potential impact but also because there was considerable reporting about this aspect. With the benefit of hindsight, however, the analysts should have been considering how to prevent foreigners from conducting terrorist attacks in the United States, even if there was little evidence on this issue.

It was also the case that crucial information, such as details on al-Qaeda's planning, was not collected. Tightly knit terrorist groups were hard to penetrate with human sources, and technical means were of limited use.

The 9/11 attacks are the most significant example since Pearl Harbor of the perils of the bureaucratic environment in which intelligence analysts work. Too few analysts were dealing with too much inaccurate or irrelevant information. Not only was there a weak tradition of cooperation, but many believed that not sharing information was required by law and regulation.

The shock of the 9/11 attacks prompted the largest reorganization of the U.S. intelligence community since the 1950s. Legislation in 2002 created the Department of Homeland Security to bring various components such as immigration, border control, the Secret Service, Coast Guard, and others under central management. Two years later, another law created the post of Director of National Intelligence to improve coordination among the various intelligence agencies.

Questions for Further Thought

How were some of the events leading up to the 9/11 attacks similar to the
situation in Tokyo before the 1995 attacks on the subway?

In retrospect, what is right – in terms of being accurate and useful – about
the August 6, 2001, item from the President's Daily Brief? What is wrong
or inadequate about it?

Much of the standard analytic framework for indications and warning was
derived from observing a nation's transition from peace to war. How would
this framework have to be changed to anticipate terrorist attacks?

The official response to 9/11 focused on reorganization. Is the structure of
intelligence organizations the only problem, or even the main one?

Recommended Reading

Coll, Steve, *Ghost Wars: The Secret History of the CIA, Afghanistan, and Bin Laden from the
Soviet Invasion to September 10, 2001*, New York: Penguin, 2004.

Gunaratna, Rohan, *Inside Al Qaeda: Global Network of Terror*, New York: Columbia University Press, 2002.

McDermott, Terry, *Perfect Soldiers: The Hijackers – Who They Were and Why They Did It*,
New York: HarperCollins, 2005.

National Commission on Terrorist Attacks Upon the United States, *9/11 Commission
Report: Final Report of the National Commission on Terrorist Attacks Upon the United
States*, New York: W. W. Norton, 2004; available online at: http://www.9–11commission.
gov/report/index.htm.

Riedel, Bruce, *The Search for Al Qaeda: Its Leadership, Ideology, and Future*, Washington,
DC: Brookings Institution Press, 2008.

Sageman, Marc, *Leaderless Jihad: Terror Networks in the Twenty-First Century*, Philadelphia,
PA: University of Pennsylvania Press, 2008.

Sageman, Marc, *Understanding Terror Networks*, Philadelphia, PA: University of Pennsylvania Press, 2004.

Wright, Lawrence, *The Looming Tower: Al-Qaeda and the Road to 9/11*, New York: Alfred
A. Knopf, 2006.

37

Anthrax Attacks

O N OCTOBER 2, 2001, A PHOTO EDITOR FOR AMERICAN MEDIA INC. checked into a hospital in Boca Raton, Florida (which is not far from Fort Lauderdale and Delray Beach), complaining of flulike symptoms. After a series of tests, doctors diagnosed that he had inhaled spores of anthrax, a disease not seen in its natural form in the United States since 1976, and one of the most destructive biological warfare agents. The photo editor died on October 5, and, in the meantime, a second employee of American Media was hospitalized with symptoms of inhalation anthrax. An investigation revealed that the anthrax spores had reached the American Media offices through the mail, but the original letter and envelope had since been destroyed, and it was impossible to determine any further details about who had mailed it. Postal officials decided against closing down the postal system because they were concerned that such a move might generate panic.

Because of the unusual nature of the disease and the timing – just three weeks after the 9/11 attacks – terrorism was the initial hypothesis. One of the employees of a tabloid published by American Media recalled that the paper had recently published an article that had mocked Osama bin Laden. Another editor at American Media had a spouse who was a real estate agent who had rented apartments to several of the future hijackers.

Further investigation revealed that in June 2001, Ahmed al-Haznawi, a Saudi national in the United States on a tourist visa who would later be one of the nineteen hijackers, went to a doctor's office in Fort Lauderdale seeking treatment for a skin lesion. He was accompanied by Ziad Jarrah (a Lebanese citizen who was attending a local flight school), who would be another one of the hijackers. Material from the wound was never tested in a laboratory, but the doctor's description of the lesion was consistent with cutaneous anthrax.

That same summer, Mohamed Atta, an Egyptian citizen living in Delray Beach and taking flight training nearby, visited firms in the area that did crop dusting. He examined the aircraft that were used for crop dusting, and later he inquired about obtaining a loan to purchase a plane suitable for this purpose. That summer Atta also visited a local doctor to get treatment for a skin rash.

On October 12, news reports revealed that letters containing anthrax spores had been received several weeks before at the New York City headquarters of the television news organizations ABC, CBS, and NBC, as well as at the offices of the *New York Post*. Several staffers of the media firms developed cutaneous anthrax, but none died. The letters to NBC and the *Post* were recovered. They had been mailed from Trenton, New Jersey, on September 18, and inside was the following short, hand-written message, which was identical in each letter:

09-11-01
This is next
Take Penacilin [*sic*] Now
Death to America
Death to Israel
Allah is great

On October 15, staffers in the Hart Senate Office Building in Washington opened a letter addressed to Minority Leader Thomas Daschle that contained anthrax spores. This letter had also been mailed from Trenton, with a postmark of October 9, and it included a similar hand-written message.

9-11-01
You can not stop us
We have this anthrax
You die now
Are you afraid?
Death to America
Death to Israel
Allah is great

The text of the notes accompanying the later attacks appeared to confirm the hypothesis that these were terrorist attacks, although by mid-October, of course, all of the original hijackers were dead. After U.S. forces toppled the Taliban government of Afghanistan in the fall of 2001, investigation of al-Qaeda camps where most of the hijackers had trained revealed facilities where primitive efforts had been made to manufacture chemical and biological weapons, although no actual weapons of mass destruction were found.

Quick action was taken to administer antibiotics to persons on Capitol Hill who might have been exposed, and no one died. Countermeasures for postal workers were not taken as quickly. Two men who worked in a mail-handling facility in Washington died from inhalation anthrax, and several postal workers in New Jersey developed the symptoms of cutaneous or inhalation anthrax, but survived. In November, a second letter, addressed to Senator Leahy and postmarked 9 October in Trenton, arrived at the Hart Office Building. Its danger was realized, and it was sent to a laboratory for study before it could harm anyone.

On October 31, a female hospital worker in New York City died of inhalation anthrax, and, on November 21, an elderly widow in rural Connecticut also died of the disease. Nothing was ever found linking these women to the other targets, and they may have just been random victims of mail that passed though post offices at the same time as the infected letters.

A total of twenty-two people were diagnosed with anthrax, eleven with the cutaneous variety and eleven with inhalation anthrax. Of those with cutaneous anthrax, all survived; of those with inhalational, five died.

As the investigation continued, the original terrorism hypothesis was dropped, even though references to anthrax were found on a laptop computer seized during the 2003 arrest of Khalid Sheikh Mohammed, the mastermind of the 9/11 attacks. By the time the 9/11 Commission Report came out in 2004, there was no mention of this possibility.

Instead, attention shifted to the view that the attacks had to be the work of an insider from a biological weapons program. The type of anthrax used in the attacks was an exceptionally refined and lethal type suitable for military use. It is available from U.S. Army stocks, but also from other laboratories. Whoever prepared the anthrax used in the 2001 attacks had to have considerable knowledge of biological weapons and special facilities for preparation and storage. U.S. officials working on defending the country against biological weapons also acknowledged that, prior to October 2001, their planning had focused on the potential danger of aerosol spray as a means of spreading biological weapons, not on the postal system. According to experts in the field, there are fewer than fifty people in the United States who have the skills needed to manufacture weaponized anthrax.

Starting in 2002, the Federal Bureau of Investigation (FBI) inquiries focused on Dr. Steven Hatfill, a researcher at the U.S. Army's biological weapons center at Fort Detrick, Maryland. He was a vocal critic of U.S. policy toward biological terrorism, warning that an attack was imminent and that the United States was poorly prepared to deal with it. Hatfill sued the government for violating his privacy because of the way in which officials conducted the investigation, and in June 2008 the government admitted that Hatfill was not involved in the anthrax attacks and agreed to pay him $5.8 million as part of an out-of-court settlement. After six years, one of the largest and most complex investigations in FBI history appeared to be at a dead end.

Meanwhile, in 2006, investigators had shifted their attention to Dr. Bruce Ivins, another researcher at Fort Detrick. Ivins had access to anthrax, worked extra hours at night in his laboratory at the time of the attacks, and was concerned that funding was being dropped for the anti-anthrax vaccine on which he was working. Ironically, he had even helped the FBI investigate the case, including one of the letters that had been sent to the Senate. Newly developed forensic technology enabled the FBI to trace the anthrax that was used in the 2001 attacks to the lab in which Ivins worked. He also had a record of mental problems. Ivins killed himself in July 2008 as the Justice Department was preparing to indict him. A few days later, the government announced that he was the only perpetrator of the 2001 attacks and closed the investigation.

Not everyone believes that the anthrax case has been solved, however. People in Congress, the scientific community, among Ivins's coworkers, and in the press claimed that the case was only circumstantial and that there are still unexplained loose ends. For example, Ivins was never definitively linked to the letters that had been mailed from Trenton. There were many other questions: Could the anthrax be traced to other individuals or laboratories besides just Ivins's? Could the trace to his lab be the result of his assistance with the Senate letter?

Questions for Further Thought

How strong was the evidence of a link between the 9/11 plotters and the anthrax attacks? How was it not convincing?

Is there another hypothesis, besides Ivins, that would better fit the disparate evidence? What else would an analyst need to know to formulate and assess a range of alternative hypotheses?

What questions and techniques from counterintelligence investigations might be helpful in resolving this case?

Recommended Reading

Cole, Leonard A., *The Anthrax Letters: A Medical Detective Story*, Washington, DC: National Academies Press, 2003.

Thompson, Marilyn W., *The Killer Strain: Anthrax and a Government Exposed*, New York: HarperCollins, 2003.

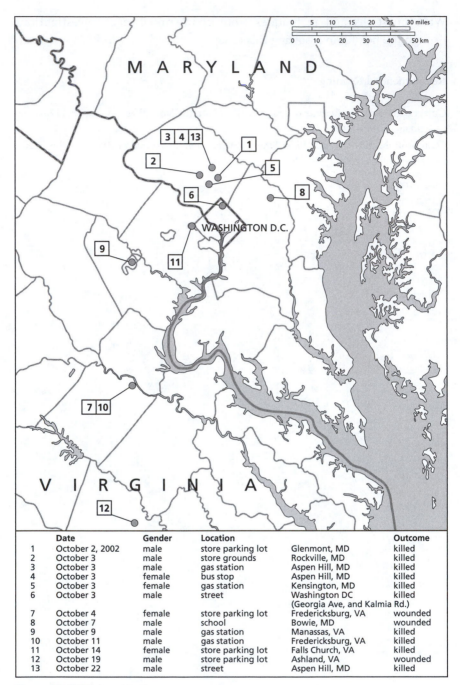

	Date	Gender	Location		Outcome
1	October 2, 2002	male	store parking lot	Glenmont, MD	killed
2	October 3	male	store grounds	Rockville, MD	killed
3	October 3	male	gas station	Aspen Hill, MD	killed
4	October 3	female	bus stop	Aspen Hill, MD	killed
5	October 3	female	gas station	Kensington, MD	killed
6	October 3	male	street	Washington DC (Georgia Ave, and Kalmia Rd.)	killed
7	October 4	female	store parking lot	Fredericksburg, VA	wounded
8	October 7	male	school	Bowie, MD	wounded
9	October 9	male	gas station	Manassas, VA	killed
10	October 11	male	gas station	Fredericksburg, VA	killed
11	October 14	female	store parking lot	Falls Church, VA	killed
12	October 19	male	store parking lot	Ashland, VA	wounded
13	October 22	male	street	Aspen Hill, MD	killed

Figure 28. DC Sniper Attacks

38

DC Snipers

AT 6:02 P.M. ON WEDNESDAY, OCTOBER 2, 2002, A 55-YEAR-OLD WHITE MAN who worked for the federal government was shot to death with a high-powered rifle in the parking lot of a grocery store in Glenmont, Maryland, just north of Washington, DC. A police station was just across the street from the scene of the crime, and an investigation began immediately. The police found a witness who remembered seeing two African-American males in a large, dark car leaving the scene, but there was no other information with enough detail to be useful.

The following day, the investigation became much more urgent when five more individuals were shot and killed in the Maryland suburbs north of the capital city using the same modus operandi – a high-powered rifle fired from a distant, unknown location. The victims were a mixture of age, gender, ethnicity, and occupation. All of the attacks took place outside, but they were at various types of locations including a car dealership, two gas stations, and a shopping mall. Witnesses provided no precise information about a possible perpetrator, but an individual did report seeing a white box truck speeding away from the scene shortly after one of the incidents. Again, there was no other evidence at the scene that was helpful.

What kinds of questions and analytic frameworks would help in catching the perpetrator as quickly as possible and preventing further killings?

Investigators usually start by using models of criminal behavior, based on many past cases. For example, they try to find some kind of connection between killer and victim, because most murders are committed by a person who knows the victim. What, however, could connect such a wide range of victims? In serial killings, another thing that investigators look for is commonalities among the victims that might point toward a possible motive. The Maryland victims, however, were a wide variety of individuals. Moreover, there was nothing to suggest the standard motivations that investigators usually find, such as greed, power, revenge, hate, or escape. Based on records of many cases over a long period of time, there were a number of hypotheses that accounted for the vast majority of crimes; these hypotheses could hopefully provide context and guidance for the Maryland investigation. These included accident, suicide, robbery, domestic violence, or even terrorism. Again, none of the standard investigative categories seemed to fit.

On Friday, October 4, for the third day in a row, there was another shooting. This time it was in a parking lot, and the female victim survived the attack. Again, witnesses provided virtually no useful information. There were no shootings over the weekend.

Now that they had a major serial killer to deal with, police officials in Montgomery County, Maryland, took the lead in organizing the investigation. They took the usual steps, such as offering a reward for information, as well as setting up an operations center with computers, copiers, faxes, phone lines, and television monitors. At the operations center, incoming data from sources, such as crime scene reports or tips from the public, were first prioritized to determine what was accurate and useful. Then there would be checks of records related to the content of the tip, such as databases covering vehicles, weapons, and criminal records. If promising leads emerged, they would be turned over to a team of officers for follow-up in the field or to analysts to see if there were links to other leads.

The local police also established contact with state and federal agencies with more resources, such as the Bureau of Alcohol, Tobacco, Firearms, and Explosives (ATF), the Federal Bureau of Investigation (FBI), the U.S. Marshals at the Justice Department, the Immigration and Naturalization Service (INS), the Secret Service, and the Maryland State Police. The ATF assumed responsibility for analyzing bullet fragments gathered as a result of autopsies and, in time, determined that the same weapon was involved in all of the attacks. The FBI's Behavioral Science Unit provided a profile that assumed that there was a single perpetrator and said that the individual probably had had recent setbacks in his domestic life and had a fascination with guns; they were not sure about the individual's race, however. The FBI also provided a geographic profile based on the time, date, and location of the various incidents. None of these efforts provided any usable leads.

Then, on Monday, October 7, a thirteen-year-old student was wounded outside his school in Bowie, Maryland, east of Washington. A search of the area produced the first concrete clue: a "death" tarot card, with "Call me God" hand-written on one side and "For you Mr. Police, Code: Call me God, Do not release to the press" on the other. There were no fingerprints, deoxyribonucleic acid (DNA), or other identifying data on the card. The police, assuming that the suspect would use this as authentication in any contact, did try to keep the message secret, but a media frenzy regarding the case was already well under way and a distorted version of the message quickly became public. Media commentators also added to the confusion by speculating on various theories, such as that the killer was a white male with military experience.

Three more people were killed and one wounded between October 9 and 19. All four attacks in this phase took place in Virginia at various locations south and west of Washington. During one of these incidents, a witness claimed to have seen an olive-skinned individual leave the scene driving a light-colored van.

In the meantime, law enforcement officials continued to use traditional methods. They solicited tips from the public but found that all were inaccurate and often involved turning someone into the police to settle a score. They also conducted massive roadblocks and traffic stops but realized that they were not really sure what they were looking for. The available facts simply did not fit any previous pattern that would help in identifying a suspect. The police had to conclude that their best hope was that more incidents would present more clues or lead to mistakes by the killer. Interagency cooperation, which had started out being so promising, slipped into disputes over turf and sharing information.

After the October 19 shooting, the authorities recovered a second written message. This one asked for $10 million, which was to be deposited to an account linked to a credit card that had been stolen the previous March. After some confusion, the authorities were finally able to establish direct telephone contact with the shooter on October 21, but were unable to prevent another death, the thirteenth shooting and tenth killing, the following day. The October 22 killing was accompanied by a third note.

Finally, on October 23, pieces that would lead to a solution began to fall into place. An individual in Tacoma, Washington, had been complaining about suspicious activity, including target shooting in his backyard, by a neighbor, John Muhammad (1961–2009). Muhammad had a troubled personal and business life and had been involved in numerous petty crimes. Fingerprints left at the scene of a September shooting incident in Montgomery, Alabama, belonged to Lee Malvo, who was traveling with Muhammad. A blue Chevrolet Caprice with New Jersey tags was registered to Muhammad. Early on the morning of October 24, an alert traveler reported a suspicious car at a rest stop near Frederick, Maryland. The vehicle had the New Jersey plates. Police arrived shortly afterward and arrested Muhammad and Malvo.

It turned out that there had been several missed opportunities in the case. There had been several shooting incidents before October 2, but these had not been linked to Muhammad and Malvo, or to the other incidents. A witness had seen Muhammad and Malvo leave the scene of one of the first attacks, but could give only a general description. Police looking for stolen cars had stopped Muhammad, but because a records check revealed nothing more than a spousal protection order from his estranged wife, they let him go. The dark Caprice had been mentioned in the press as a clue, but police had not focused on it as being any more important than many other reports. Muhammad had made several calls to the tip line using the tarot card code, but they had been lost in the flood of thousands of other calls. All of these are significant in retrospect, but at the time were part of a flood of other leads.

The DC sniper case is another example of the limitations of traditional law enforcement's investigative methods. Procedures that have worked in hundreds, or even thousands, of cases do not always fit. The case also shows how difficult it is, with finite resources, to follow up on every lead. Inevitably, valuable time is spent on what turn out to be dead ends, and valid clues get little or no attention.

Questions for Further Thought

How have investigative procedures improved, or not, since the Lindbergh kidnapping?

How big a role did cognitive biases play in this case? What about other factors that have effected investigations in the past, such as the media or luck?

What are some analytic techniques that might have helped to catch the snipers earlier?

Recommended Reading

Horowitz, Sari, and Ruane, Michael E., *Sniper: Inside the Hunt for the Killers Who Terrorized the Nation*, New York: Random House, 2003.

Moose, Charles A., and Fleming, Charles, *Three Weeks in October: The Manhunt for the Serial Sniper*, New York: Dutton, 2003.

Part VII

Medicine and Business

ONE OF THE MAIN CHARACTERISTICS OF THE CONTEMPORARY WORLD is globalization, or that things all over the planet are connected in ways that might not be obvious at first and that offer both danger and opportunity.

Effective analytic techniques are useful not only in national security and law enforcement. Medical diagnosis and deciding what to prescribe, for example, are based on hypotheses, multiple sources of information, and evaluation of data, as well as the physician's skill and experience. The risks of misdiagnosis, as well as inappropriate medicines and procedures, also have to be taken into account. Physicians readily admit that this process is as much art as science, with intuition playing a major role.

In the business world, reliable information and context about factors such as supply and demand in the present and the future have always been important for the bottom line. Business functions such as market research, risk analysis, and protecting against industrial espionage have parallels in national security analysis. The implications of technological change are also a major concern. Companies, it turns out, can be as susceptible to surprise and uncertainty as are political leaders or military commanders, as demonstrated in the global economic crisis of 2008.

Although analysts working in national security, law enforcement, medicine, and business have much to learn from each other, there are also important differences. Both medicine and business are different from political and military intelligence because, among other things, the stakes are rarely as high, and it is not legal for them to use clandestine means to collect information.

39

Severe Acute Respiratory Syndrome

I N JANUARY 2003, THERE WAS PUBLIC PANIC IN SOUTHERN CHINA IN RES-
ponse to the rapid spread of a serious respiratory disease. People in large
numbers were buying both modern medicines and traditional herbal cures,
but nothing seemed to work. Local health officials came up with a diagnosis
of what they termed "atypical pneumonia," even though the disease did
not respond to antibiotics that would normally have been effective against
pneumonia. Provincial and national governments released little information
beyond claiming that there had been only a handful of deaths and that the
situation was under control, so the outside world had little sense of what
was happening. In the months that followed, approximately 5,300 people in
China became infected, 349 of whom died.

Over the winter, the situation continued to worsen, and by late February
the disease had spread to Hong Kong. Officials there were already dealing
with an outbreak of avian influenza and were worried that the new disease
might be influenza. Symptoms, or indicators, of what they feared might be
a new wave of influenza included fever, dry cough, and body aches, which
were typical of several diseases such as pneumonia and influenza. The new
ailment, however, was more serious, acted more quickly, and spread more
rapidly. Hong Kong is, of course, a major transportation hub, and travelers
passing through the city spread the disease to elsewhere in China, as well as
to Canada, Singapore, and Vietnam.

When the mystery disease became more than just a local problem, epidemiologists began applying their standard methods of investigation. The
key questions they asked were the following: What is the cause? How is
it transmitted? How long is the incubation period during which carriers
are unaware that they have the disease? What are the symptoms when it
becomes evident? What treatments are effective? As part of their investigation, doctors in Hong Kong tested a traveler from southern China for avian

flu; the test came back negative, but this result did not trigger any particular alarm.

By the middle of March the disease was spreading rapidly in Hong Kong, particularly among health workers and young people, who would not normally have been susceptible to respiratory disease. In one Hong Kong hospital, the staff tried to help a patient who was having difficulty breathing by using a nebulizer, which pushed medication into his lungs using a fine mist. This perfectly normal treatment turned out to be a terribly wrong thing to do, as it later turned out that the unknown disease was actually spread by droplets from the carrier's lungs, so every time he exhaled, he transmitted it.

With the disease spreading and the number of deaths mounting, the level of risk of a global pandemic was increasing, so the United Nations (UN) World Health Organization (WHO) got involved, focusing on the issue of transmission. On March 12, 2003, scientists at the WHO put out an alert about the increasing spread of "atypical pneumonia" and recommended isolation of patients with the disease as a precaution. Three days later, worried that, in a globalized world, air travel was an especially efficient way to spread infectious diseases, WHO officials issued an emergency travel advisory. They decided to call the disease Severe Acute Respiratory Syndrome (SARS) and admitted that there was still much that they did not know about it. WHO doctors believed, however, that the incubation period was approximately ten days, during which time carriers could spread the disease without knowing that they had it.

In Hong Kong, authorities closed schools and started tracing the contacts of persons who exhibited symptoms of SARS. Voluntarily, large numbers of people stopped going to places where crowds gathered, such as movie theaters and restaurants. The eventual totals in Hong Kong were some 1,750 individuals who became infected, with 299 deaths.

Canada was the only country outside Asia in which a significant number of people became infected with SARS. Response there was delayed because the first victim, a woman returning from Hong Kong in February 2003, died without having gone to a hospital or having been diagnosed as having the disease. Her son, who had not traveled to Hong Kong, checked into a hospital and spread the disease through the Canadian health care system. An accurate assessment of the threat in Canada was not made until late March. After Canadian authorities grasped what was going on, they issued a travel advisory and isolated thousands of potential carriers. By July, the spread was under control, but approximately 250 had been infected, of whom 43 died.

All this time, the government of China had been strikingly unhelpful. Concerned that changing their line about "atypical pneumonia" might undermine Chinese prestige, officials continued to maintain that the disease was neither avian flu nor SARS, that the situation was under control, and that there was no need for outside involvement. It was not until late April that China became more cooperative, after the Minister of Health and the Mayor of Beijing were fired.

In the meantime, scientists all over the world had been trying to identify the mystery disease so that effective means to contain it, and hopefully cure it, could be found. One problem was that initially there had not been much interest in the hypothesis that it was a new disease. Some investigators, however, kept an open mind and considered a range of possibilities. Since mid-March, a team in Hong Kong had been working on a virus that they had managed to isolate for study. Viruses are extremely primitive forms of life that require a host in which to survive. They also mutate rapidly, meaning that preventative vaccines have to constantly be redesigned to keep up with new forms.

At first the team was not sure that they had made the right identification, because their sample was not acting as fast as SARS did in its human hosts. Therefore, they conducted a second test; this time, they received results closer to what they were looking for. To obtain further verification, they observed whether blood from victims would produce antibodies when mixed with the sample under investigation, and it did. They also used blood from individuals who did not have SARS, and there was no increase in antibodies. Now they felt confident that they had identified the virus that was causing the disease. When they examined it closely, they determined, on March 21, that it was, in fact, a new disease. Other laboratories were soon able to confirm the results.

Now the key question was this: Where had the virus originated? Again, there was a range of hypotheses, with some scientists publicly proposing that the virus had come from a weapons program or from outer space. Investigators in southern China determined, however, that there had been isolated cases there since November 2002, and that approximately a third of the early victims were individuals who sold exotic animals as food for humans. It was suspected that the virus had developed a mutation that enabled it to spread to humans who were in close contact with the animals – but not by eating their meat.

By early July 2003, countermeasures (such as isolation and close observation of air travelers) stopped the spread of SARS, and the number of cases started to decrease. In the end, approximately 8,000 were infected, of which a little more than 1,700 died. Effective analysis had informed the decisions and quick action that had prevented a global pandemic. It is worth considering what the scenarios could have been if the doctors in Hong Kong and the officials at the WHO had not been so quick and accurate in their work.

The SARS case is an excellent example of asking good questions and being open to other lines of questioning. It also demonstrates the value of anomalies and disconfirming evidence. Initially, insufficient weight was attached to the fact that the disease did not respond to the usual antibiotics that would have been effective against pneumonia, along with the fact that it was striking an unusual group of victims. As a result, countermeasures were inappropriate, and the disease spread. Later, the scientists in Hong Kong who were the first to correctly identify the disease used the correct procedure under the scientific method and sought to disprove their hypothesis.

The work of epidemiologists is of special interest to intelligence analysts. As they track infectious diseases, epidemiologists often do not know what they are looking for or what the outcome of their inquiries will be. Epidemiologists have a methodical approach, in which they start by defining the problem, reviewing the literature, and planning what they will need in the way of funds, personnel, and time. They are careful to consult a number of sources, such as other experts, physicians' reports, public records, interviews with the public, and the results of laboratory experiments. All data are carefully collected, reviewed, and analyzed before a report is written.

More broadly, there are also lessons from medical diagnosis, which is the process of identifying a disease based on factors such as the medical history of patients and their families and of patients' complaints. Physicians also examine vital signs (such as pulse and temperature) and the results of physical examinations and laboratory tests. They also depend on their own experience. This is what intelligence analysts call "all-source analysis." Although much of the physicians' work of assessing indicators and drawing inferences is similar to intelligence analysis, there are also important differences. For example, physicians have a much more extensive and detailed database of case information to use as foundations for their judgments, and they recommend a specific corrective action.

Professionals in the medical field, like intelligence analysts and people in general, can make mistakes, of course. Diagnoses are often based on factors such as outdated information, personal experiences that are only a limited sample, and sales pitches from vendors of medicines and equipment. As seen in the SARS case, the wrong diagnosis or analytic framework can have serious consequences. Studies show that formulae based on large databases on the relationships between symptoms and diseases are more accurate than the judgments that physicians make in their heads.

Questions for Further Thought

How was the SARS case similar to, or different from, a counterintelligence or law enforcement investigation?

What was the quality of the evidence? Was it sufficient?

What kind of precedents did the SARS investigators have? Were they helpful?

What are some contemporary problems to which some of the systematic investigative procedures used in the SARS case might usefully be applied?

Recommended Reading

Abraham, Thomas, *Twenty-First Century Plague: The Story of SARS*: Baltimore, MD: Johns Hopkins University Press, 2005.

Groopman, Jerome, *How Doctors Think*, Boston, MA: Houghton Mifflin, 2007.

McLean, Angela, *SARS: A Case Study in Emerging Infections*, Oxford: Oxford University Press, 2005.

World Health Organization, *SARS: How a Global Epidemic Was Stopped*, Geneva: World Health Organization, 2006.

40

New Coke

C OCA COLA IS, OF COURSE, ONE OF THE LARGEST AND BEST KNOWN companies in the world. In the 1980s, however, it was losing market share to Pepsi, its traditional rival. Pepsi was conducting an extensive and successful advertising campaign, trying to attract and lock in young consumers by making Pepsi look hip and stylish.

To respond, Coca Cola executives decided to change its taste; Pepsi was sweeter, so perhaps what Coke needed was a sweeter version. The company had already introduced Diet Coke and Cherry Coke, and concluded that it could safely tinker with the basic recipe of its premier product.

Coca Cola did some market research into customer attitudes, but the approach continued to focus on the issue of taste. For example, its researchers conducted taste tests, and many consumers said that, in fact, they preferred New Coke to the original. There was some inconsistent data, however, with focus groups indicating that there would be some anger at the change in product. In addition, surveys did not have the same results. In any case, executives did not make it clear to consumers that New Coke was to be a replacement for the original.

Neither the researchers nor the executives realized that taste was not the main issue. Instead, many consumers' strong attachment to Coke was based on emotion; they saw it as an icon of Americana. The researchers also made a fundamental mistake by not understanding that it was a modest number of loyal customers who purchased most of the Coke. Put another way: If they were displeased, they would take strong action.

Coca Cola executives did not address the gaps, anomalies, and errors in their research. In their minds, the key decision had already been made, so they went ahead with the introduction of New Coke in April 1985. The introduction was followed by a storm of protests by the loyal consumers and a huge amount of negative publicity. Loyal customers started to hoard the old Coke, and some even talked about a class action lawsuit to get the product reinstated. The introduction of New Coke became famous as one of the worst decisions in business history. The company eventually recovered from the embarrassment, and it has maintained the original Coke as part of a continuously evolving line of products.

From the beginning, Coca Cola executives were trapped by the fact that they were asking the wrong questions. They focused on the issues of taste and advertising, but people who drank Coke, especially its loyal fans who purchased a lot of the soft drink, saw the issue as one of maintaining a global symbol of the American way of life.

Coca Cola compounded the initial error by conducting sloppy market research and acting in haste. Research was not done in a rigorous fashion, and no effort was made to resolve contradictions in the data. Moreover, they apparently did not consider the implications of their being wrong.

Successful market research is based on the scientific method. Its systematic approach begins with identifying the problem (such as how to improve market share, change a brand's image, design a new technology, or get support for fighting a hostile takeover bid). It is likely to be useful to conduct a literature review or consult experts in the field to determine what is already known about the problem. Then researchers find a methodology that is appropriate to the problem (survey, focus groups, interviews, etc.). Next they carefully collect relevant data (if taking a survey, e.g., determine the appropriate sample). Then they verify the data (by collating and cross-checking, using a variety of sources, such as public records and outside experts). They identify and deal with any gaps or inconsistencies in the data. Finally, the researchers formulate a number of hypotheses and test them using the valid data.

Questions for Further Thought

Would careful research, as conducted by marketing professionals, have helped the Athenians to avoid being duped by the Egestaeans?

What cognitive biases might have been involved in the Coca Cola executives' approach? What assumptions?

Think about a current problem. How would you design a plan to analyze it using the steps used in market research?

Recommended Reading

Hayes, Constance L., *The Real Thing: Truth and Power at the Coca-Cola Company*, New York: Random House, 2004.

Malhotra, Naresh K., *Marketing Research: An Applied Approach*, London: Pearson Educa-
   tion, 2003.
Oliver, Thomas, *The Real Coke, the Real Story*, New York: Random House, 1986.
Pendergast, Mark, *For God, Country, and Coca-Cola: The Unauthorized History of the Great
   American Soft Drink and the Company that Makes It*, New York: Collier, 1993.

41

Japan in the U.S. Car Market

THE AUTOMOBILE INDUSTRY IS A QUINTESSENTIALLY AMERICAN ONE, conjuring up images of prosperity, mobility, and technology. Although Americans did not invent the car, companies such as Ford, Chrysler, and General Motors mastered production and sales. These firms became huge and profitable leaders in the industry, not only in the United States, but throughout the world. In recent decades, however, Japanese automobile companies have steadily increased their share of sales in the U.S. domestic market, which was once dominated by the big three American companies. How have the Japanese managed to accomplish this?

As early as the 1950s, the Japanese car companies, working with analysts in their government, were studying a scenario for the future that would be shaped by likely trends in areas – such energy pricing, technology, and shipping – which they believed would be drivers of change over time. They also made an in-depth study of the car market in America. Their analysis convinced them that the American companies were unwilling to endanger their short-term profits by spending money on innovations or improvements in quality. Moreover, the Japanese believed that over the long term the price of oil would increase, leading American consumers to be more interested in vehicles that were more efficient, generated less pollution, and required less maintenance, while still selling for a reasonable price. The Japanese believed that there could be great opportunities for them in such a scenario and that greater efficiency would enable them to take advantage of those opportunities. It turned out to be a prescient analysis.

Initial Japanese steps to enter the U.S. market were faltering, however. When Toyota tried to sell small cars in the 1950s, it failed; Americans still loved their big cars. Managers in the Japanese auto industry tended to have engineering backgrounds, so they bided their time, focusing on improving their ability to produce a quality product. They had a long-term, strategic perspective.

Among other things, the Japanese looked for ways to improve production methods that had been pioneered in the United States. In fact, continuous improvement – not waiting to act until something had gone wrong – became integral to their approach. They controlled costs through measures such as reducing inventories and developing just-in-time delivery of parts. They also kept labor costs low by promising lifetime employment. Efficiency was enhanced by training workers to have a variety of skills, work as teams with a considerable degree of autonomy, and have an understanding of the entire production process. Famously, individual workers could shut down the assembly line if they detected an error, which reduced the number of defective products shipped. All along, the Japanese car makers were relentlessly focused on finding out what consumers wanted and then providing it.

In the 1970s, the developments that the Japanese had anticipated decades before started to take place. The price of oil increased by more than 500 percent in the wake of the Arab embargo after the Yom Kippur War and the fall of the shah of Iran. Environmentalism and energy conservation became important issues. In addition, the cost of shipping by sea dropped dramatically.

The Japanese car manufacturers started to export large numbers of cars to the United States and found a ready market. Now U.S. consumers were more interested in durable, reliable vehicles that sold at a reasonable price, and the Japanese offered a wider range of vehicles beyond just small cars.

The Japanese did not become complacent; they continued to improve their products and adjust their strategy. In the 1980s, for example, they responded to political and economic pressures by shifting significant amounts of car production to plants in the United States. They continued to expand their offering, making better versions of vehicles that had been pioneered by U.S. firms, such as sport utility vehicles, minivans, and pickup trucks. For the future, the Japanese have already started the next phase of competition by taking the lead in offering energy-efficient hybrid gas/electric cars.

Meanwhile, in Detroit, where managers tended to have financial backgrounds, the emphasis was on short-term profits rather than long-term market share. By the early twenty-first century, U.S. firms were cutting jobs and posting huge losses. Many observers maintained that U.S. companies seemed to have lost the ability to produce cars that large numbers of customers wanted to buy. This situation left American auto makers vulnerable when the uncertainties of a major global economic crisis came in 2008, after which two of the big three, GM and Chrysler, declared bankruptcy.

As a result, the Japanese, who had had less than 4 percent of the U.S. car market in the early 1960s, are now major players. Toyota is vying with Ford to be second behind GM in sales of automobiles in the United States. Honda and Nissan also have significant, and increasing, shares of the U.S. market. On a global scale, Toyota has already become the largest seller of cars.

Analysis was not the only element of Japanese success; there was also skilled engineering and efficient production. Nonetheless, the Japanese made excellent use of analytic techniques, such as creating scenarios and identifying trends to anticipate the future. From the beginning, they also saw producing and selling cars as a multidimensional problem with economic, ecological, and political aspects, among others. They also thought in terms of the entire process and were willing to make changes. Although their approach was based on traditional Japanese values, they also remained open-minded and eventually developed a global perspective. It is also worth noting that their successful anticipation of major trends was based on the collection of a variety of data – but all from open sources.

Questions for Further Thought

What analytic insights about the vulnerabilities of economies, such as those gleaned from picking targets for the Allied bombers in World War II or identifying weaknesses in the Soviet economy, would be helpful in assessing current and future risks in the world economy?

What are some similarities between the global automobile industry and the international trade in illegal narcotics? Some differences?

What are some global trends, perhaps hard to detect at present, which will provide significant marketing opportunities in the future? What could be the political and security implications?

Recommended Reading

Chang, C. S., *The Japanese Auto Industry and the U.S. Market*, New York: Praeger, 1981.

Halberstam, David, *The Reckoning*, New York: William Morrow, 1986.

Hino, Satoshi, *Inside the Mind of Toyota: Management Principles for Enduring Growth*, Andrew Dillon, trans., New York: Productivity Press, 2006.

Magee, David, *How Toyota Became #1: Leadership Lessons from the World's Greatest Car Company*, New York: Penguin, 2007.

May, Matthew E., *Elegant Solution: Toyota's Formula for Mastering Innovation*, New York: Free Press, 2007.

Further Recommended Reading

Anderson, Terence, Schum, David, and Twining, William, *Analysis of Evidence, 2nd* ed., New York: Cambridge University Press, 2005.

Betts, Richard, *Surprise Attack: Lessons for Defense Planning*, Washington, DC: Brookings Institution, 1982.

Boba, Rachel, *Crime Analysis and Crime Mapping: An Introduction*, Thousand Oaks, CA: Sage Publications, 2005.

Cradock, Percy, *Know Your Enemy: How the Joint Intelligence Committee Saw the World*, London: John Murray, 2002.

Diamond, John, *The CIA and the Culture of Failure: U.S. Intelligence from the End of the Cold War to the Invasion of Iraq*, Stanford, CA: Stanford University Press, 2008.

Dvornik, Francis, *Origins of Intelligence Services*, New Brunswick, NJ: Rutgers University Press, 1974.

Hughes-Wilson, John, *Military Intelligence Blunders*, New York: Carroll & Graf, 1999.

Janis, Irving, *Victims of Group Think*, Boston, MA: Houghton Mifflin, 1972.

Jervis, Robert, *Perception and Misperception in International Politics*, Princeton, NJ: Princeton University Press, 1976.

Jervis, Robert, *Why Intelligence Fails*, Ithaca, NY: Cornell University Press, 2010.

Kam, Ephraim, *Surprise Attack: The Victim's Perspective*, Cambridge, MA: Harvard University Press, 1988.

Keegan, John, *Intelligence in War: Knowledge of the Enemy from Napoleon to al-Qaeda*, New York: Alfred A. Knopf, 2003.

McDowell, Don, *Strategic Intelligence: A Handbook for Practitioners, Managers, and Users*, Lanham, MD: Scarecrow Press, 2009.

Moore, David T., *Critical Thinking and Intelligence Analysis*, Washington, DC: Joint Military Intelligence College Press, 2006.

Neilson, Keith, and McKercher, B. J. C., eds., *Go Spy the Land: Military Intelligence in History*, Westport, CT: Praeger, 1992.

Neustadt, Richard E., and May, Ernest R., *Thinking in Time: The Uses of History for Decision Makers*, New York: The Free Press, 1986.

Noftsinger, John B., et al., *Understanding Homeland Security: Policy, Perspectives, and Paradoxes*, New York: Palgrave, 2007.

Ratcliffe, Jerry H., *Intelligence-Led Policing*, Portland, OR: Willan, 2008.

Vertzberger, Yaacov, *Risk Taking and Decision Making: Military Intervention Decisions*, Stanford, CA: Stanford University Press, 1998.

Winks, Robin W., *Cloak & Gown: Scholars in the Secret War, 1939–1961*, New York: William Morrow, 1987.

Index